"Perhaps nothing is more important in psychology than the understanding of oneself as well as the ability to take the perspectives of others. This book offers a groundbreaking, cutting-edge, empirically-based contextual behavioral perspective on the self. For example, the authors show how perspective-taking is developed using basic science, going far beyond theory of mind and demonstrating how this knowledge can be directly applied to work with schoolchildren and in clinical settings. If you want a single book that includes both rigorous science and direct clinical applications on the self, look no further!"

—JoAnne Dahl, PhD, associate professor in the department of psychology at the University of Uppsala, Sweden

"This remarkable edited book offers a dense and tantalizing pragmatic analysis of the self and consciousness. It is one of the best contemporary evidence-based accounts of the nature of human consciousness that I have seen, period. A must-read for anyone curious about the human condition, especially readers interested in language and cognition, acceptance and mindfulness-based approaches, positive psychology, and newer third-generation behavior therapies."

—John P. Forsyth, PhD, professor of psychology and director of the Anxiety Disorders Research Program at the University at Albany, State University of New York

"In this authoritative volume, the world of self, identity, mindfulness, and emotional disturbances is infused with exciting new theories, methods, and results. The chapters illustrate how this mixture of science and application provides the potential for designing new therapies and improving the quality of people's lives."

—Todd B. Kashdan, PhD, professor at George Mason University and author of *Curious?* and *Designing Positive Psychology*

"This book on recent advances in our understanding of the concept of the self exemplifies the saying that "there is nothing as practical as a good theory." The authors cover modern scientific findings and, more remarkably, manage to illustrate how these findings are relevant for psychological treatment. A must-read for anyone with an interest in the concept of the self, scientist and clinician alike!"

—Niklas Törneke MD, author of *Lea*

D0916706

# The Self and Perspective Taking

## Contributions and Applications from Modern Behavioral Science

Louise McHugh, PhD
Ian Stewart, PhD

CONTEXT PRESS
An Imprint of New Harbinger Publications, Inc.

Distributed in Canada by Raincoast Books

Copyright © 2012 by Louise McHugh and Ian Stewart
       New Harbinger Publications, Inc.
       5674 Shattuck Avenue
       Oakland, CA 94609
       www.newharbinger.com

Cover design by Amy Shoup;
Text design by Tracy Carlson;
Acquired by Catharine Meyers

FSC
www.fsc.org
MIX
Paper from
responsible sources
FSC® C011935

Library of Congress Cataloging-in-Publication Data

The self and perspective taking : contributions and applications from modern behavioral science / [edited by] Louise McHugh and Ian Stewart.
    p. cm.
 Includes bibliographical references and index.
 ISBN 978-1-57224-995-0 (pbk.) -- ISBN 978-1-57224-996-7 (pdf e-book)
 1. Self. 2. Developmental psychology. 3. Mind and body. I. McHugh, Louise. II. Stewart, Ian, 1971-
 BF697.S4253 2012
 155.2--dc23
               2011039764

13    12    11

10   9   8   7   6   5   4   3   2   1

First Printing

# Contents

Louise McHugh *University College Dublin*
Ian Stewart *National University of Ireland, Galway*

## Part 1
## Approaches to the Self

### Chapter 1
Ian Stewart *National University of Ireland, Galway*
Jennifer Villatte *University of Nevada, Reno*
Louise McHugh *University College Dublin*

### Chapter 2
Kennon A. Lattal *West Virginia University*

# Part 2
# Perspective Taking: Developmental and Clinical

# Part 3
# The Self: Content and Processes

# Part 4
# The Self: Mindfulness and Transcendence

# Foreword

"In the deep darkness God suddenly raised his head and listened." So begins "The Invaders," one of Ted Hughes's short stories for children from *Tales of the Early World* (Farrar Straus & Giroux, 1991) about how creation came into being. In these stories, God—who often had terrible trouble with his mother—creates animals, sometimes without thinking very clearly, and then has to deal with the consequences.

In "The Invaders," the whole earth is shaken by a sinister, howling whisper from outer space that threatens destruction of everything: "I am taking over the earth. All creatures shall be my slaves and food. I am your new Master and I am coming. I need blood. I need food." God is sick with anxiety. He has a feeling that an awful battle is about to commence, and he is not at all sure he can win. After failing to reassure the animals, God decides to arm them: tusks to the elephant and wild pig, claws to the bear and leopard, horns to buffalo and rhinoceros, teeth to... well, you can imagine. After an extraordinary climax during which the voice gets louder and louder and the animals line up around God in battle formation, there is deathly silence. Then, one by one, the animals begin to scratch. God scratches, too. The earth has been invaded—by fleas.

In this simple story, Hughes has given us a new myth for our time: of creation or evolution bequeathing us—*human* animals—with protective mechanisms to fight an enemy that turns out not to be fightable using the tools we have been given. This is central to understanding how our notions of self function (and do not function). The book you hold in your hands is a gold mine of perspectives, discussion, experimental data, and interpretation that together clarifies why the self can get us into difficulties. Here are reviewed different historical and philosophical ideas about the self, the development of self-identity, neuroscientific studies, and pathology of the self and how the modern adaptation of ancient traditions of insight (mindfulness), wisdom (clear seeing), and ethics (actual behavior that promotes wholeness) are addressing such pathology.

The book traces the history of the self within psychological science. It follows how William James distinguished "me" from "I" and further distinguished different aspects of "I": the material, the social, and the spiritual. It shows how the self seemed to disappear from view within psychology until its resurgence in the humanistic movement of Abraham Maslow and Carl Rogers, and its cognitivization with Ulric Neisser and colleagues within the new field of cognitive psychology from the late 1960s onward, and its clinical counterparts of Aaron Beck and colleagues. It also shows us a parallel stream of literature, distinguishing between the minimal or momentary self on the one hand and the conceptual or narrative self on the other, and examining how these distinctions link to language.

Language, of course, is the aspect of human behavior against which most blame is laid for producing confusion. It is an extraordinary evolutionary inheritance that achieves so much yet is often used to fight battles for which it is the wrong weapon. It seems certain that through language we create our selves—and thus become an entity that appears to go beyond the moment-by-moment co-arising of mind and body states, giving us the sense that we have privileged and private information about the nature of things. In this way, we create a self, extended over time, in which the present is left as an almost nonexistent moment between the voracious tendencies of a past and a future to create endless stories about us.

In this way, "selfing" arises from a variety of tools that emerge from genetic inheritance combined with learning history, and is then exaggerated and becomes problematic when the "selfing" attempts to solve a problem it has itself created.

The great feature of this book is its drawing together of an international field of experimental and clinical scientists, each of whom has something important to contribute to the historical, philosophical, neuroscientific, and psychological debates. What is particularly refreshing is to see scientists who are clear about their axioms and starting assumptions, the root metaphors of their field: in this case, that act and context are inseparable, that the goal of the field is prediction and influence of behavior, and that the truth criterion is whether such prediction and influence actually and demonstrably takes place. Here is clearly stated the core idea of self in this field, that it results from our responding to our own responding, that the discrimination of one's own responding must be a verbal discrimination, and a critical learning is the learning to respond in accordance with deictic frames (*I-you*, *here-there*, and *now-then*) that provide the basis for perspective taking.

And then the research starts. There are data to be reported and discussed: data from children and adults, from the clinic and the lab. In every chapter, the data are always related back to the context of real life. Here we see why children below the age of three cannot understand the rules of hide-and-seek—or at least cannot understand our (adult) rules. We see how difficulties arise when there is a deficit in self-agency and self-ownership (in psychosis) and when products of relational responding are treated as objectively true (in many emotional disorders such as anxiety and depression) and become, in the words of the authors, verbal cages of their own making. Here we see the basic building blocks of (and how to gain experimental control over) the critical variables involved in perspective taking, theory of mind, and beliefs about self and other. We see what happens when perspective taking does not develop, or is broken. We read about autistic spectrum and psychosis, about social anhedonia, and about anxiety and depression. And we discover how people may free themselves from their verbal cages through acceptance and commitment therapy or mindfulness, approaches that encourage people to see how, when an evaluation (*I-here-now*) is discriminated as just an evaluation, it acquires different relational functions, and they may even drop outside of language-driven relationality altogether.

Why is this book important even for those readers who do not take the same philosophical position? First, it provides a useful corrective. Self-report, according to this position, is not a privileged read-out of introspection, but indexes environmental influences. Second, it provides testable hypotheses about the critical variables that underlie the development of hugely important abilities such as perspective taking and theory of mind. Third, it helps to explain the inescapable traps into which we fall if we start a language-based battle within ourselves. So the metaphors of self-control and willpower that each of may have used (for example, about being captain of our own ship) may be useful fictions, but here we see them stripped bare. If someone says "I cannot live with myself," it may surely be legitimate to ask who is the "I" with whom "myself" cannot live, but this is only to ask the question as a koan. It is more legitimate to show the way we have tricked ourselves into imagining that if we can frame a question, there must be an answer.

The tricks that language can play on us are inexhaustible, so the methods we use to better understand these tricks and deal skillfully with them will also be inexhaustible. These authors show us a way forward, and if we follow where they lead, we will discover both deeper understanding and extraordinary practical wisdom.

—Mark Williams, PhD, FBA
Professor of Clinical Psychology
Wellcome Principal Research Fellow
University of Oxford

# Preface

Louise McHugh *University College Dublin*

Ian Stewart *National University of Ireland, Galway*

Understanding oneself and being able to take the perspective of other people are complex and related forms of cognition that have been the subject of much psychological and philosophical debate. This book presents a number of different theoretical and empirical orientations to the self and perspective taking (PT) within contemporary behavioral science with a particular emphasis on the approach adopted by proponents of contemporary contextual behavioral psychology. In addition to presenting modern theory and research on the self, the book will also include a substantial focus on how theoretically grounded and pragmatically oriented research is being applied to training self-understanding and PT in typically developing children as well as to remediating deficits in self-understanding in the clinical arena.

The book will be divided into four parts: (i) "Approaches to the Self," (ii) "Perspective Taking: Developmental and Clinical," (iii) "The Self: Content and Processes," and (iv) "The Self, Mindfulness, and Transcendence."

The first part, "Approaches to the Self," will comprise two chapters that provide some important background to the remainder of the book. Chapter 1 provides an overview of different approaches to the self including very early theories as well as more recent humanistic, developmental, and cognitive neuroscientific conceptions. It describes the philosophical assumptions underlying these approaches and then contrasts them with those of contextual behavioral psychology. It then gives a concise introduction to the approach to self provided by the latter that should constitute useful background for the reader in the remaining parts of the book. As described in the first chapter, one of the keystones for the contextual behavioral approach to self is the behavior analytic and more specifically Skinnerian conception of self as responding to one's own responding. In chapter 2, Kennon Lattal, the researcher who provided the first empirical demonstration of this approach, gives a concise yet comprehensive review of behavior analytic theory and research on the self. Behavior analysis is an area of psychology not traditionally noted for its contribution to complex topics such as the self, but in more recent times an amount of research has emerged from this domain which has provided the foundation for a substantial quantity of the theoretical and empirical work included in this book.

Part 2, "Perspective Taking: Developmental and Clinical" includes four chapters that focus on PT as a key repertoire underlying the development of the self. Chapter 3 provides an overview of perspective-taking research within mainstream psychology where it has been mainly conceptualized under the rubric of "theory of mind" (ToM) as well as within the more recently emerged contextual behavioral approach, which sees it in terms of a learned repertoire of *deictic* (PT) relations. Much of the early empirical work has shown that the deictic framing approach correlates well with findings from within ToM; however, more recent applied deictic framing research has begun to show potentially useful novel insights and applied uses of the deictic framing conception that arguably go further than previous ToM-based work. The next three chapters provide greater detail on perspective-taking research. Chapter 4 reviews research on precursors to PT including, in particular, joint attention and social referencing. Gary Novak, the author, and his colleagues have developed a behavioral systems approach to development more generally and it is under this rubric that he presents the findings of this work. In chapter 5, Martin Doherty, a researcher at the cutting edge of experimental work on ToM, presents a theoretical and empirical review of research in this area. Doherty's conceptual approach to PT is rooted in mechanistic cognitive assumptions, which differ from those of the contextual behavioral approach adopted elsewhere; nevertheless, the wealth of data that he presents provide potentially useful insights and clues to those coming from alternative traditions including contextual behavioral psychology. Chapter 6, the final chapter in part 2, discusses mainstream and contextual behavioral research into deficits in PT in adult and child clinical populations, with a particular focus on individuals with schizophrenia and anhedonia. The authors of this chapter have conducted research in which deficits in PT uncovered in previous research have been replicated and further explored in terms of deictic framing. As the authors suggest, these preliminary results are promising and point the way to further work on possible remediation of these deficits.

Part 3, "The Self: Content and Processes" comprises three chapters focusing on the self in the context of psychotherapy. Chapter 7 focuses on the role of the self in acceptance and commitment therapy (ACT), an application of contextual behavioral science in the therapeutic domain and one that has garnered an increasing level of empirical support across diverse forms of pathology. As outlined in this chapter, the contextual behavioral analysis of self is central in the ACT explanation of processes of pathology and therapy. Chapter 8 examines the self as a context for rule following. It examines the various patterns of rule (verbal prescription) following that people learn and how acting in accordance with rules especially as they pertain to the self is a ubiquitous feature of human existence. This chapter explains how certain patterns of rule following can lead to psychopathology while other healthier patterns provide the basis for a fulfilling vital life. The third and final chapter in this part presents the self as conceptualized within modern cognitive behavioral therapy (CBT). The self in traditional CBT is conceptualized in accordance with mechanistic cognitive assumptions in terms of particular content (i.e., "schemata") which needs to be organized in a particular way in order to facilitate psychological health. As pointed out by the authors, these assumptions are different from those which underlie the contextual behavioral approach underlying ACT. However there are important insights to be gleaned from this approach, particularly with respect to the illumination of the myriad ways in which behavior can succumb to particular "self-content." In addition, as this chapter shows, CBT research and theory as regards the self is moving in interesting new directions which may be more congruent with current contextual behavioral scientific approaches, such as the importance of meta-cognition and the effects of implicit or "unconscious" processes.

The final part of the book ("The Self: Mindfulness and Transcendence") examines the self in relation to issues of mindfulness and spirituality. Thus, we are presented in both of these chapters with a naturalistic scientific approach to areas traditionally perceived to be beyond the purview of scientific research. Chapter 10 uses the contextual behavioral approach to self as a starting point and the psychological flexibility model of change processes in ACT as an organizing framework to explore the relationship between self and mindfulness processes. Chapter 11 presents a naturalistic scientific approach to issues of spirituality and transcendence, explaining in particular how deictic framing can lead to both individual and group level transcendence thereby giving rise to the intimately connected and mutually supportive phenomena of spirituality, empathy and prosociality.

The theory and research presented throughout this book constitute good examples of the promise of current behavioral science in its investigation of complex issues of human psychology. The phenomena of self and perspective taking, intimately related as they are with so many other key phenomena—education, understanding, awareness, compassion, cooperation, psychological flexibility, empathy, and spirituality—seem particularly important and it thus seems especially important that we understand them. Research from a pragmatic contextual behavioral perspective is at an exciting stage of development and we think that the findings of current work hold out the promise of a deeper and more practically oriented understanding where these key aspects of human psychology are concerned.

—Louise McHugh and Ian Stewart, April 2011

# Part 1

# Approaches to the Self

# Chapter 1

# Approaches to the Self

Ian Stewart *National University of Ireland, Galway*

Jennifer Villatte *University of Nevada, Reno*

Louise McHugh *University College Dublin*

## Introduction

The self is a concept that is widespread in modern psychology. It first received substantial treatment by William James in the late nineteenth century, and since then has played either a central or supporting explanatory role in several major theoretical approaches to human behavior including psychodynamics, humanism and positive psychology. Despite the popularity of "self" as an explanatory concept within these approaches, however, it has arguably remained ill-defined in operational terms.

Recently, however, a strand of behavioral psychology, namely functional contextualist behavior analysis, has emerged that has begun to provide an account of human language and cognition characterized by precision, scope and depth. This approach offers a more comprehensive exploration of complex phenomena such as the self than might be found within traditional behavior approaches, but nevertheless retains the empirical grounding and scientific rigor of the latter. As regards the self, this approach provides an increasingly well supported account offering new insight into this phenomenon.

In this chapter we discuss and compare the self as conceptualized within mainstream and functional contextualist approaches. In this way, the context for the emergence of the functional contextualist approach including both connections and contrasts with older traditions will be made available. We begin with an overview of a number of mainstream approaches to the self.

# Mainstream Approaches to the Self

## Early Theorists

Perhaps the first theory of the self in modern psychology was that of William James (e.g., 1891a, 1891b) who famously differentiated between "me" (the known self, or object) and "I" (the knowing self or subject). He saw the latter as multifaceted, including the material self, social self and spiritual self. The material self was everything a person might call his own (e.g., his body, family and property); the social self was the self as known by others (and thus we have as many social selves as social relationships); while the spiritual self was a person's states of consciousness or subjective reality. Contrasted with the "me" (known self) was the "I" (knowing self). James saw the "I" as "pure ego" or consciousness. From his pragmatic perspective, this aspect of self was a highly adaptive, uniquely human product of evolution. Despite its importance though, he found it difficult to describe, often comparing it to philosophical and religious notions of "soul," "spirit" or "transcendental ego."

Charles Cooley (1902) introduced the concept of the looking-glass self whereby an individual's sense of self emerges on the basis of self-beliefs created by her impression of how others see her. According to this theory, we become to a very large degree what we think other people think we are. This conception emphasized the importance of early care-giving and educational contexts as well as the critical role of social comparison in the development of self, and drew attention to the influence of significant others including caregivers, siblings, teachers, and peers on the development of identity.

James (1896/1958) had differed from Cooley with respect to the development of self. He asserted that a sense of self emerges in a child through direct imitation of parents and influential others rather than through realization of what others' opinion of her must be. For both theorists, however, the emergence of self-identity is deeply influenced or arguably even fully determined by the beliefs and actions of others. George Herbert Mead (e.g., 1934) asserted this also. According to his symbolic interactionist perspective, people act toward things and events in their environment based on their symbolized meaning and these meanings are derived from social interaction and modified through interpretation. However, Mead's concept of the role of social influence in the development of self was fundamentally more radical than those of his predecessors since for him the self was not a private mental process, but wholly a product of interaction with the social world. In this way he put a profound emphasis on the social psychological nature of self to an extent that neither previous theorist had done.

## Humanistic Psychology

In the period from the 1920s to the 1950s, psychology was dominated by behavioral approaches which for philosophical and theoretical reasons paid little attention to the concept of the self. Even when behavior analysts such as Skinner did consider it, they approached it very differently from other perspectives and thus, the fully complex self as considered by James and other theorists did not receive much attention during this period.

The concept of the self came to prominence again in the 1950s with the rise of humanistic psychology. The latter is often seen as a reaction to decades of behaviorist influence. Proponents of humanism tended to classify behaviorism as narrow and deterministic, arguing that it omitted core aspects of human psychology, including the self. One of the pioneers of this movement was Abraham Maslow (e.g., 1954), who stressed the importance of individual subjectivity and of human potential for growth, creativity, and free choice. He outlined a concept of a hierarchy of human needs that must be satisfied, starting with basic physiological and safety needs and progressing up through needs for affection, esteem and, right at the top, "self-actualization," or development of one's full potential. He saw the latter as the ultimate goal of each individual and thus for him the self was of central theoretical importance. The self and self-actualization were also central within Carl Rogers's (e.g., 1961) approach. According to Rogerian theory, the self is a subjective phenomenon that is key to personality and of primary importance in explaining human behavior and psychological adjustment. It develops based on interaction with the environment, including especially significant others, and as the person strives to satisfy universal needs for consistency, congruence with reality, and positive regard from oneself and others. From this perspective, each person has an innate tendency toward self-actualization and growth and these can be realized given appropriate environmental and especially interpersonal conditions. This account links a number of key ideas on the self from earlier theories, such as the importance of subjective experience, interpersonal relationships and human needs and was so influential it became known as "self theory."

One of the results of the emergence of the humanistic movement was an enthusiastic revival of interest in the 1960s and 1970s in the concept of the self as a motivational agent. This resulted in increased efforts by many psychologists, including clinicians and educators to promote an emphasis on the importance of a healthy self-concept and positive self-regard or self-esteem. Despite this enthusiasm, however, empirical research on the relationship between self-esteem and adaptive functioning has not been encouraging. For example, after a thorough review of self-esteem studies in various areas of psychology, Baumeister, Campbell, Kreuger and Vohs (2003) reported that self-esteem does not lead to better performance or to higher levels of interpersonal success.

## Recent Approaches

One of the immediate consequences of research showing the lack of an expected causal connection between self-esteem and important psychological outcomes was a decline in the popularity of humanistic psychology and the self-esteem movement. However, perhaps at least partly as a legacy of humanism, interest in the self and self-related variables among psychological theorists has continued strongly up to the present. A number of features of relatively modern mainstream approaches to self should be noted. First, they typically reflect the dominance of cognitive psychology over the decades since the 1950s by conceptualizing the self in information-processing terms. For example, in the clinical arena, approaches based on traditional cognitive behavior therapy (CBT; see chapter 9, present volume) tend to describe the self in terms of cognitive structures known as schemata that allow organization of self-relevant information. Second, whereas early theorists including James defined and used self-concept in general terms as global perceptions of self-worth, or self-esteem, many modern theories focus on the self as complex and multifaceted. For example, it has been suggested that individuals perceive themselves primarily in terms of the various facets of their self-system, each facet carrying a different description and evaluation; that self-concept can differ across differing domains of functioning; and that it is our self-concept in specific areas of our lives that is most likely to guide us in those areas (see Shavelson & Marsh, 1986). Third, and perhaps most important may be the fact that modern approaches are more empirically oriented than earlier approaches which were often more philosophical than scientific.

Two areas of empirical research within mainstream psychology that have attempted to investigate the self and its characteristics are (i) comparative and developmental approaches to the origins of self and (ii) experimental cognitive and neuroscientific exploration of the nature of self. We will consider these in turn.

## ORIGINS AND DEVELOPMENT OF SELF

As regards the origins of the self, one focus of research has been emerging differentiation between self and environment. For example, according to Maccoby (1980), one key way infants learn to distinguish between themselves and the world is via body-specific associations between their actions and sensory experiences. For instance, when a child bites his own fingers, he feels sensations not felt when he bites other people's fingers or other objects. Similarly, when he cries, the felt sensations arising from production of those cries become associated with the sound. These associations help to define the "bodily self." For Piaget (e.g., 1970), self-awareness develops gradually through a process of adaptation to the environment. As the child explores objects and accommodates to them, thus acquiring a "sensory-motor schema," she also learns about herself. For instance, when she tries to fit a large rubber ball in her mouth but fails she learns something about herself as well as the ball, and this enhances discrimination between bodily self and environment.

Perhaps the most extensive research on early developing awareness of self is on self-recognition. Visual self-recognition has been studied extensively in both humans and nonhumans. Many nonhumans react to mirror images as if they were other animals. Higher primates including chimpanzees react this way initially, but eventually, they display behavior that some researchers call self-recognition. For example, Gallup (1977) reported that chimpanzees with full-length mirrors on the walls of their cage eventually began to respond to the images as reflections of their own behavior. After several days of mirror exposure, each chimp was anesthetized and bright red spots were painted on their heads in places they could not see without a mirror. After waking, they were placed in a room without a mirror to see how often they'd touch the painted spots. When the mirror was replaced they began to explore the spots twenty to thirty times more than previously. A modified version of this procedure has been used in a number of studies (e.g., Lewis & Brooks-Gunn, 1979) with children from six to twenty-four months. A caregiver places a spot of rouge on a child's nose while pretending to wipe the child's face and the child is then observed how often the child touches their face both before and after being placed in front of a mirror. Touching the spot in front of the mirror is never seen in children under fifteen months; 5 to 25 percent of children between fifteen and eighteen months old touch it; while 75 percent of those between eighteen and twenty-four months old do so.

Many theorists suggest that passing the mirror test is evidence of a self-concept. Gallup (1998) infers that passing this test is evidence not alone of self-awareness, but also of theory of mind (ToM), the ability to infer mental states in others. He argues that self-awareness is an expression of a process that allows organisms to use their own experience to model that of others and cites in support the mirror studies as well as neuropsychological studies that link right prefrontal cortical activity with both self-awareness and ToM. Daniel Povinelli, however, who has examined self-recognition in both chimps and human infants, disagrees with the contention that either has a deep understanding of behavior. In Povinelli (1998) individual children were videotaped as an experimenter placed a sticker on their head. Then, later, they were shown either (i) a live video of themselves or (ii) a recording made minutes earlier in which the experimenter could be seen putting the sticker on their head. Two- and three-year-olds responded differently depending on which video they saw. With the live video (equivalent to looking in a mirror), they reached up and removed the sticker. However, with the recording, only about one-third did so. Furthermore, this was despite knowing what the sticker was, and recognizing themselves in the recording. When asked who the child in the recording was, they replied "Me"; however, this reaction didn't seem to extend beyond recognition of facial and bodily features. When asked "Where is the sticker?" they often referred to the "other" child in the third person, saying it was on his or her head. However, most four-year-olds reached up and removed the sticker after watching the recording. Furthermore, they no longer used the third person in their description.

According to Povinelli, these results indicate that genuine "autobiographical memory" or a consistent sense of self appears to emerge in children between age three and a half and four and a half years and not at two years or under as suggested by Gallup. In other words, it is only then that a relatively sophisticated sense of self starts to emerge. This conclusion is further supported by research by John Barresi and colleagues (c.f. Barresi, 2001) indicating that it is only by age four that children begin to develop a concept of self extended into the future. Povinelli's results also suggest that passing the mirror test is based on recognition of self-behavior as opposed to a more sophisticated sense of self.

The emergence of a more sophisticated sense of self has been investigated by asking children of various ages questions about how they think of themselves. Flavell, Shipstead & Croft (1978) investigated development of the psychological self in children from two and a half to five years old by asking questions to ascertain how they thought of themselves. On the basis of the replies, children from three and a half years on seemed to have a concept of a private, thinking self distinguishable from the bodily self while by age four they appeared to develop ToM (see also chapters 3 and 5, current volume).

Children also develop an increasingly sophisticated categorical understanding of the self. According to Damon and Hart (1988), children under seven tend to define the self in physical terms (e.g., hair color, height, favorite activities and possessions). Inner psychological experiences and characteristics aren't described as distinct from overt behavior and external physical characteristics. From middle childhood on, however, self-descriptions include increasing references to internal, psychological characteristics (e.g., competencies, knowledge, emotions, values and traits). School is a particularly important context for development of the self-concept. This context highlights others' expectations about how the self should develop and provides a social context in which new goals are set and comparisons with others are prompted.

## COGNITIVE AND NEUROSCIENTIFIC INVESTIGATIONS OF SELF

Another domain of mainstream empirical work into the self is that of cognitive science, an interdisciplinary approach whose adherents share a conceptualization of the human mind as information processor and which

9

includes cognitive psychologists as well as philosophers, anthropologists, artificial intelligence researchers, linguists, and neuroscientists.

Shaun Gallagher (2000) discusses two conceptions of self that have received attention within cognitive science—the minimal self and the narrative self. The former concerns that which is specific and essential to the self, and is typically seen as devoid of temporal extension, while the latter is seen as a content rich, more or less coherent image of self involving personal identity and continuity across time.

Research on the minimal self in cognitive science is based on the idea that the self is a special and executive part of the cognitive architecture and the task is to understand how it functions and discover its neural location. The question of the specialness of the self has received attention from researchers for many decades. T. B. Rogers, Kuiper and Kirker (1977) suggested they had provided evidence in favor of the view that self is special by showing that memory for previously presented trait adjectives was better if they had been processed with reference to the self than if processed for general meaning only. However, an alternative to the self-as-special explanation was that the effect is simply based on "depth of processing" related to the extensive quantity of self-related information available.

As these competing accounts give rise to identical predictions (i.e., enhanced memory), they cannot be distinguished using overt behavioral measures. Hence the potential advantage of neurocognitive imaging research to allow examination of possible neural substrates of self. Kelley et al. (2002) used fMRI to identify the neural signature of self-referential neural activity. In a standard self-reference paradigm, participants judged trait adjectives in one of three ways: self ("Does it describe you?"), other ("Does it describe George Bush?"), or case ("Is it presented in uppercase letters?"). Results showed the self condition was best for memory and the case condition worst. More importantly, however, fMRI analysis was used to test competing explanations for the self-reference effect. Results showed that self trials were distinctive for medial prefrontal cortex (mPFC) activity, suggesting this region might be involved in the effect. Macrae, Moran, Heatherton, Banfield and Kelley (2004) provided further support for this by showing that mPFC activity can contribute to formation of self-relevant memories.

The results described seem to link the self primarily with the mPFC; however, in fact studies investigating the neural substrate of self have identified a range of alternative regions that might also be involved. For example, Vogeley et al. (2001) used fMRI to study the common and differential neural mechanisms underlying self-perspective (SELF) and ToM, which involves modeling the mental states of others (see e.g., H. L. Gallagher & Frith, 2003). They found that whereas ToM seemed located predominantly in the anterior cingulate cortex, SELF led to activation there but also in additional areas including the right temporoparietal junction, the precuneus and the right premotor and motor cortex, each of which is relatively removed from the mPFC region. Hence, the evidence seems to indicate that self-relevant processing is more widely dispersed than suggested above. Indeed, Northoff and Bermpohl (2004) present a review of domains associated with self-processing in the neuroimaging literature and suggest that "a remarkable variety of domains and cortical regions" is implicated. However, they maintain the concept of the core self by arguing for an integration of processes in distinct regions. They suggest several key subprocesses involved in processing of self-referential stimuli including representation, monitoring, evaluation and integration which they suggest take place in the orbitomedial prefrontal cortex (OMPFC), supragenual anterior cingulate cortex (SAC), dorsomedial pre-frontal cortex (DMPFC), and posterior cingulate cortex (PC) respectively. In this theory, the core self is the integration of processes occurring within these cortical midline structures and deals with self-referential information relayed from non-core regions. In fact this theory is similar to the previous one in that it maintains the central concept and agrees on the importance of the mPFC region as a neural substrate for self, albeit expanding the province of self to other regions.

While Northoff and Bermpohl (2004) respond to findings indicating "a remarkable variety" of domains associated with self by suggesting core self as an integration of domains, LeGrand and Ruby (2009), whose more recent review implicates an even greater diversity of regions, respond in a wholly different way. They argue that much neuroscientific work has not been targeting the self in its specificity; this work has focused on self-related content, but such content is not truly self-specific. In their view, what makes a process self-specific is not the content or object of process-ing but rather the subjective perspective brought to bear. The latter is not intrinsically self-evaluative but rather relates any represented object, self-related or otherwise, to the representing subject. They suggest, based on previous work on first- and third-person perspectives (e.g., Ruby & Decety, 2004; Vogeley et al., 2001) that this self-specific subject-object perspective has its neural basis at the sensorimotor level in the integra-tion of data from processes of efference, the motor command of the sub-ject's action, and reafference, the sensory consequence of that action in the world, and that research interested in self-specific processes should focus on substrates of these.

The suggestion of the importance of subjective PT as a focus for investigation of self-specific processes is anticipated by earlier theoretical and empirical work discussed in S. Gallagher (2000). This describes the "immunity principle" as one possible encapsulation of the minimal features of the experience of self. This principle declares that when a person uses the word "I" as subject in a sentence (e.g., "I think it is raining") then they are immune from making a misidentification error about the subject; in other words they cannot be wrong that it is they who are doing what they claim to be doing. Based on suggestions by Feinberg (1978) and Frith (1992), however, one possible exception to this is schizophrenic "thought insertion" in which the person seems to experience his own thought as coming from someone else. Thus, he may claim that he is not the one thinking a particular thought when in fact he is; this is a violation of the immunity principle and a serious aberration from typical self-experience. According to this conception of self, there are two key features that mark out an action, including cognition, as a self-action and thus enable the experience of the minimal self. These are self-ownership (feeling that my body is involved in the action), and self-agency (feeling that I am causing the action). Frith (1992) provides a neurocognitive model of typical minimal self and its absence in schizophrenia involving a network of comparator mechanisms underpinning self-ownership and self-agency that are localized in the cerebellum and in the supplementary motor, premotor and prefrontal cortices respectively. According to this model, phenomena such as thought insertion or perceiving one's own actions as alien result when the neural feedback mechanisms responsible for self-ownership and self-agency do not cohere such that some thoughts that appear to be owned by the self do not appear to the behaving person to have been self-caused.

The immunity principle conception of minimal self is based on the behaving person having a basic level of language and hence a conceptual framework. However, a further question is whether a core self even requires language. Shaun Gallagher (2000) suggests that evidence of a nonverbal self existing from early infancy is provided by empirically controlled demonstrations of neonatal facial imitation argued to require the ability to distinguish self from non-self among other cognitive capacities. Conclusions such as this might certainly be questioned even by other cognitive scientists; however, for many of the latter in particular, the basic question raised is still relevant: Need models of core self based on self-perspective, including those suggested by Frith (1992) and more recently LeGrand and Ruby (2009) necessarily involve language?

For many cognitive scientists, including Shaun Gallagher, the non-necessity of language readily coheres with the concept of a minimal or core self. However, Shaun Gallagher (2000) also discusses a very different concept referred to as the narrative self, an entity extended in time, with an identity, past memories and future plans, which would require language. Philosophers have posed questions regarding the nature of an apparently continuous self. For example, is the narrative self composed of a succession of transitory selves somehow united by "real" connections or are transitory selves merely abstractions from the temporally extended genuine self? Dennett (1991) has argued that the former position is more consistent with neuroscientific results that suggest the absence of a real, neurological center of experience and thus of biologically based simplicity of experience at one time or temporally extended identity. However, he argues that humans do have language and with language we create our selves verbally, thus extending our biological boundaries to encompass a life of meaningful experience. In his account, our self-invention is automatic and we're not totally in control of the product; the self is an abstract "center of narrative gravity" consisting of the abstract and moveable point where the various narratives concerning the individual, both fictional and biographical, both self and other-produced, meet up.

The idea of self-as-narrative finds support in both cognitive psychology and neuroscience. Regarding the former, Neisser (1988; Neisser & Fivush, 1994) describes the extended and conceptual selves as two important forms of self, and explains them in terms of memory and language processes. In the area of neuroscience, Gazzaniga (e.g., 1995; 1998) has suggested, based on studies of split-brain patients, that a key function of the left neural hemispheric "interpreter" is to weave together autobiographical fact and inventive fiction to produce a personal narrative that enables the sense of a self extended over time.

At this point we have examined approaches to the core self and approaches to the narrative self. To some extent the core self and the narrative self may be considered wholly different conceptions of the self. However, another way of seeing them is as distinct yet equally important modes of self. One example of the investigation of separate modes of self is provided by Farb et al. (2007) who used fMRI to examine monitoring of both enduring self-traits ("narrative" focus) and momentary experience ("experiential" focus) both in novices and in people trained in mindfulness. In the novices, experiential focus produced reductions in mPFC activity associated with a narrative focus. In the trained group, experiential focus produced more distinct and pervasive reductions in mPFC activity along with increased activity of a right lateralized network including lateral PFC as well as viscerosomatic regions including insula, secondary somatosensory cortex and inferior parietal lobule. Analyses of functional connectivity between regions showed also a strong correlation between right insula and mPFC activity in novices that was absent in the mindfulness group. These findings indicate a neural dissociation between two distinct forms of self-awareness, narrative self and immediate self, that are usually integrated but that can be separated via mindfulness training. Some might interpret the immediate self as similar to the core self. In any event, these findings cohere with suggestions (e.g., S. Gallagher, 2000) of the importance of deliberately examining the narrative mode of self while also providing useful investigation of the features of a more "present-centered" mode.

## SOCIAL CONSTRUCTIONISM

Orientations to the concept of self have also included social constructionism. According to social constructionism, the language we use is fundamental to construction and maintenance of self. A person's description of herself changes depending on whom she talks to. As she selects what to say she actively constructs a self in the context of the other. Hence, in this approach, the self is not a static entity but a dynamic process.

One prominent social constructionism theorist who has dealt with the self is Harré. According to Harré (e.g., 1989), subjective experiences of selfhood are founded on beliefs about personhood that are implicit in our language. For example, the words "I" and "me" suggest that each of us is represented by a coherent agency (the "self") that organizes our psychic life and causes our behavior. However, there is no such thing as an objective self. Concepts such as "self," "ego" and "mind" are hypothetical constructs that shape our psychological reality. Instead, according to Harré (e.g., 1995), what "I" actually does is specify a location for the acts performed by a speaker.

Similarly, J. Potter and Wetherell (1987) argue that the very experience of being a person, the kind of mental life one can have, perhaps even how we experience sensory information, are dependent on the particular representations of selfhood that are available in our culture. Since these differ from culture to culture, it follows that members of different cultures will experience being human ("selves") in different ways.

# Approaches to the Self: Philosophical Assumptions

What we have seen thus far are some key contributions of mainstream psychology to understanding the self. A range of different theories, research domains and philosophical orientations have been presented. A key aim of this chapter is to present the self as conceptualized in functional contextual psychology, a newly emerging orientation that differs at a fundamental philosophical level from mainstream approaches and whose analyses of phenomena including the self are starting to provide new insights. In order to explain this approach and its relation to other traditions, we start by examining philosophical assumptions.

## Worldviews

Scientific accounts, including those of psychology, are ultimately based on worldviews, which encompass philosophical assumptions (Pepper, 1942). Differences in worldview and thus basic assumptions can produce fundamental differences in approach. The novel approach to self being introduced here is based on the worldview of functional contextu alism, while the mainstream approaches discussed previously are based on alternative worldviews, including most prominently mechanism but also organicism and descriptive contextualism. In what follows we will consider a number of the key worldviews underlying different approaches to self and how differences in worldview influence differences in approach.

### MECHANISM

Mechanism is unquestionably the predominant worldview within science including psychology. Many of the most well known and influential approaches within psychology, including the predominant paradigm of cognitive science, are based on mechanist assumptions. All worldviews, including mechanism, are characterized by a root metaphor or commonsense way of understanding the world, and by a truth criterion, which is a method of distinguishing what counts as true. In the mechanistic worldview, the root metaphor is the machine; the world is like a machine made of parts and forces and the scientific task is to analyze the parts and forces to explain how the machine works. The truth criterion is correspondence between one's theory about the mechanism and empirically measured reality.

15

The archetypal example of mechanism in psychology is cognitive science, whose proponents tend to understand human behavior in terms of the metaphor of the human as information processor. For cognitive psychologists, for example, the scientific task is to develop increasingly accurate models of the mind as a machine that processes sensory input and puts forth output in the form of behavior. Cognitive neuroscientists generally share these assumptions but they additionally attempt to localize these processes in the brain.

One effect of the analytic character of mechanism is its tendency toward reductionism in which the action of the whole is explained by reference to the working of the parts. However, though such an approach is useful in some domains such as the physical sciences it is arguably not so useful in others such as psychology. The idea that human behavior might be wholly explainable in terms of neural processes provides one example of reductionism in the latter. The arguments against this include the suggestion that analyzing human behavior at the neural level can obscure rather than aid effective understanding and explanation of complex behavior, particularly if environmental influences, for example, are downplayed or omitted. We will return to this argument later.

With regard to the self, mechanistic theories have often seen it as an executive component of the mind, performing key processing functions with respect to information from the external world. The Northoff and Bermpohl (2004) theory of the self as multicomponent information processor constitutes an obvious example. This theory was one of a number discussed earlier which focused on locating a "core self," with the suggested idea of self as a core component of the information-processing machine, perhaps overseeing its operation. Other theories offered alternative conceptions of the role of self, suggesting, for example, that it is not an active executive overseeing processing, but might be a product of processing—an abstract representation of multiple sources of experiential information (e.g., Dennett, 1991). Despite such differences with respect to the importance of the self within the cognitive architecture, however, these different approaches still share mechanist assumptions. For instance, they share the assumption that objects worthy of investigation have an essential reality. To those concerned with the "core self," for example, the self is assumed to have an essence that the researcher needs to identify. For those who deny the reality of a core self, there are still essences that are worthy of study, but the self is simply not one of them.

The idea that the task of science is to uncover the essential nature of reality is an implicit feature not just of mechanism, but of a number of worldviews. Though it might seem an uncontroversial position, it is in fact not philosophically unproblematic. For instance, in order to verify whether theory and reality correspond one must have atheoretical access to ontological reality, which is argued to be impossible. There is also the pragmatic argument that this assumption adds nothing but can distract from the real and urgent task of solving pressing human problems. The latter is one that we will return to later in the discussion of contextualism.

## ORGANICISM

A second major worldview in psychology and one relevant to theory and research on the self is organicism. The root metaphor is the developing organism and the truth criterion is coherence between features of the account. This worldview has its origins in the rise of the biological (life) sciences, in which the study of the growth and development of organisms through various stages of the life cycle is a key focus.

With respect to the self, an organicist approach assumes that given the right conditions and minimal interference, it should develop in the same ordered, sequential manner in everyone. A number of the self-relevant developmental theories reviewed earlier note stages of development of the self (e.g., Flavell et al., 1978). Humanism also provides examples of organicist assumptions. In Rogerian theory, for instance, the self and self-concept are assumed to develop in close harmony if conditions of acceptance, empathy, and genuineness are provided; otherwise they will diverge and development will be suboptimal.

The truth criterion for organicism is coherence. It is assumed that the object of study invariably develops according to certain identifiable stages in an overarching pattern and that the scientific task is to accurately characterize the stages by identifying their order, timing of emergence and features to render a complete and coherent account. Theories of the self such as those of Flavell et al. (1978), for example, also clearly share these assumptions.

An implicit assumption within organicism, as in mechanism, is that the job of the analyst is to uncover reality. In organicism, the aim is to provide an account of the development of the object of study with complete coherence among all elements, with the assumption that there is one ultimately correct account. The problematic aspects of this ontological assumption that apply to mechanism also apply to organicism. In addition, the emphasis in organicism on normative stage-based development means that once regularities are discovered across members of a species with respect to a particular phenomenon then this may establish assumptions about the pattern of growth and discourage further work aimed at, for example, accelerating progress or suggesting alternative sequencing of stages.

By this point, we have reviewed mechanism and organicism as two major worldviews within psychology that have influenced theory and research on the self. The relatively novel approach to the self which is a key focal point of this book is based on an alternative worldview referred to as contextualism and more specifically, functional contextualism. The latter differs from alternative worldviews in at least one key way in that it orients scientific activity to the achievement of practical outcomes to an extent that others do not. In order to explain this assertion, we will first introduce contextualism and its two main varieties in psychology, namely descriptive and functional contextualism.

## CONTEXTUALISM: DESCRIPTIVE AND FUNCTIONAL

The root metaphor of contextualism is the event or act in context. From this perspective, act and context are inseparable; for example, according to Biglan (1995):

> [A]n act in context is initially experienced as a whole; the behavior of the person and the context are fused. The very quality of the act is a function of its context. Going to the store is different from going to the bank; raising one's hand to get attention is different from raising it in the act of stretching. (p. 32)

The truth criterion of contextualism is successful working; if a theoretical explanation of an act or event allows us to achieve a predetermined goal then it is true, otherwise not. This has a number of important implications. One is that contextualism, in contrast with other worldviews discussed is aontological; truth does not depend on uncovering the nature of reality. A second is that there can be as many varieties of contextualism as there are predetermined goals. In psychology there are two main forms of contextualism, namely descriptive and functional (see e.g., Hayes, 1993), each with a different analytic goal.

The goal of descriptive contextualism is a personal understanding of psychological events. Achievement of such a goal is difficult to measure or share and thus basic questions arise regarding the possibility of scientific progress. The early theorists of the self, namely, James, Mead and Cooley, and the more recently arrived social constructionists have all been categorized as descriptive contextualists (Hayes, 1993) and indeed a consistent feature in all of these cases is the lack of progressive basic or applied research. This is consistent with the assumptions of descriptive contextualism but is not satisfactory for those psychologists who wish to achieve practical change. The latter tend instead to adopt the assumptions of functional contextualism.

The goal of functional contextualist psychology is prediction and influence of behavior. Hence, while it eschews along with descriptive contextualism the implicit pursuit of a correspondence between theory and ontological reality, in contrast with the latter its explicitly stated goals are decidedly pragmatic. In fact, the practically oriented truth criterion of functional contextualist psychology is a key feature of this approach which determines its unique character and wholly differentiates it from other approaches to psychology. In what follows we will first discuss functional contextualism in psychology, and show how its truth criterion differentiates it from alternatives. We will then present a brief overview of the functional contextualist approach to the self.

## FUNCTIONAL CONTEXTUALISM IN PSYCHOLOGY

From our perspective, behavior analysis represents functional contextualism in psychology. Both the root metaphor and truth criterion of the latter are inherent aspects of behavior analysis. The core behavior analytic unit, the operant, reflects the act in context, the root metaphor of contextualism. The stimulus and response in the operant are mutually codefining, since a particular response (e.g., walking to the shops) is always defined based on its stimulus consequences (e.g., reaching the shops), while a consequence is defined as such only in relation to the response. Hence, act and context are inseparable, a key feature of the contextualist worldview. The truth criterion of contextualism, namely, successful working toward a particular goal, is also explicitly behavior analytic. Skinner (1974) suggested that "[scientific knowledge] is a corpus of rules for effective action and there is a special sense in which it could be true if it yields the most effective action possible" (p. 235); furthermore, he stated that the goal of behavior analysis was "to predict and control the behavior of the individual organism" (1953, p. 35), indicating that it is functional contextualist.

The pragmatically oriented functional contextual character of behavior analysis based on its explicitly adopted goal of prediction and influence is the key to understanding how this approach differs from others within psychology. Whereas behavior analysis requires practical intervention as a sine qua non of truth, approaches based on alternative assumptions do not, and this makes the theoretical explanations provided by each very different. For example, one important difference is in relation to mentalism. In a mentalistic explanation, the cause of behavior is attributed to a mental state; for example, "she gave up due to low self-esteem." From a behavior analytic perspective, adequate explanations of behavior must include manipulable environmental variables to allow for behavioral intervention. A mentalistic explanation such as just provided is inadequate because the cause of behavior is attributed solely to a mental state that cannot be directly manipulated, leaving no possibility of intervention (e.g., Hayes & Brownstein, 1986). Thus, for behavior analysis this explanation is ruled out. However, because alternative approaches based on mechanism or organicism do not require the possibility of behavioral intervention they do not rule out such explanations.

In relation to the self, for instance, this has often been conceptualized historically as a unified conscious agent causing behavior. This is a classically mentalistic and indeed dualistic conception that has influenced modern scientific conceptions, at least implicitly. For example, mechanistic cognitive science has often seen the "core self" as an executive overseer and instigator of mental activity (e.g., Northoff & Bermpohl, 2004). Though this approach is more sophisticated than the dualistic idea of self as a conscious agent directing behavior, nevertheless self is still a key yet nonmanipulable causal variable. The self as conceptualized within organicist humanism is neither conscious agent nor executive. For example, Polkinghorne (2001), refers to a "natural tendency or force [actualizing] the fullness of an individual's personhood"; nevertheless, here also, the self is a nonmanipulable variable.

What behavior analysis describes as mentalistic explanation is acceptable within mechanistic cognitive science because truth in the latter is satisfied by predictive verification alone. Mentalistic explanations which ascribe causal influence to an executive self are acceptable because they allow prediction even while inadequate for purposes of intervention. Another philosophically based difference between behavior analysis and cognitive science is the relative acceptability of reductionist analysis. The latter fits with the analytic character of mechanism, in which the parts are primary and the whole is derived. Thus, in cognitive science, the self is often explained as a part of the organismic machine, whether as executive overseer or as product of information processing. Furthermore, sometimes the self is further broken down into subprocesses (e.g.,

Northoff & Bermpohl, 2004). From a contextual behavior analytic perspective, however, reductionist analysis is typically seen as inappropriate. In contextualism, the whole is primary and the parts derived and thus contextualist analyses of behavior, whether self-related or otherwise, remain at the level of the whole organism. Furthermore, given the truth criterion of behavioral influence, reductionist analysis per se is of no benefit and even subordinated to the goal of behavioral influence; it may be less useful than analysis at the whole organism level.

The pragmatic truth criterion of behavior analysis also leads it to reject the organicist emphasis on stage-based maturation. From the behavioral perspective, it may sometimes be useful to group correlated response patterns (e.g., in childhood). However, too rigid an emphasis on stages including such features as timing and sequence may inhibit exploration of and intervention vis-à-vis the behavior-environment relations causing the patterns seen.

Finally, the functional contextualist roots of behavior analysis also distinguish it from approaches to self based on descriptive contextualism (e.g., social constructionist theory). Descriptive contextualist approaches seek subjective understanding of self as opposed to prediction-and-influence with respect to self-relevant behavior; hence, they tend to be more philosophical than scientific in their approach. This contrasts sharply with approaches based on each of the other paradigms discussed, including behavior analysis, which, in service of its goal of behavioral influence, advocates empirical scientific research as the most efficient means to discover effective and comprehensive methods for intervention.

# A Behavior Analytic Approach to Self

Having thus discussed behavior analysis as a form of functional contextualism and compared it in this respect with other theories based on alternative paradigms, in the following section we introduce the behavior analytic approach to the self. Particular elements of this approach will be laid out in much greater detail in later chapters in the current volume. However, in the current chapter a broad overview will be given, to introduce the current conception and allow comparison with the approaches to self discussed previously.

## Self as Responding to Own Responding

Initial conceptions of the self within behavior analysis (see chapter 2 of the present volume) have focused on the core idea of responding to one's own responding. The archetype of this approach was provided by Skinner (1974) who wrote:

> There is a difference between behaving and reporting that one is behaving or reporting the causes of one's behavior. In arranging conditions under which a person describes the public or private world in which he lives, a community generates that very special form of behavior called knowing (pp. 34–35).

This concept, which has been empirically modeled in nonhumans (e.g., Lattal, 1975) provides an important foundation for a behavioral approach to self; however it is not enough. A second key element is that the discrimination of one's own responding must be a verbal discrimination; in other words, it must involve language.

## Relational Frame Theory

A functional contextualist approach to language known as relational frame theory (RFT; Hayes, Barnes-Holmes, & Roche, 2001) has been used to extend and transform the concept of responding to one's own responding to provide a more complete account of self. RFT explains language in terms of learned patterns of relational responding referred to as relational frames. The latter are forms of contextually controlled operant behavior that people learn through multiple exposures to interactions with their native language community in which these patterns feature. Learning to relate names and objects as the same as each other is perhaps the earliest and most basic type of framing; in this case, in the presence of contextual cues such as "name of," children learn to relate particular sounds to particular objects. Many other frames are learned subsequently, such as, for example, opposition (e.g., "Day is opposite of night"), comparison (e.g., "An elephant is bigger than a mouse") and deictic (e.g., "I am here, but you are there") and there is an increasing quantity of empirical evidence showing that these patterns of framing can be established and influenced (e.g., Dymond & Barnes, 1996; Roche & Barnes, 1997; Steele & Hayes, 1991).

Despite their diversity, all relational frames involve three defining features. (i) *Mutual entailment* refers to the fact that a relation in one direction between two stimuli entails or automatically gives rise to a second relation in the opposite direction. For example, if a verbally able child is given two previously unknown foreign coins and told that coin 1 is worth more than coin 2, then she may derive that coin 2 is worth less than coin 1. In other words, the first relation entails the second one and this works whichever is trained first (i.e., it is mutual). (ii) *Combinatorial entailment* involves the combination of two relations to form a third. For example, given three foreign coins, if coin 1 is worth more than coin 2, and coin 2 is worth more than coin 3, then coin 1 can be derived as worth more than coin 3, and coin 3 as worth less than coin 1. (iii) *Transformation of function* is extremely important as regards the psychological relevance of relational framing since it is the key process according to which language can influence our behavior. In technical terms, if two stimuli, A and B, participate in a relation, and one stimulus (e.g., A) has a psychological function, then under certain conditions the stimulus functions of B may be transformed in accordance with that relation. For instance, imagine a young child has previously experienced buying candy in the store using a particular coin. Through basic conditioning processes (i.e., association with access to candy) coins of this particular type have acquired an "appetitive" function (i.e., they are desirable). If the child is then shown two novel coins and told that a new coin is worth more than the first and is then given a choice as to which she wants, then she will likely choose the new one, despite the desirability of the original coin and the fact that she has had no experience with the new one. This is because the psychological functions of the new coin have been transformed through comparative relations such that it is now more appetitive (desirable) than the original one. It bears repeating that this transformation of functions effect is crucial in explaining the effect of language on behavior.

From an RFT perspective, once the individual begins to relationally frame through her interactions with the socioverbal community, she will thereafter continue to elaborate the network of stimuli that are framed for her and thus the functions of her environment will be transformed in increasingly complex and diverse ways. Thus, the world becomes increasingly verbal and she can never "escape" from language unless under very unusual circumstances. Naturally, even her own behavior becomes part of this network of relationally transformed stimuli and indeed, given how much access she has to it both directly through her own experience as well as through the reflection of that experience by other members of the verbal community, verbally responding to her own responding will become a core aspect of her world. Verbal responding to one's own responding is how the self is conceptualized from a functional contextualist behavior analytic perspective. This conceptualization reflects important aspects of mainstream theories but also, by facilitating research and intervention, represents an important advance both theoretically and empirically on those previous approaches.

## A Preliminary RFT Model of Self

Dymond and Barnes (1994) provided the first empirical demonstration of the RFT model of self. The initial part of the study involved establishing contextual control over relations of coordination (sameness) between arbitrary nonsense syllable stimuli. The stimuli used and relations thus established may be represented this way: A1-B1-C1, A2-B2-C2, A3-B3-C3. Empirically established and controlled coordinate relational responding has been extensively studied and is typically referred to as "stimulus equivalence." The demonstration of the model required a number of additional critical elements. Participants were trained to emit two self-discrimination responses on two time-based schedules of intermittent reinforcement. If they did not make a response then choosing B1 was reinforced whereas if they made at least one response then choosing B2 was reinforced. Subsequently they were tested for transformation of the functions of stimuli coordinately related to B1 and B2, respectively, namely, C1 and C2, such that if no response was emitted then choose C1, whereas if at least one response was emitted then choose C2. All four participants showed the predicted transformation of functions, thus providing a basic empirical model of verbal self-discrimination. Subsequent studies showed transformation of self-discrimination functions via additional frames, namely, comparison (more / less) and opposition (Dymond and Barnes, 1995, 1996).

## Verbal vs. Nonverbal Self-Discrimination

The RFT perspective on human self-awareness is that the person is "not simply behaving with regard to his behavior, but is also behaving verbally with regard to his behavior" (Hayes & Wilson, 1993, p. 297). The above studies showed transformation of self-discrimination functions via relational frames and thus provide simple models of verbal self-knowledge, or the symbolization or description of one's own behavior, which is the core of the RFT approach to self. In one sense this approach reflects traditional theories of self which suggest the importance of self-description but in another it advances beyond those theories in a key way by allowing empirical modeling of this process at a basic level.

From a theoretical perspective, verbal self-knowledge via relational framing is a two-edged sword. It can be important and beneficial to human beings while it can also be a cause of pain and suffering (e.g., Hayes & Gifford, 1997). Verbal self-knowledge is potentially important because a verbal description of one's own behavior, and especially the contingencies controlling it, can alter relevant behavioral functions. For example, in developmental tests of delayed gratification, young children are typically told that they can have one edible reinforcer (e.g., candy) immediately or two if they wait for several minutes. RFT would suggest that a sufficiently verbally advanced child might relationally frame this situation in accordance with IF...THEN frames such that "waiting" is co-ordinately framed with "more" while "not waiting" is framed with "less." This may make it more likely that they wait. Alternatively, imagine a child who takes the smaller amount anyway. Their capacity to describe their own behavior and to compare it with the alternative (e.g., "I didn't wait and now I have less than I could have gotten") may well make the edible less reinforcing through transformation of function.

This analysis suggests the verbal processes that may be involved in self-regulation of behavior. The analysis is consistent with the Skinnerian idea that "a person who has been 'made aware of himself' by the questions he has been asked is in a better position to predict and control his own behavior" (Skinner, 1974, p. 35). However, RFT argues that this is true only to the extent that a person is verbally self-aware through relational framing with regard to his own behavior. Nonverbal self-awareness should not allow for self-regulation as described here.

Verbal self-knowledge can also be a cause of suffering. The bidirectionality and transformation of functions that characterize relational framing mean that verbal reports (e.g., spoken descriptions or even simply thoughts) of past painful events that one has experienced can themselves be painful. In the case of someone who has experienced a traumatic event, for example, a description of the event is in coordinate relations with the event itself and thus negative functions of the latter will transfer to the description. This is painful, yet it can also be useful to deliberately engage in description of such experiences since it can help decrease the aversiveness of stimuli connected with that event (e.g., cars for someone who has been in a car accident) and thus facilitate psychological recovery. This is the basis of a variety of psychotherapeutic techniques such as desensitization.

The distinction between verbal and nonverbal self-discrimination is simply a starting point for what is in fact a multilevel analysis of the phenomenon of the self. As the child's verbal repertoire develops through interactions with their socioverbal environment, they are taught to respond in accordance with a repertoire of deictic relational frames that builds on their ability to verbally discriminate behavior and which provides the basis for perspective taking (PT), described next.

## Perspective Taking

Relational frame theory argues that learning to respond in accordance with deictic frames is a core part of the development of self. The three key deictic frames are I-YOU, HERE-THERE and NOW-THEN (see, e.g., Hayes, 1984). These frames are unlike most others in that they seem not to have formal or non-arbitrary counterparts. Frames of coordination and difference, for example, are based, respectively, on physical sameness and difference. However, deictic frames cannot be traced to physical dimensions; though physical properties will be involved in any particular instance of deictic framing, they are incidental to the relational pattern (for example, the words "here" and "there" are typically used with respect to specific physical locations, but the physical features of those locations are irrelevant with respect to the appropriateness of the use of the words). Hence, these frames must be taught through demonstration and multiple exemplars of the relational pattern, without reliance on formal properties. According to D. Barnes-Holmes, Hayes, and Dymond (2001), "[a]bstraction of an individual's perspective on the world, and that of others, requires a combination of a sufficiently well developed relational repertoire and an extensive history of multiple exemplars that take advantage of that repertoire" (pp. 122–123). In the course of interactions with the verbal community, the child will gradually learn to appropriately respond to and ask questions such as the following: "What are you doing here?", "What am I doing now?", "What will you do there?", and so on. The physical environment in which such questions are asked and answered will differ across exemplars, but the required relational patterns of I-YOU, HERE-THERE and NOW-THEN will be consistent and, thus, as in the case of the learning of other relational frames, these patterns will be abstracted over time.

There is evidence that PT frames develop over time (e.g., McHugh, Barnes-Holmes, & Barnes-Holmes, 2004a). Furthermore, evidence of the development of PT skill demonstrated by studies such as McHugh et al. is broadly consistent with that shown by researchers operating under the rubric of ToM (see e.g., Baron-Cohen, Tager-Flusberg, & Cohen, 2000), the most well known mainstream account of PT ability. Thus, here again, evidence from the contextual behavioral approach to an important psychological phenomenon parallels that provided by a mainstream account. At this point, the reader may wonder why the ToM account, if it is relevant to the development of the self, was not presented earlier in the context of other mainstream approaches; however, in fact, this account is not explicitly connected with the self in this way. It is only in the context of the RFT approach, in which the development of PT is seen as critical to the construction of self, that ToM research is seen as directly relevant. This is one important contribution of RFT. Furthermore and as with other domains, the pragmatic foundations of the former allow it to progress beyond the predictive models of the mainstream account in order to positively influence psychological development. With regard to PT, for example, a number of more recent studies have demonstrated that deictic frames can be trained in young children (e.g., McHugh, Barnes-Holmes, & Barnes-Holmes, 2004; Heagle & Rehfeldt, 2006).

According to RFT, once the deictic frames of I-YOU, HERE-THERE and NOW-THEN are established in a person's behavioral repertoire they become an inherent property of most verbal events for that person. In this account, when an individual talks to another person, it is from the perspective of I located HERE and NOW about events occurring THERE and THEN. Even in the context of the simple greeting "How are you?" for example, I am asking HERE and NOW about the situation of YOU (the listener) located THERE (a few feet away) and THEN (when you reply). The same analysis applies to situations in which I talk to myself. If I criticize myself with the statement "That was stupid," after making a mistake, for example, then I, HERE and NOW am judging myself THERE and THEN (making the error). In summary, deictic frames establish a constant division between the speaker, who is always HERE and NOW and the spoken about, which is THERE and THEN.

# The Three Selves

RFT also suggests that, in combination with an extended relational repertoire, PT framing can establish three functionally different types of self: (i) self as the *content* of verbal relations (the conceptualized self); (ii) self as an ongoing *process* of verbal relations (the knowing self); and (iii) self as the *context* of verbal relations (the transcendent self) (Hayes, 1995).

## THE CONCEPTUALIZED SELF

Self-as-content, or the conceptualized self, consists of elaborate descriptive and evaluative relational networks that a person constructs about themselves and their histories over time. As soon as verbal humans become self-aware, they begin to interpret, explain, evaluate, predict, and rationalize their behavior. They organize these descriptions and evaluations of their own histories and tendencies into a coherent network; a consistent presentation of a "self" that generally persists across time and situations.

The conceptualized self is well-elaborated, touching on every verbally known aspect of life and integrating self-knowledge of one's current and historical feelings, sensations, preferences, abilities, thoughts, interactions, learning; in fact, all of one's conscious experiences. It is also multilayered, since contingencies support different depths of self-knowledge in different contexts. For example, a person might explain a given instance of behavior to his boss in a very different way than he would explain it to his therapist. Also, the way he might present himself or even think of himself might be very different with different people (e.g., friends, family, work colleagues) based on differences in history with different individuals.

Self-evaluations are always made HERE and NOW about our behaviors that occur THERE and THEN. However, we rarely attend to the process of interpreting and evaluating as it happens in the present moment. Difficulties occur when products of relational responding (e.g., thoughts, judgments, comparisons, beliefs) are treated as objectively true and inherent aspects of the real world, a process referred to within the contextual behavioral based psychotherapy of ACT (acceptance and commitment therapy; e.g., Hayes, Strosahl, & Wilson, 1999) as *cognitive fusion*. This can be problematic when self-evaluations come to appear as historically rooted and unchangeable; our stories may become rigid and ossified and no longer simply describe our past behavior, but also guide our future behavior in directions that maintain the coherence of the story. This may result in our ignoring or discounting contradictory evidence, selectively attending to and amplifying confirmatory evidence, and acting in ways that are consistent with our story about who we are and how we came to be that way.

Conceptualized self-stories can lay a trap in that they can appear to explain the causes of a person's past behavior. A person might say things like, "I failed that exam because I'm stupid," or "I didn't get out of bed today because I'm depressed." This kind of reasoning, though common, can create a self-amplifying feedback loop where one seems to lose the ability to change what one does, because what a person does is who they are and who they are is what they have done in their past. This implies that the only way to change the future is to change the past, which is impossible, and thus this line of thinking can effectively lock a person into a verbal cage of their own making. Fusion with a conceptualized self may thereby maintain dysfunctional patterns of behavior. Indeed, empirical evidence suggests that this is the case, since persons who feel they have good, sensible reasons for being depressed have poorer responses to empirically validated treatments for depression (Addis & Jacobson, 1996).

## THE KNOWING SELF

Self-as-process, or the knowing self, is the ongoing, verbal discrimination of psychological events as they occur in the moment. Statements that reflect the self as a process of knowing typically begin with phrases such as "I feel," "I think," and "I wonder." The knowing self feeds the conceptualized self (e.g., in order to know that "I am a depressed person," I must first know that I frequently feel sad and have low energy across many contexts) and is also necessary to contact a transcendent sense of self-as-context, since a self-monitoring repertoire is required to observe the observer.

The knowing self is extremely useful in behavioral regulation both for the socioverbal community as well as for the individual themselves. Regarding the former, it allows other members of the verbal community to predict an individual's behavior without knowledge of the individual's learning history. For example, if a person says that she feels anger toward another then this may allow other people to predict how she might act toward that person in particular contexts. Self-as-process is also critical in the psychological development of the individual themselves. In order to respond effectively to one's own responding, one must first be aware of the response and its impact. For example, understanding and responding to my thoughts and feelings about other people's behavior in a fluid and flexible manner is critical in the context of establishing personal relationships. Hayes et al. (2001) describe the importance of self-as-process as follows:

> The reason that [self-as-process] is important is that much of our socialization about what to do in life situations is dependent upon this verbal process. Emotional talk is perhaps the clearest example. While conditions, such as anger, anxiety, or sadness, are quite varied in the histories that give rise to them, they are quite similar in the social implications that are verbally related to them... [I]ndividuals who are not able on an ongoing basis to describe and categorize their own behavior...have no way of relating their socialization about what to do in life with the highly individualized and changing circumstances in which they find themselves. (p. 127)

Self-rules would also be much less effective without self-as-process. From the RFT perspective, self-rules are an important topic because verbal humans likely produce vast numbers of self-directed rules that guide their behavior every day. Some are simple and trivial (e.g., "I should take a left turn at the shop"), while others are complex and profound (e.g., "I must do something meaningful with my life"); however, the effect of self-rules is undoubtedly significant. Self-rules are relevant with respect to both self-as-content as well as self-as-process. In regard to the former, for example, a person may prescribe a rule for himself based on his concept of himself (e.g., "I won't bother applying for courses in that area because I'm not intelligent enough to pass them"). However, self-rules produced on the basis of self-as-process are particularly important because they guide individuals' behavior in an ongoing way in potentially important life situations. Such rules might include the appropriate way to act in the presence of particular feelings in particular contexts (e.g., affection with an intimate other) and might be relatively useful (e.g., allowing oneself to be more open to one's feelings) or potentially disadvantageous (e.g., avoiding deep feeling).

Threats to the development of a knowing self include inadequate training by the verbal community, such as when awareness and expression of emotions, thoughts, and sensation are punished, ignored, denied, or contradicted. This is frequently observed in the case of child neglect or abuse. A neglected child may not learn to accurately describe sets of emotions and sensations he experiences as "hunger" or "boredom" or "fatigue" if there is no one to ask questions and teach him to label these experiences in a way that allows him and others to respond to these experiences effectively. Similarly, a child who experiences pain and fear at the hands of her mother and is met with the response, "Mommy loves you and would never do anything to hurt you," may not learn to accurately predict or describe her psychological experience.

Weak self-knowledge may also be the result of experiential avoidance, or the tendency to avoid or escape from difficult psychological events even when doing so results in negative consequences. As suggested previously, self-knowledge of aversive events is itself aversive, which means that humans cannot always avoid or escape pain situationally. Since we can't escape our own psychological experience, we attempt to avoid awareness of the experience. Chronic experiential avoidance of this nature results in difficulty observing and describing one's thoughts, emotions, and sensations (e.g., alexythymia, anhedonia, amotivation) that is characteristic of such psychological disorders as depression, post-traumatic stress disorder, and borderline personality disorder.

Other difficulties linked to deficits in the self-as-process repertoire include an inability to persist in or change focus (e.g., attention disorders, obsessive self-focus leading to phobic anxiety), the dominance of a conceptualized past and future whereby the present moment is lost to worry and rumination (e.g., anxiety and depression), and the dominance of framing events in terms of judgments about their affective relevance to self (e.g., narcissism, depression, anxiety, personality disorders).

## THE TRANSCENDENT SELF

Self-as-context, or the transcendent self, is the invariant in all self-discriminations. If someone answers many different questions about themselves and their behavior then the only aspect of their answering that will be consistent across time is the context from which the answer is given, that is, "I, HERE and NOW." Since self-as-context is an abstraction from the content of verbal responding it is "content-less" and thus constant and unchanging from the time it first emerges. It is itself a product of verbal responding yet as a verbal category which applies to everything that a person has ever done it incorporates both the nonverbal self (as behavioral stream resulting from direct psychological processes) as well as the verbal self (as both object and process of knowledge gained through relational framing) and can thus provide the experiential link between nonverbal and verbal self-knowledge.

Self-as-context is often referred to as the transcendent self, because it is difficult to describe or contact verbally, even though it is a product of relational framing. It cannot be experienced as an object because experiencing it would necessitate adopting a perspective on it that was not one's own perspective, which is impossible. Hence, it is not thing-like and thus can be described as limitless, unchanging, and ever-present. For these reasons, it is often linked with spiritual and religious concepts and experiences.

The self-as-context has important implications for how humans experience and regulate psychological pain, since this sense of self is not threatened by aversive content in the way that the conceptualized or knowing self can be. It allows a person to confront deep emotional pain and facilitates willingness, compassion, and intimacy.

A weak self-as-context repertoire results in a variety of social and psychological problems, including an unstable identity or sense of self (as seen, for example, in borderline personality and dissociative disorders), fear of annihilation in the face of aversive private experiences, difficulties with intimacy or connecting with others, social anhedonia, stigma or objectification of others, and a lack of empathy or self-compassion.

## The Three Selves and Other Perspectives

Thus, we have described three different "selves" that are distinguished within the current approach. How do these concepts compare with approaches to self seen within alternative psychological approaches?

The conceptualized self corresponds to the "me" or "empirical self" of William James, the self-concept of humanistic psychology (e.g., C. Rogers, 1961) and the narrative self of S. Gallagher (2000) or Dennett (e.g., 1991). In addition, the suggestion that psychological problems can result when the conceptualized self becomes rigid and guides behavior in unhelpful ways has important similarities with the humanistic concept of incongruence, whereby the self-concept diverges from the "true" self and causes psychological maladjustment. In contrast with humanistic and other approaches, however, the current approach offers environmentally based explanations of the early origins of self and of self-related psychological maladjustment in adulthood that can facilitate research and intervention to an unmatched degree.

Many religious and psychotherapeutic traditions stress the importance of self-as-process as a means of achieving openness, sensitivity or wholeness. One of the aims of a therapeutic relationship, for example, is to help the person "get in touch with their feelings" or, in RFT terms, to establish framing with respect to emotional terms that coordinate with those in operation in the human verbal community more widely. This emphasis on the knowing self was originally confined to the humanistic psychology movement but it has become recognized as important by other therapeutic (e.g., CBT) and nontherapeutic (e.g., I/O) approaches within psychology also.

Evidence from neuroscience supports the self-as-concept versus self-as-process distinction. Recall that Farb et al. (2007), discussed earlier, for example, found evidence for two neutrally distinct, but habitually integrated forms of self-reference. The narrative (conceptualized) self, which integrates experiences across time (NOW-THEN) and place (HERE-THERE) from a single perspective ("I") was described by Farb et al. as a higher order mode of self-reference that may be overlearned and made automatic through practice. Meanwhile, the experiential self (self-as-process) which was derived from neural markers of transient body states was a more basic mode of momentary self-reference characterized by neural changes supporting awareness of the psychological present.

It has already been suggested that the phenomenon of self-as-context is related to spiritual and religious experience. Within psychology, a concept that is directly relevant is peak experience. The latter, which has been described within humanistic and transpersonal psychology, is characterized by participants as mystical, revelatory and personally illuminating. Humanistic psychological perspectives describe an increase in frequency and quality of such experiences as an important characteristic of self-actualization (e.g., Maslow, 1964). In addition, more recently, proponents of transpersonal psychology (e.g., Wilber, 1997) have advocated the deliberate exploration of such experiences to enable continuing psychological development. Such experiences are interpreted by the current approach as temporary experiences of pure "content-less" self-as-perspective. Thus, the nature and origins of this experience are explained as a product of perspective-taking processes that are themselves forms of (deictic) relational learning. Thus, this approach can provide a bottom-up understanding of peak experience and other forms of "revelatory" insight and also of the types of practice that can contribute to reaching self-as-context including mindfulness for example. In relation to the latter, there is increasing empirical evidence both at a basic scientific level (e.g., Farb et al., 2007) as well as via practitioner research (e.g., J. Miller, Fletcher, & Kabat-Zinn, 1995) that mindfulness is a practice that can promote psychological health as well as providing the basis for increasing insight into one's psychological processes. From the current perspective, mindfulness involves deliberate ongoing responding in accordance with "self as process" which strengthens the operant of taking perspective on one's own behavior as well as weakening the functional context for fusion with the kinds of ongoing thoughts that might otherwise simply become part of the increasingly expansive self-as-content relational network. Both these processes make the temporary content-less perspective of self-as-context more likely. What is perhaps particularly important about descriptions such as this is that they involve specification in empirically supported technical terms of the processes involved in mindfulness and self-as-context in a way that can facilitate further research into and refinement of these concepts, which is arguably unique to the current approach.

## Conclusion

This approach to self both shows similarities with traditional approaches as well as contributing unique insight into self-development. For example, with respect to the initial development of self-awareness, the current approach agrees with previous accounts on the importance of discriminating self-behavior from other aspects of the environment; however, it is unique in highlighting and empirically modeling the verbal dimension of this self-discrimination. The current approach also agrees with alternative approaches that have suggested the importance of the subjective "I" (e.g., James, 1891a), and on the gradual development of levels of PT ability (e.g., Baron-Cohen et al., 2000); however, it is unique in suggesting that the construction of the subjective "I" happens as part of the development of PT ability and that the latter is based on the development of particular patterns of contextually controlled relational responding. As another example, the current approach agrees with the importance of such apparently ephemeral and difficult-to-capture concepts as "transcending the ego," but it provides a well-defined and bottom-up approach to understanding the development of the ability to do this.

Perhaps the most important and novel aspect of this approach however, is that, in accordance with its underlying philosophical assumptions, it specifies variables that facilitate prediction and influence over the development of appropriate self-descriptive behavior at each level of the analysis. Examples of such variables include, for example, contextual cues for relational responding (e.g., coordinate, deictic and analogical) and (typically social) reinforcement for accurate self-description at different levels of the development of self (for example, discrimination of self from environment, discrimination of self from other, and discrimination of content from context).

This key feature of the current approach means that it readily facilitates intervention with regard to self-related problems, whether in respect of the delayed development of self and PT in autistic populations, for example, or of self-related psychotherapeutic problems as treated by clinicians using acceptance and commitment therapy for instance. Furthermore, it allows ongoing research to refine theory and thus yield improved interventions. For example, the last several years in particular have seen a considerable quantity of empirical work on PT frames, both in terms of assessment and training of the basic frames in young children (e.g., Rehfeldt et al., 2007) and in terms of investigation of therapeutically relevant patterns of behavior such as empathy in adults (e.g., Vilardaga, Estevez, Levin, & Hayes, in press). An area with future potential is work on self-rules, for example, which both theory and empirical research suggest have a substantive effect on human behavior (e.g., Lowe, 1979). The current approach facilitates a functional conceptualization of self-rules and the way they can affect behavior and might thus afford a unique perspective on data obtained during talk-aloud procedures (e.g., Ericsson & Simon, 1993), for example.

In summary, based on its unique philosophical and theoretical underpinnings, the functional contextual behavioral approach has tremendous potential with respect to the psychology of the self. It shows agreement with previous mainstream approaches with regard to many key features of the self; however, it also provides a unique conception of this phenomenon characterized by novel theoretical and practical insights and, based on its close link with a vibrant program of empirical research, has the potential to become increasingly influential with respect to self-related theory and application in the future.

# Chapter 2

# Self in Behavior Analysis

Kennon A. Lattal *West Virginia University*

One's environment is a key to one's identity.

Soonmi ~451 (in *Cloud Atlas* by David Mitchell)

## Introduction

As in many other areas of psychology, self is a topic of interest in behavior analysis. Because definitions of self derive from assumptions about the determinants (i.e., the nature) of human behavior, there is no general agreement on its definition, a point confirmed by inspection of both psychological (e.g., English & English, 1958; Wolman, 1973) and general (e.g., Random House Dictionary of the English Language, 1966) dictionary descriptions of the term. Rather, self is more usefully given meaning by examining the conditions under which it is used within a particular psychological framework or worldview. This review considers conditions under which self is used in behavior-analytic conceptual analyses, methods, research, and application. In so doing, the review's broader goal of providing a behavior-analytic description of self will be achieved.

## Conceptual Analyses of Self

Self often is preceded by the article "the." This article, however, suggests that (a) self is an entity—a thing, a noun that often requires a definite article and (b) there is a single, all-encompassing "self." These same points are expressed in many formal definitions of the term. English and English (1958), for example, included the following under their definition of self:

> [i]n technical discussion two distinct concepts appear and reappear (and are too often confounded): (A) the self as the subject, the agent, the individual person, the living being; or as a specific part of that being; and (B) the self as the individual that is somehow revealed or known to himself (p. 485).

Parts of (A) at least imply that the self is not only an entity, but also an agent of behavior. Summarizing this view, Skinner noted that "[t]he organism behaves, while the self initiates or directs behavior" (1953, p. 284). As with many hypothetical constructs that are inferred from behavior, the self as an entity or an agent is suspect, or worse, in behavior analysis because it denigrates or ignores the environment as the source of control over behavior. Considered as a hypothetical construct, self often is reified, becoming an entity. Once reified, it too often becomes the cause—the agent—of behavior. This in turn results in the all-too-familiar problem of circularity and the creation of what Skinner (1953, p. 285) called an "explanatory fiction": evidence for the self is the observed behavior, which is then said or assumed to be caused by the very agent that the behavior defines.

Part (B) of English and English's (1958) definition suggests awareness or knowledge, or lack thereof, of one's actions or the consequences of one's actions. In this regard, Skinner observed that there "appear to be two selves acting simultaneously and in different ways when one self controls another or is unaware of the activity of another" (1953, p. 284). Self-awareness is an important parameter of self within behavior analysis, but, as will be shown below, it is addressed functionally, without the implicit dualism suggested by Skinner's analysis. Because Skinner was the first to do so, his analysis seems a logical starting point for considering self from the standpoint of behavior analysis.

## Skinner on Self

Skinner devoted two chapters to self in *Science and Human Behavior* and, later, another in *About Behaviorism*. His analysis in those chapters and in other writing precludes self as either an entity or an agent: "A person is not an originating agent. He is a locus, a point at which many genetic and environmental conditions come together in a joint effect" (1974, p. 168). Skinner's observation also implies historical causation, which is central to a behavior-analytic worldview. Such causation further obviates the need to posit internal, proximally contiguous causes of behavior such as selves.

Skinner does, however, speak of the same individual functioning as both speaker and listener. He discussed these functions in part under the topic of self-editing in *Verbal Behavior* (1957). In his analysis, the speaker composes verbal responses and then listens to them before they are manifest as overt verbal behavior. He suggested that covert speech is released (his word) when a subvocal trial run of the material does not generate conditioned aversive stimulation. Such stimulation would have been present had the speech been punished previously, leading him to conclude that the "speaker usually rejects a response because it has been punished" (p. 371). He went on to speculate that the effect of external punishment of verbal behavior is to cause it to drop "below the level of scope or energy at which it affects the surrounding world" (p. 376) so that the effect is that the speaker talks to himself. Skinner also addressed self-strengthening of verbal behavior, where other activities strengthen the speaker's verbal behavior with the effect of "increasing the supply of behavior to be composed and edited" (p. 403).

Later in his career, Skinner returned to the laboratory to consider what is meant by "having a self-concept." Epstein, Lanza, and Skinner (1981) first trained pigeons to peck a small blue sticker attached in random places on their bodies. Then each pigeon was trained to peck briefly on a blue dot of light only when they could see it in a mirror placed in the experimental space. When the blue sticker subsequently was placed in a location on the pigeon's body such that it could be seen only in the mirror, each pigeon pecked at the location of the sticker on its body. An infant's (Amsterdam, 1972) or chimpanzee's (Gallup, 1970) recognition of itself in a mirror has been offered as evidence of a nascent self. Epstein et al.'s experiment begged the question of what is meant by a self-concept, and also whether what is called a self-concept is cognitively and developmentally emergent or learned.

# Self-Awareness

## THE LANGUAGE OF SELF-AWARENESS

The terms awareness, consciousness, and mindfulness often are used interchangeably to describe aspects of a person's behavior under the control of other aspects of the same person's physiology, their behavior, or effects of such behavior on other people or things. A person often is said to be aware, mindful, or conscious of himself (though self-conscious has a double meaning in everyday use) or his actions. From a behavior-analytic perspective, two potential problems exist with these vernacular descriptions. The first is that the target is the person and not the person's behavior, as in someone who is "aware of herself." Such a description suggests the self as an entity of which the person is informed. Self-awareness as a state then may be considered a prerequisite for certain kinds of behavior. For example, good social skills sometimes are said to require an awareness of the effects of one's behavior on others, implying that self-awareness is a prerequisite for social competence. Like many other psychological terms (e.g., attention [Ray, 1969]), self-awareness is not a cause of behavior. Rather, it is simply a description of what many consider an important set of responses. In the example, self-awareness is an element of what are labeled "good social skills." The second problem with the descriptions of each of these terms is their accompaniment by the verb "to be." Using this verb also creates a state of awareness, consciousness, or mindfulness, or lack thereof, which in turn controls the behavior. The result can be the reification described previously.

These same terms, however, also can be used in a descriptive sense to label a person's behavior with respect to her own body, other behavior, or effects on the environment. Thus, in the case of humans to be mindful or aware of oneself means that some other response (typically, though not always, verbal) is under the discriminative stimulus control of one's own physiology, behavior, or effects on the environment, as when Epstein et al.'s (1981) pigeons responded to their own mirror images (see also Thompson, 2008).

## SELF-AWARENESS AS DISCRIMINATIVE STIMULUS CONTROL

Zuriff (1986, pp. 237–238) observed that a straightforward discrimination of the sort just described might be a direct response to a stimulus, without "awareness." He proposed self-awareness to be a second, higher-order, discrimination in which the first discrimination comes under the control of another (verbal) response. In his example, in the presence of an apple one might say "I see an apple." The higher-order response might be "I am aware that I see an apple" such that the second discrimination is or is not under the control of the first. This distinction, then, allows for situations where one might do something with or without awareness. To borrow further from Zuriff, eating an apple while awake likely might be reported as "Yes, I am aware I ate the apple." But, eating an apple while sleepwalking might be done without awareness, that is, by reporting that "I was unaware I ate the apple." Zuriff's two-level description of self-awareness is in effect a conditional discrimination—a four-term contingency—in which a discriminative stimulus controlling the response-reinforcer relation is itself brought under discriminative stimulus control.

## THE DEVELOPMENT OF SELF-AWARENESS

Used as described above, self-awareness implies that there is a history of reinforcement or punishment for accurately labeling controlling environmental antecedents or consequences of one's own behavior or one's own physiology. Such a history comes about "only after the society has reinforced verbal responses with respect to one's behavior as the source of discriminative stimuli" (Skinner, 1945, p. 551). One empirically investigated example of such a circumstance is correspondence learning. Risley and Hart (1968), for example, first allowed young children to play with different toys. Later, when the children were asked which toy they played with earlier, the accuracy of their reports was low. During an intervention condition, correspondences between the toy the child played with and her report of playing with that toy increased when such correspondences were followed by candy treats. Several variations of the procedure using different modalities and types of responses in the two phases (e.g., "saying" and "doing") suggest its generality (see review by Lloyd, 2002). Lattal and Doepke (2001) suggested that such correspondence may be considered a type of conditional discrimination where what one says or does serves as a discriminative stimulus for a subsequent report of the earlier activity. Just such a sequence of events is what is involved in self-awareness.

Skinner's (1945) analysis of how private events come to be identified involves the reinforcement of correspondence, and further suggests its role in the development of self-awareness. In the case of private stimuli, Skinner noted that appropriate verbal and nonverbal responses to such stimuli may be shaped by the differential reinforcement of successive approximations to an appropriate correspondence between the private event and the overt response to it. Thus, if a child has an earache, correspondence between the site and type of the pain and the verbal response is shaped. Thus, of the many verbal responses possible to the earache, the ones that are reinforced by others, and thus become more likely to occur, are those that correspond to the type of pain. Private stimuli, unlike external ones, cannot always be verified with precision. As a result, there typically is greater variability in the labeling of these stimuli than of external ones. In the case of self-awareness shaped in this way, the variability across people in "being attuned to one's body" may reflect different histories of correspondence learning. The expression "self-awareness" may be applied in the same way to external events, such as reinforcing correspondence between what one sees in their self and what others see. Being "aware of one's strengths and weaknesses" or of "the effect of one's behavior on others," for example, may be considered a description of the correspondence between present verbal or motor behavior and a prior history of successes and failures (that is, reinforcement and punishment) of different response classes.

## A CONTINUUM OF SELF-AWARENESS

The opposite of self-awareness is when a person is said to be unaware, unmindful, or unconscious (though unconscious also is used in other ways) of their physiology, their behavior, or effects of their behavior on the environment: colloquially, clueless. Used in the descriptive, behavioral sense already described for awareness, these terms also describe not a state, but the diminishment or absence of conditional discriminative stimulus control of the sort defining self-awareness. As Hineline put it, "acting unconsciously implies the absence of...a repertoire of self-description—no more, no less" (1984, p. 184).

Unconscious actions may have different antecedents. In some instances, it may be that the antecedents simply cannot be identified by the person behaving either because they lack the necessary reinforcement history to identify them or because the effect of the person's behavior could not be identified (that is, anticipated) at the time it occurred. Alternatively, behavior labeled unconscious may have such an extensive history of reinforcement that it becomes "automatic" and therefore not a source of discriminative control over verbal behavior. It is not uncommon at some point after such an act to not be able to report having done it (e.g., turning off a burner on the stove or locking the house door). Such behavior most likely once was tacted easily, but with an ever-growing history of such actions, the discriminative control of those actions over the verbal responses describing those actions diminishes and may even disappear. In this latter sense, the vernacular "acting unconsciously" can imply fluency.

## Self-Expression

Self-expression can refer to the unique aspects of a person's behavioral repertoire, things that distinguish the person from others. It is not the outward manifestation of a homunculus residing within the person, but rather it is behavior that is a function of the individual's unique behavioral history. Even contingencies that operate in common ways across individuals in a culture are structured such that variation is likely. A contingency typically specifies rather precisely the targeted response, but such precision in both laboratory and extra-laboratory settings leaves the remainder of the individual's repertoire free to vary. It is this repertoire that is unspecified and often unhampered by the specific contingencies on a particular response class, which is the wellspring of what is called self-expression. In the case of people, for example, social norms/contingencies dictate that clothes be worn in public. Beyond this minimal contingency, considerable variation in apparel is apparent. Even in situations where the contingency includes specification of the type of clothing, there often is latitude for the individual's unique history to be manifest. Handwriting, speech patterns, mannerisms, proclivities and idiosyncrasies that contribute to one's individuality and self-expression all develop where social and other contingencies specify a minimal response but leave other aspects of behavior to vary. Such variation is a treasure trove of individuation worthy of exploration and promotion in how behavior analysts talk about and respond to questions of self.

## Self and Behavior-Analytic Research Methods

Both general and psychological dictionary definitions of self include "individual" as part of the definition. The analysis of individual behavior is the hallmark of behavior-analytic research (e.g., Sidman, 1960). Regardless of whether individual and self are isomorphic, behavior analysts have methods that carry the self label.

## Self-Experimentation

Within the framework of a set of methods broadly concerned with behavior of the individual and nuances of individual differences in the control of behavior by contingencies, specific methods for self-experimentation have evolved. These methods are the logical extension of the focus on individual-subject behavior outlined above. They involve the individual as both subject and experimenter, arranging contingencies and delivering reinforcers while concurrently behaving according to those arranged contingencies. In a sense, self-experimentation also is a variety of self-reporting (see section on this latter topic below). Watson and Tharp (2006) described both general and specific methods for self-experimentation and Neuringer (1981; Roberts & Neuringer, 1998) further developed both the methods and rationale for it. The methods have found particular favor in the area of self-management/self-modification, which is a subarea of self-experimentation distinguished only by the application of self-experimentation methods specifically to behavior of social or personal significance to the individual.

Subject-as-experimenter raises questions about objectivity and consistency of implementation of procedures, expectancy effects, reliability of measurement, and generality of findings (the latter in part because the N usually is 1). Despite these limitations, self-experimentation has garnered a wide following both as classroom projects and more generally as a method for at least complementing other approaches in ameliorating problem behavior.

Neuringer's (1986) experiments both illustrate the utility of self-experimentation and suggest how some of the seemingly inherent limitations might be constrained. Neuringer asked the question of whether a human can respond randomly. To answer it, he attempted to enter randomly sequences of numbers into a computer. After several such entries, the computer compared his entries to a mathematical definition of randomness and provided feedback to Neuringer. Over time, his numerical selections became random, an outcome others had claimed was not feasible (e.g., Wagenaar, 1972). By using the computer to both record the data and determine/provide the feedback, two major tasks that are questionable in most self-experimentation tasks were made more transparent and objective.

## Self-Reporting

Self-reporting is used to obtain additional information over the course of an experiment and as a potential substitute for actual exposure to contingencies. With respect to the first use, the additional information may either corroborate or supplement "hard" data. Lane, Cherek, Lieving, and Tcheremissine (2005) investigated the effects of marijuana on human forgetting during a conditional discrimination task. In addition to obtaining physiological measures of the effects of the two dosage levels of the marijuana, each subject rated several statements related to its effects (e.g., "I feel a typical marijuana high"). The ratings of each item were significantly different from one another across control and drug conditions (see Hayes [1986] for a discussion of in situ self-reporting).

Self-reports have been used in other experiments as a nominal substitute for responding under the control of contingencies. In a typical procedure, a subject chooses between small-immediate and large-delayed rewards (e.g., Rachlin, Raineri, & Cross, 1991). Self-report sometimes is used instead of contingency exposure because the rewards under study can be prohibitively large (e.g., £1000) and the delays can be long (e.g., years). Johnson and Bickel (2002) compared choices between small-immediate and large-delayed rewards within individual subjects when the rewards (ranging from £6.50—£162.33) were either real or hypothetical. The delay was increased systematically from 0-s to 6 months. The resulting delay discounting functions were similar for both real and hypothetical rewards and the data from both were comparable to previous results obtained using nonhuman subjects. In the absence of evidence that self-reports of likely behavior are equivalent to what actually happens under the same contingencies, such data can only be regarded as a form of verbal behavior and not necessarily reflective of how the reporter actually might respond under the contingencies being probed.

---

# Self in Behavior-Analytic Research and Application

Self in contemporary behavior-analytic research and application functions as both a dependent and an independent variable. The most obvious example is self-control, where self-control is an index of behavior subject to influence by various environmental and physiological variables and, particularly in applied research and practice, where self-control techniques allow individuals to control their own behavior. Self-reporting also functions as a dependent variable, changing as a function of different environmental circumstances.

# Self in the Experimental Analysis of Behavior

### SELF-AWARENESS

In several experiments, various aspects of the organism's own behavior have been established as discriminative stimuli that controlled choice responses. Lattal (1975), for example, arranged a conditional discrimination task such that a sample key always the same color was associated on different trials with a requirement that a pigeon peck a response key once to produce a choice component. On other trials, withholding pecking the key for 10 s was required to produce the choice component. Once in the choice component, a peck on one of the colored keys was reinforced if a peck in the sample component had resulted in the choice component and a peck on the other colored key was reinforced if no response in the sample component had resulted in the choice component. Accuracy of greater than 85 percent was obtained by both pigeons used in the experiment. The results thus are consistent with Zuriff's (1986) suggestion, described above, that self-awareness might be the outcome of a first- and second-order discrimination and therefore also with Lattal and Doepke's (2001) suggestions about correspondence as a conditional discrimination. The pigeons' behavior first had to come under control of the two contingencies in effect in the sample component and then that behavior had to be tacted correctly for reinforcement to occur. Skinner (1953) observed that "the behavior which we call knowing is due to a particular kind of differential reinforcement" (p. 287). Experiments like Lattal's suggest at least that knowing about one's behavior in relation to other environmental events can be discerned even in nonverbal organisms when contingencies are appropriately arranged.

### SELF-CONTROL

In the experimental analysis of behavior, the analysis of self-control involves manipulating environmental and physiological variables that control choices of larger delayed reinforcers over more immediate smaller ones. In a seminal experiment by Rachlin and Green (1972), pigeons initially chose either a 1.5-s reinforcer available immediately after a peck to one of two available response keys or a 6-s reinforcer available only after a 6-s delay from the response selecting that alternative. The pigeons exclusively chose the immediate reinforcer until a lengthy period was introduced prior to allowing the choice. Under these conditions, preferences shifted to the delayed, larger alternative. Making the analogy even more precise, Grosch and Neuringer (1981) conducted a creative series of experiments with pigeons that paralleled Mischel's (1974) analysis of self-control in children, with similar results.

More generally, self-control is said to occur when a person engages in behavior in the short term that has no immediate consequence or that results in the short-term loss of reinforcers in favor of longer-term gain for such behavior. Simple examples including foregoing immediate pleasures such as eating an extra piece of a yummy dessert cake or remaining inside one's warm abode on a cold morning in favor of the longer-term gains, respectively, of weight control by resisting the temptation of the extra fat-and-cholesterol-riddled dessert or cardiovascular health by foregoing the warm abode and braving the cold to undertake that seven-mile run.

In ordinary use, constructs like self-control and willpower suggest that agents of the individual are conspiring or even competing with one another somewhere else, in one of those other universes of discourse, to control choices. The behavior-analytic alternative account is a historical one, in which one's prior history of reinforcement for weight or exercise control, established over an extended period, is responsible for the healthier choices. Similarly, the choice of the extra dessert or warm abode suggests to a behavior analyst not a weak self-agent, weak control over that agent, or a person who is not the "captain of their own ship," but either a different history of reinforcement or current circumstances controlling the other choices.

## SELF-REPORTING

Experimental analyses of self-reporting have focused on its function as a dependent variable, as a measure of how other environmental variables influence self-reporting. In a series of experiments, Critchfield (e.g., 1993) investigated self-reports "as behavior subject to the same fundamental influences as any other" (1993, p. 495). Humans first completed a delayed matching to sample (DMTS) task in which a sample stimulus array was presented briefly, followed by a delay interval that was followed in turn by the opportunity to choose between one of the stimuli in the preceding sample array and one or more distracter stimuli. Immediately after the choice, the subject was asked to self-report whether they made the correct choice or not. This in turn was followed by feedback indicating whether the choice was correct or incorrect. If the latter, further feedback was given as to whether the response was too fast or too slow. The number of sample and comparison stimuli appearing on each trial was manipulated across conditions. Self-report accuracy varied as a function of choice accuracy in the DMTS task, the number of stimuli comprising either array, and DMTS speed and accuracy. Such results reveal the self-report to be malleable, influenced by the environmental circumstances under which it is made. Self-reports thus investigated index environmental influences and not introspective reflection.

## Self in Applied Behavior Analysis

### SELF-CONTROL AND SELF-MANAGEMENT

Most research involving self-control in applied behavior analysis involves the implementation of procedures that treat it as an independent variable, where "the dependent variables are indices of other...behaviors, for example, time-on-task, teachers' ratings of classroom behavior, and creative writing skills" (O'Leary & Dubey, 1979, p. 449; Rosenbaum & Drabman, 1979; see also Dziadosz & Tustin [1982] for an example of self-control treated as a dependent variable in an application context). Designed to give the individual greater autonomy, self-control or self-management techniques include ones that focus on either antecedent events or consequences.

Self-management has both advantages and disadvantages relative to behavior management by others. It can influence behavior accessible only to the individual, target behavior missed by independent observers, promote generalization and maintenance of behavior change, and facilitate efficiency and effectiveness of the individual in group endeavors by distributing responsibilities for supervising and providing feedback among the group members (Cooper, Heron, & Heward, 2007). In addition, self-management has the potential benefit of continuous (24/7) maintenance of the intervention. The limitations of self-management have been discussed above and include lack of objectivity in assessing behavior, often no interobserver reliability of data, variability in implementing and maintaining contingencies, and lack of generality. Both advantages and limitations are taken into consideration when implementing and evaluating the following interventions involving self-management.

## SELF-MANAGEMENT OF ANTECEDENTS

This involves establishing or rearranging environments to minimize or maximize the likelihood of certain subsequent responses. It includes manipulating establishing or motivational operations as well as establishing stimulus control over behavior. In the former case, self-management might take the form of eating a filling but low-calorie snack prior to going out to dinner with friends at something like "The Stuffed Pig," a buffet-style restaurant notorious for its high-calorie dishes. In the latter, it might take the form of a dieter eliminating tempting food items from the home, in line with the old adage "out of sight, out of mind," or a student designating a specific space for work such that the space functions as a discriminative stimulus for writing or studying.

**Self-reporting.** Whether described as self-recording, self-observation, or self-monitoring, self-reporting may be considered a form of antecedent self-management in that there are a number of demonstrations of its effectiveness in changing behavior and then maintaining those changes (e.g., Broden, Hall, & Mitts, 1971). It is not difficult to imagine that producing a visual stimulus in the form of a graph of one's own behavior could function as a discriminative stimulus for further action toward bringing the line on the graph either up or down, depending on the desired direction of the behavior change. Nor is it unreasonable to speculate that visual evidence of progress toward one's goals might serve to reinforce further efforts along those lines. The maintenance of behavior once it has reached its targeted levels may be influenced similarly by visual evidence of success. It is as if the maintenance of a particular weight or a particular exercise regimen results in a sort of behavioral momentum that is enhanced by continued visual evidence of the success of the behavior management program.

**Self-instruction.** Self-instruction, like any other kind of instructional control, involves the presentation of verbal stimuli intended to exert control over behavior. The only differences are that the instructions are generated by the person whose behavior they are intended to control and, as with all self-management methods, they are more difficult to analyze. It is possible, however, to assess the effects of "instructions about self-instructions" on subsequent behavior. That is, in therapeutic situations, the person sometimes is given instructions about how to instruct themselves regarding the target behavior, and a functional relation thus can be constructed between the therapist's instruction and subsequent behavior change, with the inference that behavior change results from the self-instruction.

A lack of control of one's present behavior by past behavior can be an example of absentmindedness or, more precisely, absentminded behavior. Putting down one's reading glasses, coffee cup, or some tool and later not being able to find these items is a common experience of many people. One way of increasing mindfulness in such situations might be to create a discriminative stimulus by doing something like clearly verbally labeling the act of placing the object (e.g., "I am putting my glasses on the dresser") at the time of placement so that the stimulus later might be more likely to control returning to the object's location. Conceived in this way, mindfulness may be considered to be a function of self-instruction.

## SELF-MANAGEMENT OF CONSEQUENCES

When the behaver is concurrently the observer/arranger of his own consequences, those consequences are said to be self-determined. Both reinforcers and punishers, positive or negative, in principle can be administered in this way. In practice, the process often is trickier. As a result of the latter, self-reinforcement and self-punishment have both strong advocates and detractors. For brevity's sake, only self-reinforcement is reviewed, with the recognition that many of the same observations, pro and con, could be applied to self-punishment.

Bandura (1976) defined self-reinforcement as occurring when "individuals regulate their behavior by making self-reward conditional upon matching self-prescribed standards of performance" (p. 135). He suggested that self-reinforcement occurs in many human situations, emphasizing the autonomy of the individual in establishing both the behavioral criteria for administration, including the amount delivered and the conditions under which the reinforcer is to be administered. Despite enthusiasm for the concept in some circles (e.g., Bandura; Watson & Tharp, 2006), others have been more skeptical.

The Achilles' heel of the concept of self-reinforcement was stated succinctly by Skinner (1953), who observed that the "individual may at any moment drop the work in hand and obtain the reinforcement" (p. 238), thereby undermining the contingency between responding and the reinforcer. Goldiamond (1976) elaborated on Skinner's point by noting that with self-reinforcement there also is not independent assessment of whether the response met the self-established criterion for reinforcement. Watson and Tharp (2006) discussed having others dispense reinforcers in self-management interventions, but did not regard it as a necessity.

Catania (1975; cf. Skinner, 1953) distinguished between the self-reinforcement operation or procedure and the self-reinforcement process, inviting the question: even if self-reinforcement as a procedure is possible, is the behavior change attributable to the putative self-reinforcement? For example, social contingencies arising from peer pressure or expectancy could produce results that mimic the effects of reinforcement. From a treatment standpoint, the outcome would be the same, that is, a change in behavior in the expected direction; however, the behavioral mechanisms in the two examples are quite different.

## THE ETHICS OF SELF-MANAGEMENT

In aiding in the implementation of self-management programs, as with implementing any behavior change program, the behavior analyst must be alert to the fact that most behavior selected for change is contextual and multidimensional. In terms of the individual, the value of choosing exercise in the cold versus staying in a warm room, or low-calorie food over higher-calorie food must be tempered by other contemporary and historical contextual variables. For example, encouraging or reinforcing consuming low-calorie meals with a person suspected of having an eating disorder, exercise where there are physical contraindicators, or behavior that exacerbates preexisting conditions like obsessive-compulsive behavior raises ethical questions.

In terms of their broader implications for the science of behavior, the selection of programs for self-modification are best guided by the same guidelines for any intervention: choosing what to change, and when and how to change it are all important. Selecting behavior for change without regard for its significance to the individual not only is a waste of time, but also trivializes the science. Programs that produce meaningful change in meaningful behavior, however, enhance the individual in relation to many dimensions of self addressed in this review.

---

# Conclusion

Were a reader of this chapter approached by a lexicographer of psychological terms and asked for a succinct definition of self, to be included among definitions from other perspectives, what might the response be? Here is a possibility:

*Self:* 1. The collective repertoire of behavior (colloquially: the individual) resulting from a unique genetic and behavioral history. 2. A specific behavioral repertoire under stimulus control, such that multiple selves may be described. 3. A verbal response describing aspects of one's behavioral repertoire. 4. A dependent variable: the outcome of contingencies of reinforcement and punishment. 5. An independent variable: a potential source of control over an individual's behavior.

Self is a valid and useful behavior-analytic concept when defined in these ways. Like other concepts in psychology, self becomes confusing and loses its utility when it is stripped of its environmental context in an attempt to define it as an entity with an existence independent of the very circumstances that give rise to the term in the first place.

Injecting a "self" concept into the behavior-analytic worldview has both drawbacks and advantages. On the one hand, the use of vernacular terms is problematic (but inevitable) in many sciences, where technical meaning is obfuscated by the competing history of such everyday use. Furthermore, many lay terms and terms borrowed from other areas of psychology are not defined with sufficient precision to know exactly what is meant. So it is with "self," with its myriad everyday meanings and its varied use in other areas of psychology. Without careful clarification, invoking self in behavior-analytic description can be a catalyst for conceptual confusion.

On the other hand, such term-borrowing allows behavior analysis to address concepts that are used frequently in everyday life and to connect with other points of view within psychology. Discussions of self like the one initiated by this volume minimally allow behavior analysts to both clarify their own point of view and engage in dialogue with other points of view. Although there will be obvious differences in the definition and use of the term, as suggested by the proposed definitions above, common problems and common interests may not only clarify the meaning of concepts within a viewpoint, but also have heuristic value for all viewpoints involved in such dialogue. Selfishly, then, behavior analysis has as much to gain as to give by considering how such widely used psychological concepts as self are given meaning in both behavior analysis and other worldviews.

# Part 2

# Perspective Taking:
# Developmental and Clinical

# Chapter 3

# A Contemporary Functional Analytic Account of Perspective Taking

Louise McHugh *University College Dublin*

Ian Stewart *National University of Ireland, Galway*

Nic Hooper *University of Kent*

*"You never really understand a person until you consider things from his point of view—until you climb inside of his skin and walk around in it."*

Excerpt from *To Kill a Mockingbird* by Harper Lee

# Introduction

The ability to take the perspective of others and thus anticipate their beliefs and desires is central to our social lives (Epley, Morewedge, & Keysar, 2004). Three decades of psychological research have shown that this ability starts in early infancy and develops throughout childhood and beyond (Baron-Cohen, 1994; Gopnik & Slaughter, 1991). In recent years, a novel functional analytic account provided by relational frame theory (RFT) has started to provide new insights into this ability with applications in a number of important applied domains. The key aim of this chapter is to describe the empirical research underlying this RFT-based approach, and to link it with applied work described in other chapters in the current text. It will start by describing some traditional accounts of perspective taking (PT). It will then introduce the theoretical basis for the RFT account. Finally it will present a brief overview of key RFT-based research to date.

# Mainstream Approaches to Perspective Taking

## Selman

A prominent early approach to PT was provided by Robert Selman, who described a five-stage model of the development of this ability. According to Selman (1980; Yeates & Selman, 1989), children gradually develop the ability to discriminate their own perspective from those of others and to see the relationships between these potentially discrepant points of view. His research involved presenting children with "interpersonal dilemmas" and then asking them a range of related questions (e.g., "Does X know how Y feels about situation Z?"). Responses to the latter led him to construct a five-stage model of the development of "role-taking skills," the first stage of which begins to emerge around age three and the final stage in adolescence.

Selman's work in the area of interpersonal development led to increased interest in how PT could contribute to social development. However, this account was descriptive only; it did not attempt to explain how children could take the perspective of another. At the same time that Selman was describing his model, however, another approach to PT that did purport to explain this ability was also beginning to emerge. This was theory of mind, which has now become the dominant paradigm to conceptualize PT within mainstream psychology.

# Theory of Mind

The theory of mind (ToM) approach suggests that PT is based on an ability to mentally represent the mind (including beliefs, desires, intentions, emotions, etc.) of another. This concept initially appeared in Premack and Woodruff (1978) who investigated whether chimpanzees had a theory of mind that would allow them to understand human goals. Numerous related comparative studies have followed, most of which suggest that chimpanzees lack this understanding (D.C. Penn & Povinelli, 2007; Tomasello & Hermann, 2010). Some studies suggest some social understanding in chimpanzees that begins with the observation of others' behavior, similar to how this develops for humans (e.g., Okamoto, Tanaka, & Tomonaga, 2004); however, none have identified the development in chimpanzees or other nonhumans of more complex ToM abilities such as understanding of false beliefs (see e.g., Call & Tomasello, 2008, for a recent review).

## DEVELOPMENTAL RESEARCH

After emerging as an issue in the comparative domain, the phenomenon of ToM subsequently became a topic of intense interest in the human developmental domain, where its appearance in early life was investigated. Baron-Cohen and colleagues have suggested that there are five levels in the development of the attribution of information or mental states to the self and others that range from simple visual PT to predicting actions on the basis of false belief (Howlin, Baron-Cohen, & Hadwin, 1999). At level 1 (*simple visual PT*) the person acts consistent with the principle that different people can have different views of the same situation. At level 2 (*complex visual PT*) they realize that people can see things differently. Level 3 (*seeing leads to knowing*) is based on the principle that people only know things that they have seen (M. Taylor, 1988). At level 4 the person knows that actions can be predicted on the basis of true belief (Howlin et al., 1999). Finally, at level 5, they know that actions can be predicted on the basis of false belief and that it is possible that previous beliefs (held by oneself or others) could have been false.

An extensive quantity of research has been conducted into ToM abilities in children, a review of some of which is provided in chapter 5 of the current volume. For instance, one consistent finding is that successful false belief performance tends to emerge at around age four (e.g., Perner, Leekam, & Wimmer, 1987). In addition to investigation into levels of ToM ability, there has also been theoretical speculation on and empirical investigation into possible precursors to this ability. Baron-Cohen (1991) has argued that understanding of attention, suggested to emerge between 7 and 9 months, is an important precursor to ToM while Meltzoff (2002) has focused on other suggested precursors including understanding of others' intentions and imitation (see chapter 4 of the current volume for a review of behavior analytic theory and research on precursors to PT).

## CLINICAL RESEARCH

Closely related to research into the development of ToM abilities in typically developing children is investigation of ToM deficits in children with autism spectrum disorder (ASD). For example, Baron-Cohen, Leslie, and Frith (1985) compared children with ASD with mental-age-controlled groups of typically developing and non-ASD developmentally delayed children and found ToM / PT deficits in the ASD group alone. On the basis of accumulating evidence such as this, it has been suggested that children with ASD do not have a ToM and thus have particular difficulties with tasks requiring them to understand others' beliefs and that this is a key feature of ASD.

More recent research has indicated that a number of other clinical and subclinical conditions also appear to be characterized by deficits in ToM / PT. These include most prominently schizophrenia (Corcoran, Mercer, & Frith, 1995) but also conditions related to it such as schizotypy (J.P. Chapman, Chapman, & Kwapil, 1995) and social anhedonia (Villatte, Monestes, McHugh, Freixa i Baque, & Loas, 2008) (see chapter 6 for elaboration on the link between clinical disorders and ToM / PT deficits).

## TRAINING THEORY OF MIND

In addition to assessment of ToM abilities, there has also been a limited amount of research on training ToM. For example, Clements, Rustin, and McCallum (2000) gave typically developing children between 34 and 60 months old feedback on a particular ToM task ("unexpected transfer"). One group got a detailed explanation regarding their responses while a second were simply told whether they were correct or not. Findings showed that only the explanation condition increased children's understanding of false belief. Fisher and Happé (2005) tested and trained ToM in ten children with ASD. Individual training sessions were administered with corrective feedback on all training trials. The participants were tested before and after training and at a two-month follow-up and showed significant improvements on ToM tasks compared with controls.

Kloo and Perner (2008) reviewed the literature on training ToM and concluded that multiple training sessions are required in order for training to be effective and that elaborated as opposed to brief feedback is superior. However, Knoll and Charman (2000) have questioned whether, despite their apparent success, training studies allow generalized ToM understanding. They provided children with false belief training that involved discussing the "unexpected transfer" task and reported that though participants showed improvement on this task itself, they showed none on an alternative false belief test. Begeer et al. (2010) used a randomized controlled design to test the effectiveness of a 16-week ToM treatment in eight- to thirteen-year-old children with ASD. Results showed that compared with controls, the treated children improved in conceptual ToM skills but not in elementary understanding, empathic skills, or parent-reported social behavior.

## A Contextual Behavioral Approach to Perspective Taking

Theoretical and empirical interest in perspective taking, the substantial majority of which has been conducted under the rubric of ToM, has been considerable in mainstream psychology and thus an increasing body of knowledge as to sequential development of particular skills, manifestation of deficits in particular populations, and training and remediation of skills under certain circumstances has begun to accumulate. However, from a contextual behavioral perspective, there are fundamental issues that this mainstream work does not address and that are of key importance with regard to the utility of the research generated. For instance, questions remain over the basic and functional processes that comprise PT and the most focused means of establishing these. Theory of Mind, for example, has been conceptualized as an ability that underlies perspective-taking, and the relative success of some ToM training studies in accelerating the acquisition of ToM understanding suggests that the development of this ability is to at least some extent "experience-driven." However, the exact status of ToM itself and the details of the kind of critical experience, or learning history, that might underlie it, remain unclear. As a result, training may not be targeting core response patterns, meaning less than optimal efficiency as regards required training time, for instance, and lack of generalization to other tasks or everyday contexts, as indeed has been reported.

One of the fundamental assumptions of a contextual behavioral approach to psychology is the importance of achieving both prediction and influence in the explanation of behavior. The latter in turn requires the specification of manipulable processes as a sine qua non and this affords contextual behavioral psychologists an advantage at the level of intervention. This approach has had notable success in certain domains in which it has been able to identify key causal variables and thus enabled relevant change. Up until relatively recently, it has not achieved the same level of success in domains involving more complex human behavior, such as perspective taking. However, as explained previously in this text, this has now begun to change, based on the emergence of a contextual behavioral conceptualization of human language and complex behavior, namely, relational frame theory (Hayes, Barnes-Holmes, & Roche, 2001).

# Relational Frame Theory

Relational frame theory (RFT) is a functional analytic approach that accounts for the development of language and higher cognition in terms of learned generalized patterns of relational responding referred to as relational frames. The prototypical example of such relational responding is the relation of coordination between words and their referents (e.g., [actual apple] = "apple") that children begin to learn around eighteen months. Continued exposure to the socioverbal environment produces increasingly complex patterns of generalized relational responding including more extensive examples of the frame of coordination as well as additional noncoordinate frames including distinction (e.g., "Boys are different from girls"), opposition ("Day is opposite to night"), comparison ("This car is bigger than that") and others (Hayes et al., 2001). According to RFT, all examples of this phenomenon possess the following three characteristics (see also chapter 1, current volume):

- mutual entailment (the fundamental bi-directionality of relational responding; for example, if A > [is greater than] B then B < [is less than] A)

- combinatorial entailment (the combination of already known relations to generate novel relations; if A > B and B > C then A > C and C < A)

- transformation of stimulus functions (the transformation of psychologically relevant functions of a stimulus in accordance with the underlying relation in a given context; if A > C and C is desirable then A is more desirable)

## DEICTIC RELATIONAL FRAMING

According to RFT, PT skills are based on a particular pattern of relational framing referred to as deictic framing. Deictic relational frames specify a relation in terms of the perspective of the speaker (McHugh, Barnes-Holmes, & Barnes-Holmes, 2004b). The three frames that appear to be most important in this regard are those of *I* and *You*, *Here* and *There*, and *Now* and *Then*. Unlike other frames, these do not appear to have formal or non-arbitrary counterparts and cannot be traced to formal dimensions in the environment. Instead, it is the relationship between the individual and other events that serves as the constant variable upon which these frames are based. Responding to, and asking, many questions contained within our common verbal interactions with others (e.g., "What am *I* doing *now*?" or "What are *you* doing *there*?") appear to be critical in establishing them. Each time questions such as these are asked or answered, the physical environment is different. What remains constant across these and similar questions, however, are the relational properties of *I* versus *You*, *Here* versus *There* and *Now* versus *Then*. Furthermore, according to RFT, these properties themselves are abstracted through learning to talk about one's own perspective in relation to the perspective of others. *I*, for instance, is always from this perspective *here*, but not from the perspective of another person *there*. Abstraction of an individual's perspective on the world, and that of others, requires a combination of a sufficiently well developed relational repertoire and an extensive history of exemplars that take advantage of that repertoire.

The three PT frames described above can generate a range of relational networks, including: I-Here-Now; You-Here-Now; I-Here-Then; You-Here-Then; I-There-Now; You-There-Now; I-There-Then; and You-There-Then. Many phrases common to our daily discourse are derived from these eight relational networks. Consider, for example, the phrases

"I am here now, but you were here then"; "You were there then, but I am here now"; and "You and I are both here now, but I was here then." Of course, when used in actual dialogue, these phrases would often include or substitute words coordinated with particular individuals, places and times. For illustrative purposes, consider the following example: "It is four o'clock and I am at work [Here and Now], but Fiona [You] is still at home" [There and Now]. What appears to make PT frames particularly complex and useful is that they cannot be defined in terms of particular words. That is, words such as "I," "you," "here," "there," "now," and "then" (used to describe the perspective of the self and others) are merely examples of the relational cues that control the PT frames, and a range of other words and contextual features may serve the same function. As is the case for all relational frames, what is important is the generalized relational activity, not the topography of particular cues.

From an RFT point of view, the establishment of deictic framing is critical to the development of PT as traditionally defined. Hence, there should be some correlation between competence in deictic framing and in more traditional PT tasks. Furthermore, targeting the deictic frames directly should lead to improved performances on the latter. There is already empirical evidence in both respects supporting this account.

# The RFT approach to PT: Empirical Research

## THE BASIC PROTOCOL

In contrast with mainstream approaches to PT such as ToM, the contextual behavioral RFT approach specifies the processes that give rise to PT in terms of the effects of manipulable environmental variables (e.g., use of contextual cues such as I and You), and thus it constitutes a novel and potentially powerful new approach to this ability. Empirical support for this account of PT has been accumulating over the last several years. The earliest published study in this area (McHugh, Barnes-Holmes, O'Hora, & Barnes-Holmes, 2004) developed a protocol that targeted the three PT frames of I-You, Here-There, and Now-Then, in conjunction with three levels of relational complexity, referred to as: simple relations, reversed relations, and double reversed relations. To illustrate the distinction among these levels of complexity, explicit examples are provided below.

Consider a simple I-YOU PT task in which participants were presented with the following question: "If I (Experimenter) have a pen and YOU (Participant) have a cup: What do I have? What do YOU have?" Responding correctly to this trial (i.e., "You/Experimenter have a pen and I/Participant have a cup") requires that the participants respond in accordance with the I-YOU deictic relational frame, under the contextual control of the If-Then relational frame. In effect, the If-Then frame determines the functions (i.e., the pen and cup) that become attached to the I and YOU related events in the deictic frame. The PT protocol also included simple HERE-THERE PT trials. In a simple HERE-THERE trial the participants may have been instructed as follows: "I am standing here at the yellow door, and you are standing there at the brown door. Where are you standing? Where am I standing?" A correct response on this trial requires that the participants respond in accordance with the I-YOU and HERE-THERE frames, under the contextual control of If-Then. The third simple relational task involved simple NOW-THEN relations. These trial types differed from the other simple relations in that they did not involve responding to I and YOU simultaneously. Consider the following example: "Yesterday I was shopping, today I am washing the car. What was I doing then? What am I doing now?" Once again, a correct response requires that the participants respond in accordance with the I-YOU and NOW-THEN frames, under the contextual control of If-Then.

A more complex level of relational framing is required for reversed relations. The protocol included reversed I-YOU, reversed HERE-THERE, and reversed NOW-THEN trials. Consider the following example of a reversed I-YOU trial: "If I have a pen and you have a cup, and if I was you and you were me: What would you have? What would I have?" A correct response to this trial involves a transformation of functions in accordance with a deictic relation between I and YOU. That is, the mutually entailed relation between I and YOU transfers "pen" from I to YOU and "cup" from YOU to I. Reversed HERE-THERE and NOW-THEN relations followed the same format in which transformations of functions occurred via mutually entailed relations.

An example of a reversed HERE-THERE task goes as follows: "I am standing here at the yellow door and you are standing there at the brown door. If here was there and there was here, where would I be standing? Where would you be standing?" A correct response to this trial involves a transformation of functions in accordance with a deictic relation between HERE and THERE. That is, the mutually entailed relation between HERE and THERE transfers "yellow door" from HERE to THERE and "brown door" from THERE to HERE.

The protocol also contained exposures to trials involving NOW-THEN reversals. A participant might be instructed, for example, "Yesterday you were watching television, and today you are reading. If now was then and then was now, what would you be doing then? What would you be doing now?" The correct response in this case, as with the I-YOU and HERE-THERE reversed tasks, is the reverse of the original locations. Reversed NOW-THEN relations followed the same format in which transformations of functions occurred via mutually entailed relations.

The most complex level of relational complexity was referred to as a double reversed relation, in which two relations were reversed simultaneously. Consider the following double reversed trial referred to as an I-YOU/HERE-THERE double reversal: "I am standing here at the yellow door and you are standing there at the brown door. If I was you and you were me, and if here was there and there was here, where would you be standing? Where would I be standing?" In this trial, the I-YOU reversal followed by the HERE-THERE reversal involves two mutually entailed relations between I and YOU and HERE and THERE, thus reversing the initially reversed relation. In simple terms, the participant deriving these relations ends up at the door where they originally started.

The second form of double reversed trials followed the same format except that these trials were based on HERE-THERE and NOW-THEN rather than I-YOU and HERE-THERE. For example: "Yesterday I was standing there at the brown door, today I am standing here at the yellow door. If here was there and there was here, and if now was then and then was now, where would I be standing now? Where would I be standing then?" Once again, in simple terms, the participants deriving these relations would respond by stating that they end up at the door where they started.

The findings from this study (i.e., McHugh, Barnes-Holmes, O'Hora, & Barnes-Holmes, 2004) revealed differences among participants' responses on the various frames, and on the three levels of relational complexity. Specifically, the results for relation type revealed that participants emitted more errors on HERE-THERE and NOW-THEN relations when each was compared with I-YOU relations. The results for relational complexity revealed that participants made significantly more errors on reversed and double reversed relations than on simple relations. Overall, these findings indicated that, even in adults, PT appears to consist of functionally distinct relational components.

## AN INITIAL DEVELOPMENTAL PROFILE

In a subsequent study (McHugh, Barnes-Holmes, & Barnes-Holmes, 2004a) the same relational protocol was used to provide a developmental profile of the deictic framing skills of individuals across different age groups. The findings from this study indicated a clear developmental trend in the ability to perform the relational PT tasks from early childhood to adulthood. Young children (aged three to five years) produced more errors than all of the older age groups (ranging from six to thirty years). Furthermore, these differences are broadly consistent with the mainstream cognitive-developmental literature, described above, which has reported that performances on simple ToM tasks generally develop across the ages of four and five years old, and are usually well established by age six (M. Taylor, 1988).

In order to control for the potential confound that the younger participants' poorer responding was due to the length of the statements used in the tasks, McHugh et al. (2004a) conducted a second experiment in which same-length foil statements that did not require complex relational responding were presented to the two younger groups of participants (i.e., those aged 3-5 and 6-8). An example of a foil (reversal) trial was as follows, "I'm sitting here on the blue chair and you're sitting there on the black chair. If here was here and there was there, where would I be sitting? Where would you be sitting?" Responding to this trial does not involve the level of relational responding involved in responding to a typical HERE-THERE reversal as there is no transformation of functions between mutually entailed relations required (i.e., the participant and experimenter remain in the same positions in which they began). In the case of both the 'foil' groups (i.e., the 3-5 and 6-8 year olds) fewer errors were produced than had been made by the corresponding age group given the original statements. This supports the conclusion that the errors produced by children in both age groups in the original experiment were due, at least in part, to the derived properties of the correct responses rather than statement length. [U1]

## MODELING TRUE AND FALSE BELIEF

In a more recent study, McHugh, Barnes-Holmes, Barnes-Holmes, and Stewart (2006) investigated the role of deictic framing in true and false belief understanding (ToM levels 4 and 5, respectively). To do so, they used a protocol that was modeled on the "deceptive container task" (a traditional test of true and false belief understanding) but that consisted of six trial types that differed from each other in terms of the relational frame or frames implicated (i.e., HERE, THERE, NOT HERE, NOT THERE, BEFORE NOW, AFTER NOW).

Some trial types focused on true belief understanding, in which the correct response requires prediction of responding based on a true belief. Consider the following question, for instance: "If you put the doll in the cookie jar and I am here, what would I think is in the cookie jar? What would you think is in the cookie jar?" Other trial types examined false belief understanding, in which the correct response requires prediction of responding based on a false belief. From an RFT perspective, responding in accordance with a relation of distinction or 'logical not' may be important in the latter. An example of a question used in this case was: "If I put the doll in the cookie jar and you were not there, what would I think is in the cookie jar? What would you think is in the cookie jar?" The correct response in the latter case involves indicating that I (Experimenter) will know what is inside, but you (participant) will not know, because you were not there when I put the doll inside. Other trial types focused on the temporal deictic frame of NOW-THEN. One type (AFTER NOW), assessed true belief, while another, (BEFORE NOW) assessed false belief. Consider the AFTER NOW trial "You open the cookie jar and there is a doll inside now. Now, what do you think is in the cookie jar? After now, what would you think is in the cookie jar?" This task assessed true belief because the correct response requires participants to indicate that they can act on the basis of what they have seen as true. The BEFORE NOW trial types were similar in format but assessed false belief. However, unlike the other false belief trials, they did not assess false belief by emphasizing logical not. Instead, false belief was implied in the temporal order of the events stated in the trial. Consider the following example: "You open the cookie jar and there is a doll inside now. Now, what do you think is in the cookie jar? Before now, what did you think was in the cookie jar?" This task assessed false belief because the correct answer required participants to determine that before now they could only act on the basis of a false belief (i.e., that there were cookies in the cookie jar).

Similar to the previous study that modeled and assessed aspects of perspective taking using deictic relations, McHugh et al. (2006) assessed participants in groups ranging from early childhood to adulthood, and showed a clear developmental trend in the repertoire under assessment, which this time was true and false belief understanding. This developmental trend was supported by significant differences in the number of errors between most of the age groups, and the fact that error rates appeared to decrease as a function of age. Thus this work supported and extended previous empirical research favoring an RFT approach to perspective-taking.

The studies just described both deployed a relational protocol specially designed to investigate the validity of the RFT interpretation of perspective-taking. The empirical evidence yielded developmental profiles that suggested that these repertoires emerge in a sequence indicative of PT and false belief, as traditionally defined in the language of ToM, and which characterizes the emergence of language and cognitive complexity, more generally. A third, more recent study has provided further support to the RFT account and further insight into perspective-taking processes as conceptualized by this account. In the literature on ToM, the skills of PT and false belief are believed to give rise to the more complex cognitive ability commonly referred to as deception. This phenomenon has also been modelled by RFT research.

## MODELING DECEPTION

McHugh, Barnes-Holmes, Barnes-Holmes, Stewart, and Dymond (2007) developed a relational frame analysis of deception. They used a protocol similar to that designed to examine false belief understanding; however, in the deception protocol, the three deictic frames were manipulated in conjunction with a frame of distinction, and logical not. For illustrative purposes, consider the following task, in which a participant is instructed as follows: "If I have a teddy bear and I do not want you to find it, where should I hide the teddy bear?" In this trial, the scenario depicted involves I (the Experimenter) aiming to deceive you (the participant). In an alternative though similar trial, the participant may be instructed: "If you have a teddy bear and you do not want me to find it, where should you hide the teddy bear?" Although the correct response is the same for both trials, they each require the participant to adopt a different perspective.

Findings were broadly consistent with the developmental profiles obtained from the relational PT and true and false belief protocols. That is, the deception protocol generated yet another clear developmental profile from early childhood to adulthood. However, the deception protocol, as would be predicted given its greater relational complexity, produced many more errors than the previous two protocols, and larger age differences particularly among the younger groups.

## COMPARING "I" AND "YOU" RESPONDING

One issue that emerged from initial work modeling perspective-taking as deictic relational framing, was the inability to parse out responding in terms of specific perspectives. In other words, while the early perspective protocols permitted an analysis of the specific types of frames involved in PT, they did not permit a clear-cut investigation of responding from one's own perspective, compared with responding from that of another. Differences in complexity between responding in accordance with "I" (self) and "You" (other) relations are thought to be critical in explaining the relative difficulty of false-belief tasks in which taking the perspective of another plays a central role. McHugh, Barnes-Holmes, Barnes-Holmes, Whelan, and Stewart (2007) focused on this distinction. Findings indicated a clear difference in mean response latencies for tasks that required taking another's perspective, than for tasks that required taking one's own perspective.

RFT might predict that taking the perspective of another would produce longer reaction times than taking the perspective of the self since tasks involving another's belief would appear to involve more relational framing than those involving one's own belief. Responding from the perspective of another appears to involve responding in accordance with an "If-Then" frame via a transformation of functions in accordance with a mutually entailed deictic relation between I and YOU. However, responding on the basis of one's own perspective does not appear to require this level of complexity. For example, responding on the basis of I alone does not *necessarily* involve an "If-Then" frame, which does appear to be essential with another perspective. In other words, one has to derive relations such as "If I was you, I would be thinking the same thing" in order to take the perspective of another, whereas this is not essential in taking one's own perspective. Significantly longer reaction times for taking another's perspective, therefore, are consistent with RFT predictions.

In summary, therefore, the findings from these initial studies indicated that the relational repertoires required for PT appear to follow a distinct developmental trend, and seem to be comprised of functional relational units of analysis. They also suggested how the RFT approach to PT as deictic relational framing correlates with mainstream approaches to this domain. More importantly, however, consistent with the pragmatic assumptions underlying RFT, such findings have had important implications for the design of programs to train PT.

## TRAINING PERSPECTIVE TAKING

By now, a number of RFT training studies have been conducted which have used a PT protocol similar to that employed by McHugh, Barnes-Holmes, & Barnes-Holmes (2004a) to remediate deficits in PT framing in typically developing young children (Y. Barnes-Holmes, 2001; McHugh, 2004; Heagle & Rehfeldt, 2006; Weil, Hayes, & Capurro, 2011). In the first study cited, two children were exposed to the PT protocol with corrective feedback presented after each trial. A seven-year-old girl required training on the reversed and double reversed relations in order to complete the entire protocol. A three-and-a-half-year-old boy was exposed only to I-YOU and HERE-THERE trials, and required extensive training across exemplars, also on the reversed and double reversed relations (Y. Barnes-Holmes, 2001). The second study (McHugh, 2004) again employed the refined PT protocol, with two four-year-olds, a boy and a girl. Assessment at the beginning of the study revealed that both children had a sophisticated repertoire of I-YOU and simple HERE-THERE responding and thus no training was required in these domains. However, training simple NOW-THEN tasks required extensive and systematic exemplar training. The children were also both trained in more complex relational tasks involving I-YOU and HERE-THERE relations including reversed I-YOU, reversed HERE-THERE and double reversed I-YOU and HERE-THERE.

In the third study, Rehfeldt and Heagle (2006) employed a multiple-probe design to teach PT skills to three typically developing children between the ages of six and eleven. Generalization tests of PT with respect to new stimuli and real-world conversational topics were also tested. All three children were successfully trained on the protocol and performed with high accuracy on the generalization tests.

The most recent of the studies cited trained PT in three children using a within-subjects multiple-probe design (Weil, Hayes, & Capurro, 2011). In this study, performance on ToM tasks was tested before, during, and after deictic relational intervention to determine if the latter could directly improve performance on the former. Results showed that all three children improved on ToM following the intervention. More specifically, after training in reversed relations, improved performance was demonstrated on ToM levels 3-5 while after training on double reversed relations, improved performance was shown on ToM levels 4 and 5.

### DEICTIC FRAMING IN AUTISM AND OTHER DISORDERS

Most of the early work on deictic relations has focused on typically developing children and adults. However, Rehfeldt, Dillen, Ziomek, & Kowalchuk (2007) employed a variant of the McHugh, Barnes-Holmes, & Barnes-Holmes (2004a) protocol to examine deictic relational framing in children with ASD and to compare their performance with that of age-matched typically-developing counterparts. Performance on the PT protocol was compared with that on standardized instruments commonly employed in ASD assessment including the Vineland Adaptive Behavior Scales – Interview Edition (Sparrow, Balla, & Cicchetti, 1984). Findings showed that the ASD group made more errors overall on the McHugh et al. (2004) PT protocol and that this distinction was most pronounced for reversed relations. In addition, an inverse correlation was found between percentage of errors on the Now-Then reversed relations test and the Daily Living Skills domain of the Vineland.

In addition, as briefly mentioned earlier, deficits in PT are seen in a number of clinical and subclinical conditions other than ASD including schizophrenia, schizotypy, and social anhedonia. Researchers have also begun to investigate deficits in relational framing in these conditions. Research in the area of social anhedonia, for example, has linked anhedonic behavior to deficiencies in deictic framing tasks that involve both a high level of relational complexity and an interpersonal perspective (Villatte, Monestes, McHugh, Freixa i Baque, & Loas, 2008) and shown that scores on social anhedonia measures can be accounted for by deictic framing, empathic concern, and experiential avoidance (Vilardaga, Estévez, Levin, & Hayes, under submission). Chapter 6 of the current volume provides more detail on this promising work and it mentions that future studies will aim to address deficits found in particular populations using training protocols similar to those described above.

## Summary and Future Directions

This chapter first presented mainstream theory and research on PT. As discussed, a key weakness of this prior work is that it fails to provide a useful specification of the processes involved. The functional contextualist RFT account of PT was then presented. In contrast with the mainstream approach this account does specify the processes underlying PT.

It provides a functional analytic account of this ability as deictic relational framing. Furthermore, in support of this account, a series of RFT-based research studies has shown that deictic relational framing ability correlates with PT as measured using traditional ToM tasks and that protocols based on deictic framing can be used to model various forms of PT ability including true and false belief and deception. One category of recent studies has begun to successfully establish deictic relational framing abilities where absent in typically developing children while another has begun to show deficits in deictic framing in children with ASD and in adults with clinical conditions associated with PT deficits.

The technical account provided by RFT has thus begun to gain significant empirical support. Future RFT research should continue to focus on the relationship between deictic framing and performance on traditional ToM tasks. Studies with larger populations that are matched by age, relational performance, and ToM performance are needed to further test the relation between deictic framing and PT performance measured via traditional ToM tasks as well as to provide more detailed information on processes involved in deictic framing itself. As such research continues, the present account promises future benefits at both the basic and the applied level. At the basic level it will provide increasingly detailed empirically based information on PT and skills traditionally linked to PT such as empathy and social interactions. At the applied level it promises more direct and efficient training of PT and better generalization outcomes than mainstream accounts in individuals with deficits in PT including both typically developing children and adults as well as individuals in particular subclinical and clinical categories.

# Chapter 4

# Precursors to Perspective Taking

Gary Novak *California State University, Stanislaus*

## Introduction

This chapter will examine precursors to perspective taking (PT) in infancy from a behavior analytic point of view. PT is a key repertoire that not only underlies development of an understanding of others but also is critical to development of the self. For this reason, it is important to understand its ontogenic origins. As outlined in other chapters in this volume, within the modern contextual behavioral approach adopted by relational frame theory (RFT; Hayes, Barnes-Holmes, & Roche, 2001), PT is one of a number of patterns of generalized contextually controlled relational responding ("relational framing"), involved in human language. PT is deictic relational framing, which is framing in accordance with the perspective of the speaker, and in which the person refers to their own behavior ("I") and that of others ("YOU") in space ("HERE" versus "THERE") and time ("NOW" versus "THEN"). Emergence of this ability is critical to the development of the adult human self in all its complexity, including a number of key types of "self" including self-as-concept ("Me") and self-as-perspective ("I") (e.g., McHugh, Barnes-Holmes, & Barnes-Holmes, 2004a & b). It also underlies a sophisticated understanding and appreciation of the behavior of others, including the ability to predict their behavior based on their beliefs, and the capacity to empathize with them (e.g., Vilardaga, 2009).

Though from this point of view, the PT repertoire is essentially verbal in character, it is also the case that there is a critical foundation for this repertoire in the preverbal development of the child, which might be referred to as precursors to PT. The latter emerge in the earliest stages of infancy and may be tracked throughout the period before verbal behavior begins to arise as well as during the early stages of its emergence. They include repertoires such as mutually responsive orientation, joint attention and self-referencing, which support interaction with others as well as differentiation of oneself from them and they emerge in a more or less supportive human social context in which they tend to be strongly encouraged.

As suggested, particular precursor behaviors provide a key foundation for PT. Thus, this precursor repertoire and the social contexts in which it emerges are important for that reason. The contexts giving rise to this repertoire also contribute more directly to the development of PT by enabling and supporting development of verbal behavior (relational framing) in general as well as that directly relevant to PT (i.e., deictic). The development of a verbal repertoire and the way in which PT subsequently emerges within the context of this repertoire are, as mentioned, described elsewhere. This chapter will touch on the beginnings of the development of a verbal repertoire but will mainly focus on precursors to PT as a developmental foundation. Thus, it will describe the social contexts alluded to above, some key processes at work in them and the skills that emerge from these processes.

# A Behavioral Systems Process

Mainstream cognitive-developmental approaches to phenomena such as precursors to PT can often provide useful description of behavioral changes in the young child. However, their suggested explanations of the observed patterns of behavior are typically based on mentalistic assumptions that ignore potentially important environmental variables. For example, there is an implicitly held (and sometimes explicitly stated) assumption that infants seek and interpret others' focus of attention and corresponding emotional perspective because they appreciate that people have emotions, intentions, and perspectives that differ from their own. However, this is a mentalistic explanation of attention engagement because the cause of the behavior is located not in the manipulable environment but in an inaccessible mental realm. From a behavior analytic point of view, explanation must ultimately be such as to allow both prediction and influence over responding. This is the reason for the behavioral concentration on precise specification of manipulable environmental variables. Focusing on such variables can allow for more fully complete explanations that can enable practical intervention; for instance, acceleration of learning in typically developing populations or remediation of behavioral deficits in the developmentally delayed.

In this chapter, as an alternative to the mainstream approach to the emergence of PT, I will describe a developmental process based on a behavioral systems approach (Novak, 1996, 1998; Novak & Pelaez, 2004). The latter shows how behavior and its organization in young children changes as the result of specific contingent reciprocal interactions between behavior and the environment, the latter especially, but not exclusively, consisting of sensitive caregivers. This approach takes on board the child's phylogenic and ontogenic histories as well as current social, nonsocial, and cultural environmental contingencies. It draws on skills learning models (Moerk, 2000; Novak, 1999), dynamic systems concepts (Thelen & Ulrich, 1991), and especially contingencies of reinforcement, to explain how PT develops. Most importantly, it points to manipulable environmental variables for explanation of important developmental change.

When we examine PT we are looking at organized patterns of behavior that have emerged from basic developmental processes and are embedded in social and cultural contexts. All of these levels and more (e.g., physiological) may need to be considered for a complete account. However, while development can be viewed at different systems levels, the behavioral systems perspective emphasizes learning-produced behavioral change as *the* basic process in the development of PT. The most useful tool for analysis is the four-term contingency which adds setting events (e.g., establishing operations; Michael, 1993) to Skinner's three-term contingency (i.e., discriminative stimulus, response, and consequence; Skinner, 1935). Behavioral development occurs through interactions between the ever-developing organism and the ever-changing environment (Novak, 1996; Novak & Pelaez, 2004).

# Skills Learning as a Model for Development

In the development of PT, multiple behavior-environment interactions become organized over time into behavior-environment classes, by the coalescent action of conditions organized by contingencies of reinforcement. These functional classes are assembled through a skill learning process in which multiple training exemplars are provided to the child by the environment (either self-generated or caregiver-generated). Consequences which may be automatic, intrinsic to the relation, or arbitrarily determined by caregivers or cultures select which stimulus class and behavioral class relationships emerge.

Some component of skills may be present but undetected prior to being assembled under coalescent organization. Thelen and Ulrich (1991) used the term "hidden skills" for these unobserved components of apparent skills. Hidden skills are necessary components of the development of apparent skills, but are not sufficient by themselves to produce them. When apparent skills emerge that are important for the development of other behaviors, they are called behavioral cusps (Rosales-Ruiz & Baer, 1997). For example, walking is a behavioral cusp since once it emerges it opens the pathway to a wide range of other behaviors. Walking is based on several hidden skills such as balance, alternating leg movements and so on that are necessary but not sufficient for walking to become possible. These hidden skills develop and then eventually together allow the apparent skill but the development of the former goes unnoticed until they may be recognized in the latter (Thelen & Ulrich, 1991).

## RICH SOCIALLY ORIENTED TRAINING ENVIRONMENT

The skills learning model requires a rich environment providing multiple training exemplars and contingencies, and there is ample evidence of this in both the social and ecological environments. With respect to language learning, for example, Hart and Risley (1995) examined social class differences in use of language spoken by parents to their children, and found relatively large disparities between language exposure for children in families classified as "welfare" versus children in families classified as "professional." Despite this general pattern, however, the species typical environment was sufficient for all children to learn to use language and overall, the findings of their study show parents as part of a species typical environment affording relatively consistent training opportunities and suggest that there is built-in environmental redundancy for acquisition of language and cognitive skills.

Studies such as those of Hart and Risley (1995; 1999) and of Moerk (1983, 1986, 1989, 1990) have done much to demonstrate that the learning environment of the infant is a great deal richer than the minimalist one suggested by nativists such as Brown (1973). This detailing of the infant's species typical environment is very relevant to general cognitive development including the development of precursors to PT. From their earliest days, children enter into a continual stream of reciprocal interactions with their environments, directed toward developing socially oriented skills both by their own actions and by the behaviors of a mentalistic or "mind-minded" (Meins & Fernyhough, 1999) caregiving environment.

## PARENTS AS INTUITIVE TEACHERS

Papousek and Papousek (1987) outlined characteristics that make nearly all parents "intuitive" teachers. Without training or education parents 1) keep the child awake and alert; 2) present structurally simple stimuli in learning trials; 3) repeat these learning trials many times; 4) gradually increase the complexity of the tasks; 5) provide adequate reinforcers; and 6) adapt their behavior to the child's responsiveness. Keller, Chasiotis, and Runde (1992) found evidence of the same general intuitive teaching skills across three cultures (German, Greek, and American) that they studied.

Moerk (1986) found evidence that parents are not only intuitive teachers of cognitive skills, but also sensitive and contingent ones. A number of studies looking at child-parent interactions have noted the sensitivity of most parents, as characterized by the dynamic adjustments they make in their behaviors as a function of the developmental changes in their children's responsiveness to them (Gogate, Bahrick, & Watson, 2000). An example of this is provided by the phenomenon of "motherese," which is characterized by infant-directed speech that is simplified, repetitive, higher and wider-ranging in tone, and slower in tempo, and which is believed to be universal across human cultures. Furthermore, this is not solely a language-relevant phenomenon, since some of its characteristics are also evidenced in the infant-directed behavior of nonhuman hominids (Falk, 2004). In addition, the intuitive adjustment of adult behavior to a learner has also been observed in the vocal behaviors used by human adults in dog-training (Hirsh-Pasek & Treiman, 1982).

From a behavioral systems perspective, this type of dynamic adjustment of parental behavior results from the consequences to child and parent. As both child and parent behaviors change, so do their prompting and reinforcing effects. The child provides reinforcing consequences for the parent's teaching behaviors. That is, the parent provides skill learning trials, and if the child responds with attention, positive affect, or other behaviors reinforcing to the parent, then the parent continues for a few learning trials. If the child does not respond to the parent's prompts or averts gaze, fusses, or shows other negative affect or lack of interest, then the parent changes behavior, perhaps escalating the motherese characteristics, using more visual or tactile attentional stimuli, or simplifying the trial until positive reinforcement from the child occurs as the child acquires skills. Concurrently, the parent's behaviors also set the occasion for and reinforce the child's behaviors. For example, if a child reaches for and grasps an object that the parent pointed to and named, the parent may smile, laugh, and say "good girl." If the child does not reach for it, the parent may gently grab the child's wrist and move the hand to contact the object. If the child continues to ignore the object, the parent may use "motherese" to prompt a response. If the child continues to ignore the object, the parent may prompt responding to another object or give up altogether. In addition, general setting conditions, such as whether the child is rested or sleepy, hungry or full, whether the parent is rested or tired, relaxed or rushed, and previous interactional history will serve as establishing operations that provide a context for stimulus salience and reinforcement effectiveness.

# Development of Precursors to Perspective Taking

Having discussed features of the training environment, in accordance with a behavioral systems skills learning model I will now examine stages of development of precursors to PT.

## Mutually Responsive Orientation (MRO)

Mutually responsive orientation (MRO) refers to the positive relationship that develops between children and their parents early in the child's life (Kochanska, 1997). As viewed by Kochanska and her colleagues

MRO includes mutually responsive, reciprocal interactions that enhance the development of social interactions. The reciprocal behaviors include shared positive affective behaviors and coordinated enjoyable routines (Kochanska & Aksan, 2006). These interactions that are "cooperative, trusting, reciprocal, and infused with positive feelings" (p. 1596) reinforce interactions that are attuned to the level of performance of each participant, much as partners in a dance.

Kochanska and Aksan (2004) looked at changes in parent and child bids for attention at seven months and again at fifteen months. They found several developmental changes. First, they found that parents directed more social-interactive bids and attempts to regulate mood at their seven-month-olds than at their fifteen-month-olds. As the children became more skilled socially and in their abilities to self-regulate, parents let them lead a higher percentage of social exchanges. This parallels the fading out of parent talk to children observed by Hart and Risley (1999). Child bids directed at the parents were reciprocals with a tripling of the number of positive social bids (e.g., smiling, vocalizations, etc.) and a reduction in negative social bids (e.g., crying, showing upset, etc.) and physical bids (e.g., coughing, sneezing, choking, etc.) producing a total bid increase by children as they got older. In line with a dynamical systems viewpoint, it was found that parents dominated the initiation of social events earlier on and then faded out their initiations in response to the child's increasingly capable behaviors as they got older.

As defined, the organized, dyadic system behavior comprising MRO (e.g., coordinated routines, harmonious communication, and mutual cooperation) seems to be an early developing cusp in the development of PT and related skills. Kochanska and her colleagues (Kochanska, Aksan, Prisco, & Adams, 2008) not only found evidence of MRO in children as young as seven months with their families, but also found that this type of positive interaction influenced the amount of power assertion (e.g., direct commands, prohibitions) that parents used when the children were 53 months of age, and influenced also the children's "self-regulation" (e.g., slowing down, delaying gratification) at that age. MRO has also been associated with later child cognitive-affective development described as development of the "conscience" (Kochanska, 2002; Kochanska & Murray, 2000). For example, Kochanska and Aksan (2006) found that MRO significantly affected preschool children's self-moral behaviors. Specifically, guilt as measured by gaze aversion, bodily tension, global positive and negative affectivity, confessing, and apologizing in response to a staged mishap was related to MRO levels in infancy. Moral behaviors were positively related to infant-child levels of MRO and infant temperament measures.

## Joint Attention

A mutually responsive orientation is a behavioral cusp that also contributes to the development of the crucial skills of joint attention. The latter, which was discussed previously, refers to synchronization of the child's attention with that of another person in the sharing of an object or event, under the control of eye contact and cues. Joint attention is itself a cusp because it enables the child to learn about objects in the environment from interactions with the parent.

Consider a three-year-old girl and her mother visiting family friends. As the adults sit in the living room and chat, the girl plays with a puzzle on the floor. Suddenly, a kitten runs into the room and the little girl's face lights up with surprise and pleasure. However, her next action is not to engage the kitten in play, but to look up at her mother's face while pointing to it, to see if her mother had also witnessed the animal's dramatic entrance. Gaze shifts may subsequently be combined with gestures toward the object within the visual field of the familiar face.

### GAZE FOLLOWING

Gaze following is a key skill in the development of joint attention. Carpenter, Nagell, and Tomasello (1998) found the median age for pointing following of infants in their study was 11.7 months and the median age for gaze following was 13.0 months. In order for joint attention to be functional in other contexts, the infant must be able to attend to the parent and come under the control of shifts in parental gaze rather than voice or gestures to lead to jointly reinforcing aspects of the environment. Research with nonhumans has shown that their focus of attention can come under the control of the gaze or head movements of others. These demonstrations include the use of cues among apes (Pitman & Shumaker, 2009), and control by human head movement (but not gaze alone) in domestic dogs and captive bottlenose dolphins who had previous experience in studies involving human pointing (Pack & Herman, 2004). Traditional developmentalists view early joint attention as due to either evolutionary adaptations or cognitive development that is universal in the species. However, given the very general and limited responsiveness of newborns to eye-related stimuli, it is likely that newborn preparedness to respond to facial stimuli is restricted to reflexive responding that enables responses that are automatically and socially reinforced. Joint attention would then be shaped over the first year of the child's life, first responding to it (RJA) and then initiating it (IJA).

## RESPONDING TO JOINT ATTENTION (RJA) AND INITIATION OF JOINT ATTENTION (IJA)

RJA and IJA are large and important response classes that have been extensively studied. Both entail situations in which a novel object becomes visible to at least one of a child-parent dyad, one of the two looks at the object, then makes eye contact with the other and then both look at the object. RJA occurs when the child uses the adult's cue to look at the object and IJA occurs when the child cues the adult to look at the object. Automatic reinforcement may occur from seeing the object. In addition, there may be social reinforcement, including smiling, vocalizations, and other mutually enjoyable events resulting from the development of an MRO. Before gaze is established as an effective cue, early joint attention prompting may be vocal or gestural, and as previously mentioned, in the early months the prompting is likely to be multimodal involving vocalizations and pointing to the object by the parent. In an example of multimodal motherese, parents may use exaggerated facial expressions to cue attention, and in doing so, direct attention to the face, and particularly the eyes, which soon become discriminative cues and conditioned reinforcers for attending to what the parent is viewing.

RJA involves learning that the parent's gaze shift is a discriminative stimulus that signals that an attentional response will be reinforced. In RJA, a gaze shift from the parent, such as shifting the gaze from looking at the child to looking at an object and back to the child, becomes discriminative for the child's own gaze shift that is reinforced by the object or parental responsivity. Early on in the learning of RJA, the parent is likely to use pointing or another sensory modality (e.g., saying, for instance, "Look at this!") in a type of multimodal motherese. After some number of trials in which different stimuli are presented, but gaze shift is consistently employed, the gaze shift itself comes to control the child's responding.

IJA refers to the child providing cues that function to cause the parent to participate in the joint attention pattern. Children engage in IJA when an establishing operation, such as the appearance of a novel object of interest, is effected. Under these conditions, the child learns that orienting their parent's behavior toward the object is reinforcing. It may be reinforcing for several reasons, depending on the characteristics of the establishing operation. For example, if the object is threatening, orienting the parent's attention to the object may result in the parent reducing the threat (negative reinforcement). If the object is ambiguous, orienting the parent's attention to it may have the consequence that the parent says "okay," names it, or gives it to the child to play with. B. A. Taylor and Hoch (2008) argued that RJA and IJA were largely independent response classes with RJA functioning as a tact, reinforced by social reinforcers, and IJA functioning as a mand influenced by establishing operations created by the presence of certain objects. The authors showed that both classes, initially absent in the children with autism in their study, could be taught with operant procedures.

Mundy and his colleagues have used mathematical models to evaluate reinforcer effects on joint attention. Mundy et al. (2007) looked at RJA and IJA in infants between 9 and 18 months. They found significant inter-infant variability in the amounts of both. Furthermore, between 9 and 15 months RJA showed a linear model of development. However, IJA development was nonlinear, appearing suddenly as phase shifts. Just as receptive language is observed to precede production, so RJA precedes IJA. In the long term, children's level of RJA at 12 months and IJA at 18 months predicted their language proficiency at 24 months.

Morales and colleagues (Morales et al. 2000) found systematic differences in RJA in children as early as six months of age. In a similar study, MacDonald et al. (2006) found that children with autism between 24 and 48 months demonstrated small deficits in responding to joint attention (RJA) and significant deficits in initiating joint attention (IJA), compared to typically developing children. Deficits in joint attention in children with autism have been well recorded (Carpenter, Pennington, & Rogers, 2002; Mundy, Sigman, & Kasari, 1994).

## BEHAVIORAL INTERPRETATION OF INITIATION OF JOINT ATTENTION

Dube, MacDonald, Mansfield, Holcomb and Ahearn (2004) have provided a relatively detailed behavior analytic interpretation of IJA. According to this, the initiation of joint attention in an interesting object or event momentarily establishes the reinforcing capacity of a class of stimuli (to be referred to here as adult-attending stimuli) as conditioned reinforcers. Adult-attending stimuli are primarily visual indicators that the adult is aware of the interesting event; for example, the adult's eyes are open and oriented toward it. Adult-attending stimuli indicate that the adult is attending to the event and not necessarily to the child. Adult-attending stimuli become effective as a conditioned reinforcer after a learning history in which (a) they have been reliable predictors that the adult will react to the interesting event and (b) the adult's reaction has been related to increased reinforcement. Thus, according to Dube et al.'s (2004) interpretation the IJA of gaze shifting is an observing response exhibited because of a history of producing adult-attending stimuli as immediate consequences. Adult-attending stimuli function as links in a behavioral chain: as conditioned reinforcers for gaze shifting and as discriminative stimuli indicating an increased probability of other reinforcers related to the adult's behavior with respect to the child and the interesting object or event. If the gaze shift reveals that the adult is not attending to the object or event, then additional IJA responses (verbalizations, gestures) with a history of producing adult-attending stimuli may follow.

Dube et al. (2004) continue to suggest that the analysis of the interesting event as a motivational operation is required because the child does not continually observe adult-attending stimuli whenever the adult is present. In the absence of the interesting event, adults still generate adult-attending stimuli related to various features of the environment with great frequency (adults are usually looking at something), but these adult-attending stimuli do not function as conditioned reinforcers (adults are often looking at things unrelated to the probability of reinforcement for the child's behavior). The value-altering effect of the interesting event is the increase in reinforcing effectiveness of adult-attending stimuli; evocative effect is the increase in frequency of gaze shifts that may produce adult-attending stimuli as consequences.

According to Dube et al. (2004), at the onset of an interesting event, a child may emit event-related behavior solely due to a relevant history of event-related consequences and thus engage in solidarity play. However, they may also emit both event-related behavior and IJA because of a reinforcement history that includes both event-related consequences and adult-mediated consequences (for example, the adult continues to look at the object or the adult joins in play with the object). Dube et al. (2004) also suggest that one possible class of reinforcers that may maintain IJA is negative reinforcers, the termination of a mildly aversive situation. Startling or unfamiliar objects or events may cause mild conditioned or unconditioned feelings of anxiety or uncertainty (severe feelings of fear seem likely to set the occasion for imperative behavior that would not be classified as IJA). If the child's past experience has been that the adult's behavior in such situations is a reliable guide to the level of threat, then one consequence of the gaze shift may be adult-attending stimuli indicating that nothing is amiss. If so, one possible function of the behavior would be the reduction or termination of aversive stimulation (Skinner, 1957). This operant class seems closely related to the developmental concept of social referencing, in which the child observes the emotional expressions of others to appraise events and guide action. This relation is suggested in part by research demonstrating that maternal expressions can acquire discriminative functions in an operant conditioning paradigm in 9- to 12-month-old infants (Gewirtz & Pelaez-Nogueras, 1992).

## DEFICITS IN AND REMEDIATION OF JOINT ATTENTION

Deficits in joint attention have been suggested to play a role in autism and as such have been receiving increasing attention from researchers (Carpenter et al., 2002). Dawson et al. (2004) have even argued that joint attention deficits alone can differentiate between typically developing and autistic learners. Specifically, the latter appear to lack prerequisites for joint attention including orienting to speech sounds and other social stimuli (e.g., someone pointing) as well as showing more direct evidence of deficiencies in joint attention. For example, Charman (1997) demonstrated that children with autism would look at a mechanical toy but did not exhibit gaze switches between the toy and an adult who was present.

Whalen and Schreibman (2003) provided the first study to systematically use behavioral principles to train joint attention skills in children with autism. Their results showed that they successfully established RJA skills in all five children tested while establishing targeted IJA skills in four out of five and that these skills also generalized. However, though RJA skills were still shown at three-month follow-up in three out of the four who completed training, there was a marked decrement at follow-up in IJA. One factor that may have been responsible for this was the use of "extrinsic rewards" in the IJA training procedure whereas naturalistic joint attention seems to involve the intrinsic rewards of sharing something with another. More recent studies have attempted to address this apparent shortcoming. Isaksen and Holth (2009) reported an empirical study similar to Whalen and Schreibman (2003) but in which a key additional aim was establishment of normal social behavior consequences as discriminative stimuli for positively reinforced responses. They reported that all four children who took part made significant progress in both RJA and IJA from baseline to post-training. More importantly, their results showed that both RJA and IJA were maintained or improved from post-training to follow-up.

## Social Referencing

In social referencing, the infant responds to parental cues as a guide to determining how to behave in unknown contexts (Gewirtz & Pelaez-Nogueras, 1992). Such cues include the parent's facial, vocal, and bodily expression. The reinforcing or punishing consequences of the subsequent behavior strengthen this responding as it begins to emerge and it is maintained by intermittent reinforcement.

Behaviorally, social referencing is viewed as an example of social knowledge. With experience, the child learns that if the mother is smiling when a stranger approaches, reinforcement is likely. However, if the mother is cringing, crying may prevent the stranger from hurting her. Thus, the facial expression of the mother becomes a setting event that establishes the stranger as discriminative for positive or negative reinforcement; if the mother is smiling, the stranger may evoke attention from the child; if the mother is showing concern, the stranger may evoke crying from the child.

Campos and Barrett (1984) have postulated that the responses and perceptions making up social referencing are "prewired" (i.e., unconditioned) and that social referencing mostly involves emotional components. However, results of behavioral research suggest that social referencing (whether instrumental or affective) can result from the contingency-based learning. Gewirtz and Pelaez-Nogueras (1992) conducted two experiments to see if infants could learn to respond to maternal "expressive" cues in ambiguous situations. They showed that any arbitrary stimulus could come to function as a discriminative stimulus functionally similar to the mother's facial expression in social referencing and concluded that they had provided a laboratory analogue of the way social referencing develops in the child's interactions with the parents in naturalistic settings. That is, the child learns through operant conditioning to associate the caregiver's facial expression (joy or fear) with specific consequences.

Although some have suggested joint attention as a type of social referencing, Pelaez (2009) has argued that the development of joint attention precedes and is necessary for social referencing and that social referencing is more complex. Besides responding to the gaze cues with attention as in joint attention, in social referencing the child reacts to the novel stimulus in a manner that is in accordance with the parent's expression (Pelaez-Nogueras & Gewirtz, 1997). That is, if the mother is smiling the child smiles and approaches, but if the mother has a fearful face, the child reacts accordingly. Social referencing adds to joint attention by cueing the learner to respond to a novel stimulus in a way that accords with the other's emotional expression. The latter comes to play the role of a setting event (Pelaez, 2009) or establishing operation that is developed through multiple examples into a conditional discrimination. So, over time, if the parent is smiling, then a parental gaze shift toward an object is an S+ for approach, while if they have a fearful expression, then their gaze shift toward the object is discriminative for avoidance.

Pelaez (2009) reasoned that the abilities created through basic visual discriminations such as those in joint attention and social referencing seem to be mutually dependent and critical aspects of parent-child (or other teacher-learner) exchanges. These basic skills are necessary foundations for conditional discriminations, developing language, and socializing. The emotional and social aspects of social referencing are cusps for the later development of PT, and lead to reciprocal conversation, cooperative play, and displays of sympathy and empathy. Thus, these are all social abilities that require the basics of joint attention and social referencing (Pelaez, 2009).

## Bidirectional Relational Responding

A longitudinal study of fourteen infants studied monthly from nine to fifteen months old found a common pattern of emergence of related social-cognitive skills at around twelve months (Carpenter et al., 1998). The sequence found was: communicative gestures (e.g., showing, pointing, and giving item), attention following (i.e., gaze and point following), imitative learning, and referential communication (e.g., naming objects). In addition, joint engagement, as seen in MRO, was already present in all the infants prior to the study's onset. The development of self-discriminations, MRO, RJA, IJA, and social referencing skills all constitute obvious precursors to PT. These skills also provide a foundation for an additional repertoire that is critical for the development of PT as well as cognition more generally, namely, generalized contextually controlled relational responding or relational framing, the core skill underlying generative human language. Thus, in addition to providing a foundation for verbal PT, the social cognitive skills listed above provide a foundation for verbal responding more generally.

Children learn patterns of generalized relational responding by exposure to multiple exemplars for these patterns in their socioverbal environment. The earliest such pattern that humans learn is bidirectional name-object responding. This is a precursor to the relational frame of coordination and is extremely important as it provides the foundation for linguistic reference as well as constituting a prototype for relational framing more generally. This pattern is taught in the context of the parent-child "naming game."

## THE PARENT-CHILD "NAMING GAME"

An example of typical interactions in the context of this game might be as follows. The caregiver draws the child's attention to a novel object (e.g., a banana) and tells the child the name of the object (i.e., "banana"). If the child then repeats the name or an approximation of it then the parent smiles and lavishes praise on her. This is explicit training in the discriminative response "see object A → hear and say name B." Later (perhaps immediately though perhaps not) the caregiver may also ask the child to look at or pick out the novel object in the presence of a vocal prompt (e.g., "Where is the banana?"). Once again, if the child responds by picking out or perhaps even just looking at the appropriate object then, once again, smiles and praise are provided by the caregiver. This is explicit training in the relation "hear name B → respond to object A." This type of "object-name → name-object" (as well as the opposite direction "name-object → object-name") pattern happens numerous times in the history of an infant and with different object-name combinations. Furthermore, across multiple exemplars of explicit training in both object-name and name-object elements of the game, there are particular cues present consistently such as the word "is" and other more subtle features of the game and over the course of exposure to the multiple exemplars of the bidirectional pattern these consistent cues start to acquire control over a generalized bidirectional pattern in which both name → object and object → name necessarily feature. As a result of this history, eventually the cue alone controls the production of the bidirectional pattern and the child becomes able to derive name-object if trained in object-name alone and vice versa and thus at this point the child is showing the first example of generalized bidirectional relational responding.

From the point of view of the current chapter, what is particularly important about the name-object game just described is that it depends on the child already having a relatively well established repertoire of social interactive skills including joint attention. With a strongly established joint attention repertoire, the child will readily respond to novel objects to which the caregiver draws their attention and may also initiate such games by drawing the attention of the caregiver to novel objects in the vicinity. Hence, the precursors to PT provide an important foundation for the learning of this critical repertoire, and thus, in turn for the repertoire of relational framing more generally.

## EMPIRICAL INVESTIGATION OF THE FACILITATIVE ENVIRONMENT

The history that facilitates precursors to PT such as joint attention also facilitates the multiple exemplar training of the object-name and name-object pattern. Long before they start to show elementary patterns of relational framing such as described above, children are being immersed in social interactions that strengthen some of the social repertoires that we have already seen as well as preparing them to learn object-word relations. For example, Novak and Scott-Klingbord (1998) studied the social interactions that mothers have with their infants at least as early as 6 months. There was wide variation but mothers interacting with their infants tended to use objects in multiple ways, picking up objects, manipulating objects, labeling objects, placing objects in children's hands, moving the object by moving the children's hands, and even asking the children to label the object or asking them what they "thought" of the object. Such requests occurred many months before the children would actually be able to utter their first words and demonstrate the "mind-mindedness" of parents. Other researchers have observed parents prompting preverbal infants to speak. Hart and Risley (1999) described the monologues used by parents with their preverbal children as "floor-holding" and noted that about 200 out of 350 parental utterances per hour on average were similar to the following: A parent, after the child did not respond to "That's yours," added, "Where's that big bear? Is it behind you?" (p. 38). Hart and Risley used the phrase "becoming partners" to describe the beginning of the parent-child verbal communication that started after the child had begun to use their first few words. They noted that parents asked their infants an average of 83 questions per hour (compared with 33 per hour for other adults). This kind of questioning of course plays a key role in the parent-child naming games that allow the emergence of bidirectional relational responding.

## Conclusion

The development of precursors to PT is a very important aspect of a child's early development. The setting up of social reinforcers provided by contingent, sensitive, and intuitive caregivers contributes to the development of mutually responsive orientation, receptive joint attention, and children's initiation of joint attention, which are social behavioral cusps for the development of verbal PT, as well as to the development of bidirectional relational responding, which is a crucial stage in the development of language including deictic relational framing or PT.

# Chapter 5

# Theory of Mind

Martin Doherty *University of Stirling*

## Introduction

The aim of this chapter is to provide a brief overview of research into the development of theory of mind (ToM), the uniquely human ability to understand mental states, both our own and those of others. As adults we do this all the time, usually without thinking about it. Children, however, have a very limited version of this ability. In particular, until about age four, they do not seem to understand *belief*.

Cognitive psychologists understand belief in terms of mentally represented situations, or *propositions*. Simple beliefs can, for example, represent one's current situation. My current belief that Costa Coffee is still open is about (i.e., represents) the coffee bar downstairs, and represents it in a particular way—as open. Coupled with information about my desire for an Americano, knowledge of my belief can be used to predict my behavior. Most ToM researchers think that in the normal adult, ToM beliefs and other mental states are understood in this way: mental representations of reality that determine behavior.[1] However, the child's view of the social world seems very different from our own.

One current debate in ToM research is whether children really lack adult-like understanding. A lot of exciting recent work suggests that some understanding of belief may exist in infancy. I shall defend the view that until age four, children do not understand beliefs and other representational mental states. I shall cover three key theories. The debate largely centers on a single task, the false belief task (implicit and explicit versions). The chapter will close with a discussion of developments after age four that build on a basic understanding of belief, and developments in children's understanding of nonmental perspective taking that parallel their understanding of false belief.

---

# Theory of Mind: Definition and Tasks

Interest in ToM began when Premack and Woodruff (1978) asked "Does the chimpanzee have a theory of mind?"[2] They defined ToM as the ability to impute mental states to oneself and others. Since then it has been used in a variety of ways; in particular, acquisition of ToM has been identified with success on the *False Belief task*. There is considerably more to human social understanding than understanding beliefs, of course. Nevertheless, most developmental ToM work has involved this task, which is seen as marking a critical transition in the ability to reason about the mind.

## False Belief: The Unexpected Transfer Task

In a commentary on Premack and Woodruff's study, Dennett (1978) suggested minimal criteria for ascribing a ToM. The latter is principally useful for predicting, explaining, or influencing what someone will do.

---

1    Although some philosophers claim that this is not how the mind works (e.g., Churchland, 1981), I argue that we have no other way of making sense of behavior. The philosopher Fodor has this to say: "if commonsense intentional psychology really were to collapse, that would be, beyond comparison, the greatest intellectual catastrophe in the history of our species; if we're that wrong about the mind, then that's the wrongest we've ever been about anything... We'll be in deep, deep trouble if we have to give it up." (Fodor, 1987, p. xii)

2    The answer is still a matter of debate, but is probably "no" or "it depends what you mean." See the debate between Tomasello, Call and Hare (2003) and Povinelli and Vonk (2003), or Doherty (2009) for a summary.

Behavior can often be predicted simply by knowing someone's desires, and children have some understanding of desire from late infancy (Repacholi & Gopnik, 1997). However, for accurate behavior prediction, one also needs to know what someone believes.

This can be illustrated by the False Belief task, the typical version of which is the Unexpected Transfer task (Wimmer & Perner, 1983). Children are told that Maxi puts some chocolate in cupboard A and that, while he is absent, his mother moves the chocolate to cupboard B; they are then asked where Maxi will look for his chocolate when he returns. Children four and older answer A (where Maxi believes it to be). Three-year-olds, however, answer B (where it really is). This is among the more reliable findings in psychology.

To solve the task children must consider Maxi's (false) belief. The task is designed so that predicting on this basis gives a different answer than does predicting based on current reality. Young children seem to do the latter, since they systematically get the wrong ourselves.

## False Belief: The Unexpected Contents Task

Some argue that the False Belief task underestimates children's understanding of the mind. Hogrefe, Wimmer, and Perner (1986) hypothesized that children might be more willing to attribute a false belief to another if they had recently held the same false belief. In the *Unexpected Contents* task, children are shown a candy package and asked what is inside. Having answered "candy," they are shown that it in fact contains pencils. They are then asked what someone else will think is inside when first shown it. Despite their recent false belief, children are no better at this than at the Unexpected Transfer task. Even more surprisingly, when asked to report what they themselves had thought was in the tube when they first saw it, children under four typically say pencils (Gopnik & Astington, 1988).

This can be interpreted in two ways. The radical interpretation is that we have limited insight into even our own mental states. Most people intuit that we can accurately introspect on our mental states. However, there is evidence that this ability is limited. For example, Nisbett and Wilson (1977a) showed participants one of two filmed interviews, of an actor playing a teacher. Those who saw the interviewee answer disagreeably rated his accent, appearance, and mannerisms as less attractive than did those who saw him answer pleasantly. Nevertheless, they denied that his behavior had influenced their liking of him. Instead they claimed that their dislike of his accent, appearance, and mannerisms contributed to their dislike of him—the opposite of the truth. Nisbett and Wilson (1977b) present a number of similar examples of people's inability to report on their own cognitive processes.

It should be noted that it is possible to lack introspective insight into what has caused one's own current mental states, but still be able to introspect on them; that is, you can know what you believe even if you don't know why. However, Gopnik (1993) has provocatively argued that we lack even this ability, based on children's inability to recall beliefs they just held. She claimed that we use the same ToM to explain our own behavior and beliefs as we use for others. When asked what we thought was in the candy package, we reason that if someone (us) had only seen the outside, they would think there was candy inside. Children under four are unable to reason in this way, either for others or for themselves.

The other interpretation is that this lack of introspective access only applies to previously held beliefs. Plausibly, our representation of current reality is constantly being updated and overwritten as we get new information. This includes the revelation that there are pencils inside the candy package, which overwrites "candy." When now asked what we thought was inside, since the belief has been overwritten, it must be reconstructed. Reconstruction of one's past beliefs presumably follows a similar pattern to hypotheses about other people's. There has been much debate over which interpretation is correct. Practically, however, the Unexpected Contents task is now typically used as a variant of the False Belief task.

# Theoretical Issues

At this point in the development of the field there were two tasks which plausibly measured the understanding of belief. Children become able to pass both at age four. Three broad types of theory have been proposed to explain this developmental finding.

## "Theory" Theory

This claims that *theory* of mind really is theory-like (e.g., Perner, 1991). Children predict and explain mental states in terms of a set of concepts (belief, desire, etc.) that are causally related to perception and action. This is analogous to a scientific theory. The theoretical structure needed to solve the false belief task is simple if-then reasoning using two mental state concepts and relating them to action: if Maxi *wants* his chocolate, and *thinks* it is in cupboard A, then he will go to Cupboard A. This seems to conform to the natural way of talking about this situation.

"Theory" theory advocates see successful false belief performance as the direct result of conceptual development—of becoming able to understand beliefs etc. as mental representations of the world. Development thereafter elaborates on this basic insight. This constructivist conceptual view of development is one end of a continuum of views on ToM.

## Modularity Theories

At the other end of the spectrum are mental module accounts (e.g., Fodor, 1992). They also see the structure of ToM as theory-like. However, rather than developing, the theory is instantiated in a specific brain mechanism dedicated to ToM. Everyone in the debate sees the brain as the seat of ToM; however, modular accounts differ because modules are a particular kind of processor (Fodor, 1983). A module is basically a black box, taking particular input (information on behavior) and producing particular output (descriptions of mental states). Modules are specialized, and thus can be fast and efficient. It is usually argued that they evolved, which moves the explanatory burden out of developmental psychology altogether.

The best-known modularity theory was that of Leslie (1987). This posits a single processor, the ToM mechanism, which becomes active around 18 months, and is first evident in allowing pretend play. Children can in principle understand false belief from this age, but executive function limitations mean they cannot pass a false belief task. One appeal of this theory was that it seemed to fit well with symptoms of autism (i.e., lack of pretend play and poor false belief performance). Subsequent research has shown that children with autism are capable of pretend play, although they typically do not engage in it (e.g., V. Lewis & Boucher, 1988), and there was an extended debate about how similar understanding pretense is to understanding belief (see e.g., Doherty, 2009).

The details of Leslie's original theory are unimportant. Several claims remain prominent: ToM reasoning is performed by innate specialized brain mechanisms; these switch on early; they cannot support false belief due to executive function limitations.

## Simulation Theory

"Theory" theory and modularity theory map out the extremes of the current debate. A third approach is simulation theory, which has a different take on the nature of ToM. Another natural way to talk about others' mental states is what you would do or think in their place. Simulation theory advocates argue that ToM typically involves imagining yourself in the other person's position, using your decision-making apparatus to decide how to act or think, and then attributing the result to the other. No theory is necessary. Minds are sufficiently similar that one's own mind can model other people's (Gordon, 1986; Heal, 1986).

## The Theoretical Debate

The debate over whether ToM involves primarily simulation or theory figures mostly in the philosophical literature. P. L. Harris (1992) proposed the only detailed developmental proposal. According to this, success on the false belief task shows ability to perform a simulation of a certain complexity. This fits the false belief data well. It was devised to do so, however, and distinguishing simulation theory from "theory" theory empirically is difficult (see Ruffman, 1996, for findings favoring the latter).

Recently, the debate has been enlivened by neuroscience, and in particular the discovery of mirror neurons. These neurons, found in the motor cortex of macaque monkeys, fire when the monkey produces a particular action and also when it sees the same action produced by another. Studies using fMRI have found regions of the human brain that appear to have these "mirror" properties, and single cell research in patients with epilepsy suggests humans also have individual mirror neurons (Mukamel, Ekstrom, Kaplan, Iacoboni, & Fried, 2010). These findings suggest a neural basis for simulating others. Just as simulation theory would predict, activity in our own brains mirrors the actions of others. It remains to be seen how mental states such as beliefs, which have no visual physical counterpart can be incorporated into such a theory. In addition, how these new discoveries might relate to development has yet to be worked out.

# Criticism of the False Belief Task

The claim that children do not understand beliefs until age four is controversial and theoretically loaded. Whether you find it intuitively plausible may be influenced by your recent contact with preschool children. For example, the latter love the game of "hide and seek" but seem poor at it because they don't appear to understand that the seeker is not supposed to know where the hiders are. Peskin and Ardino (2003) examined preschoolers' hide-and-seek play. Even 3-year-olds could explain the rules. Nevertheless, they played very poorly. A few told the experimenter to hide, and then also hid themselves. Others hid before the seeker had turned away, told the seeker where they planned to hide, remained in plain view, or did not remain quiet or hidden. When playing as seeker, they would tell the hider where to hide, or stand and watch while she hid. Game performance was strongly related to performance on false belief tasks. There are clear changes in everyday behavior that correspond to developing concepts of belief.

Nevertheless, there have been numerous claims that the false belief task drastically underestimates children's abilities. Underestimation of children is a constant danger in developmental psychology. For example, questions asked in psychology experiments are unusual, which psychologists often forget. Usually one asks a question to learn the answer. Psychologists (and teachers) ask questions to which they know the answer, to find out if the child knows. Preschoolers, unfamiliar with this kind of question, may interpret them in unanticipated ways. In the 1990s in particular, many studies were carried out in which the procedure of the false belief task and the form of the questions were manipulated to ensure children's understanding. There were hundreds of these studies. In some, the manipulations made no difference. In others, they made a substantial difference. Studies of both kinds were followed by replications or failures to replicate. By selectively reading studies, one could conclude that even three-year-olds can pass modified false belief tasks, or, conversely, that children do not master the task until age five. What was required was a convincing overview.

Wellman, Cross and Watson (2001) provided just that with a meta-analysis. They integrated findings from the first 15 years of false belief research (i.e., 178 studies involving over 4,000 children). Analysis showed that several factors made no difference. Whether children were asked about what someone will do, say, think or know made little difference.

Findings from the unexpected transfer and unexpected contents tasks did not differ, nor did it seem to matter whether the question concerned the child's own previous false belief or someone else's.

## Factors Affecting False Belief Performance

Six factors did affect performance though. One is likely artifactual: children do better if the target object is absent. For example, sometimes the chocolate is eaten, or the candy package's unexpected content is nothing. This is plausibly because in the standard versions children systematically give the incorrect answer—the object's actual location, for example. If the object ceases to exist, this option is removed. They may then simply guess, thus "improving" from 0 to 50 percent. Sure enough, Wellman et al. found that at best this variable raised performance to chance. Another factor was country. In Australia children did relatively well, in Japan relatively poorly. Cultural differences in ToM development may exist; however the same general pattern of development held. The precise age at which cognitive abilities develop is not usually important, within broad limits. More important is sequence.

Three other factors seem largely procedural. Children do better if there is an explicit motive—for example, if the chocolate is moved as an act of deception or there is a pencil in the tube because we needed a place to keep it. Children also perform better if they take part themselves, rather than passively watch. Performance is also better if the false belief is made more salient, by stating it or depicting it, for example. None of the factors improved 3-year-olds' performance to above chance.

The only factor to interact with age was temporal marking. Some versions of the test questions are potentially ambiguous concerning which point in time is being asked about. For example, C. Lewis and Osborne (1990) argued that for the unexpected contents task the test question, "What did you think was in here?" was insufficiently clear. Appending "before I took the top off?" clarifies the timepoint being referred to and improves performance. Siegal and Beattie (1991) produced a similar improvement in the unexpected transfer task by appending "first" to the test question, e.g., "Where will Maxi look *first?*" These questions do not always produce improvement, even when repeated by the same research groups (e.g., Peterson & Siegal, 1999). They are undoubtedly clearer, though, and have frequently been used in subsequent research. Wellman et al. found that this kind of test question does improve performance—

but only for older children. If younger children's competence was being masked by failure to understand the question, the opposite should be the case. Instead, temporal marking produces an improvement around age four.

In sum, this meta-analysis suggests the false belief task can be made slightly easier or harder, but no manipulation changes the basic pattern of development. The task has received an astonishing amount of critical attention but it remains a robust finding that older preschoolers can predict behavior based on a false belief, and younger preschoolers cannot.

# Implicit Understanding of Belief

The research discussed all concerns children's ability to make explicit predictions about what someone will do or think. As they become able to do this, they also start to be able to do other things requiring understanding of belief. They become able to explain incorrect actions based on false beliefs (Robinson & Mitchell, 1995; Wimmer & Mayringer, 1998). They become able to conceal information—such as in Peskin and Ardino's (2003) hide-and-seek task cited above. They also become capable of lying and deception (e.g., Peskin, 1992; Sodian, Taylor, Harris, & Perner, 1991). There are credible claims that competent deception can develop before false belief understanding (Newton, Reddy, & Bull, 2000); nevertheless, children are typically unable to judge false beliefs until age four.

This supports "theory" theory's claim of conceptual change around four. The ability to *use* a concept of belief seems absent before this age. However, there is recent evidence that suggests such a concept may be available before age three—as required by modularity theory. This understanding could be called implicit, meaning it cannot be used to make judgments.

The first search for implicit understanding of belief came from the "theory" theory camp. Clements and Perner (1994) set up a false belief scenario for children to watch. Sam the mouse put his cheese in a box by one of two mouseholes and went inside. While he was away, Katie mouse moved the cheese to a box by the other mousehole. The narrator announced that Sam had awoken and was planning to retrieve his cheese, and prompted "I wonder where he will look?" The assumption is that children will look to the hole they think Sam will come out of. If sensitive to his false belief, they should look at the hole he entered. If not they should look to the one with the cheese (since his stated intention is to retrieve it). Finally, they were asked the explicit false belief question "which box will he open (first)?"

The results were clear-cut. Until age 2 years 11 months, children looked to the wrong location. By age 3, however, there was a rapid rise in looking to the correct false belief location. Most children did not pass the explicit question until age 4. Two things are noteworthy: first, an implicit false belief sensitivity was evident a year before correct explicit responding, and second, this sensitivity was absent before age three. Ruffman, Garnham, Import, & Connolly (2001) subsequently examined whether the implicit / explicit discrepancy could be due to a nascent explicit understanding in which children lacked confidence. They used a "betting" procedure to gauge confidence in explicit predictions. Children who failed the explicit question were confident in their wrong answer, while younger successful children were unsure of their correct one. This suggests the hypothesis of a nascent understanding of false belief combined with a lack of confidence is incorrect.

These findings indicated that children may be able to represent another's false belief nearly a year before they can make judgments about false belief. Furthermore, this has recently been extended down to young two-year-olds by Southgate, Senju, and Csibra (2007). They showed twenty-five-month-olds a vignette similar to Clements and Perner's, with two key differences. One was that it was nonverbal: a woman watched while an object was placed in one of two boxes. Children were first shown her reaching through one of two flaps corresponding to the boxes. The flaps lit up and there was a tone just before she reached, to cue them to look in anticipation. Then the sequence was repeated, during which there was a telephone noise and the woman turned away. While she was looking elsewhere the object was removed. The tone sounded and the flaps lit up. Would the woman reach to where she falsely believes the object still is? The findings were clear: two-year-olds looked at the flap next to the box where she had last seen the object, and looked at it longer.

Southgate et al. speculate that the reason why they found anticipatory looking much earlier was due to the verbal prompt used in the earlier studies. When children heard "I wonder where he will look?" they might have interpreted the "where" as referring to the object's location, rather than the protagonist's behavior. However, there is no independent evidence that children make this kind of consistent age-related error. The other major difference between studies is that the object disappears entirely. This may be more critical, since it removes any reason to look at the "non–false belief" location.

Southgate et al.'s study is one of several recent studies showing sensitivity to belief in very young children. This began with a study by Onishi and Baillargeon (2005) with fifteen-month-old infants. In this study a woman had either seen or not seen an object moved into one of two boxes. When she reached into the box containing the object, infants looked longer if she had not seen the object move (so should falsely believe it was elsewhere) than if she had seen it move. Again, through their pattern of attention, infants seem to be distinguishing between behaviors based on true and false beliefs.

## Accounting for Implicit and Explicit False Belief Data

Integrating the findings from implicit and explicit false belief studies is a challenge for all theories. According to Baillargeon, Scott and He (2010), children fail standard ToM tasks because they require i) representation of the agent's mental state, ii) accessing this in response to task demands, and iii) inhibition of other responses. Implicit ToM tasks only require representation of the agent's mental state. The other two requirements either overload children's limited resources, and/or the neural connections needed are immature. Speculations about neural development are difficult to assess one way or the other. Claiming that dedicated neural structures are in place but not yet able to do what they are there for potentially undermines the evolutionary claim for innate ToM abilities. A ToM mechanism that cannot be used for a considerable period after it becomes active would be an inefficient use of limited resources. However, the claims about overloading children and inhibitory difficulties yield clear empirical predictions: modifying the executive demands of explicit false belief tasks should substantially lower age of success. Wellman et al.'s (2001) meta-analysis, discussed above, shows this is not the case.

Other researchers argue that implicit false belief tasks do not require children to have concepts of representational mental states. Ruffman and Perner (2005) suggested that infants may be picking up on behavioral regularities. Infants' statistical learning abilities are sophisticated (e.g., Gomez & Gerken, 2000), potentially allowing them to develop complex expectations based on behavioral regularities, without yet having abstracted mental-state concepts from this information. Regularities such as people searching for objects where they last saw them would produce success on these tasks.

Another response suggests humans have two systems for reasoning about beliefs (e.g., Apperly & Butterfill, 2009). One develops early and is limited and inflexible. This accounts for infant performance on implicit ToM tasks. The other develops slowly and is more flexible. This allows preschoolers to pass standard false belief tasks. In adulthood, both systems operate. This allows an active role for the earlier system from the start.

A third possibility is that infants' precocious abilities are based on simpler concepts that allow them to "fake it" (e.g., Doherty, 2011). For example, the implicit false belief tasks discussed can be solved with a concept of "engagement." Infants are very sensitive to what adults are engaged with, partly because this can predict if adults will interact with whatever the infant is interested in. Infants can keep track of which situations or objects people have (not) been engaged with, and make attempts to (re) engage them when this suits their interests (e.g., O'Neill, 1996). Disengagement occurs when an object an adult had been involved with changes location, so long as the adult is not present or paying attention during the change. If children are sensitive to this, both the object and the location where disengagement occurred will be more salient. This would predict an increased tendency to look at either the object, or the location the adult last had contact with it. If the object is removed, infants will look at the location, as occurred in Southgate et al.'s study.

Infant ToM research is new and dynamic. For now there is no consensus on what exactly infants are doing. In particular, a proper evaluation of the findings will require a developmental account of how early abilities relate to later ones.

# Broadening the Focus

So far I have concentrated largely on the false belief task. This task has been critical to theoretical developments in the field, and is viewed as a "litmus test" for ToM. If truth be told, though, there has been a disproportionate focus on it. However, understanding of belief is a developmental milestone from which much else develops.

## Understanding of Knowledge

Around the time children show an explicit false belief understanding, they also show some understanding of knowledge. This is unsurprising, since knowledge is defined as justified true belief. Children can judge which of two people knows the contents of a box, for example, if they know that one person has seen inside and another has not. Wimmer, Hogrefe, and Perner (1988) found 4-year-olds but not 3-year-olds were good at this; Pratt and Bryant (1990) found better performance in 3-year-olds, and this ability may somewhat precede success on the false belief task.

Though children might be able to distinguish between results of access and no access to information, they struggle to distinguish different kinds of access. Gopnik and Graf (1988) let children find out the contents of a box by looking inside, being told, or guessing. Three-year-olds were unable to say how they found out; four-year-olds did much better.

Four-year-olds' grasp of knowledge is far from perfect, however. O'Neill, Astington and Flavell (1992) showed children a box with two ways of finding out the contents—opening a window to look in, or putting a hand in to feel. They were shown pairs of objects that differed only in either color (e g , a red and a blue ball) or weight (a full and an empty piggybank). One object per pair was hidden in the box, and children had to choose whether to look or feel to find out which. Only by age 5 were they better than chance at correctly choosing whether to look or feel. Children show a similarly delayed understanding of how much informational access is needed to know something. In the "Droodle" task (Chandler & Helm, 1984), children are shown a picture, which is then covered up except for a small unidentifiable detail. Until age five, they are confident that someone who saw only that small detail could identify the picture. Although by age four children know informational access is needed for knowledge, they do not yet distinguish different kinds or amounts of information.

## Second-Order Theory of Mind

After age five, children start to be able to reason about the effects of mental states on other mental states. The second-order false belief task mentioned above (Perner & Wimmer, 1985) requires children to judge

John's false belief about Mary's belief. The stories in this kind of task are typically complicated and thus age of success is variable, but roughly children between 5 and 7 years begin to pass.

A procedurally less complex task gauging second-order mental-state reasoning involves inference. Children see a bead taken from a dish with beads of only one color, and put in a box. A doll saw the dish with the beads at the start, but not the transfer, and is told truthfully that the bead in the box is from the dish. Children are then asked if the doll would know the color of the beads in the box. Though children have no problem themselves with this inference, up to age 6 or 7 they answer that the doll would not know (e.g., Ruffman, 1996). Inference is "second-order" as it involves generating one piece of knowledge from another.

Around the same time, children start to realize that cognitive states interact with emotions. Even infants know that satisfaction of desires typically produces happiness, but understanding that emotions are based on beliefs about a situation does not develop until about five or six. P. L. Harris, Johnson, Hutton, Andrews, and Cooke (1989) told children stories where, for example, a character who liked cola was offered a cola can that without her knowledge had been filled with milk (which she disliked). Four-year-olds, though able to infer her false belief, that the can contained her favorite drink, still judged that she would be sad when first seeing it.

Hadwin and Perner (1991) replicated this finding and compared it with children's understanding of surprise. Surprise is the definitive belief-based emotion: a result of discovering your belief does not match reality. Hadwin and Perner modified the candy task, telling children about a character who, for example, found jelly beans in a chocolate-candy package. After correctly predicting initial false belief, children were asked to indicate his emotion on seeing the contents by pointing to a picture of a surprised or neutral face. Virtually no four-year-olds, half the five-year-olds, and most six-year-olds could do this consistently.

Ruffman and Keenan (1996) found similarly late development of understanding of surprise. Their study is one of the few to address whether second-order ToM reasoning differs in kind from first-order ToM, or is simply more complicated. They included a control question that matched the information-processing demands of the surprise question by requiring children to simultaneously consider the story character's previous false belief and current knowledge: "Show me the dish that John thought there would be white paper inside, but now knows that there's green paper inside." This question did not cause problems, even for the six-year-olds, who in this study showed little understanding of surprise yet. Ruffman and Keenan argued that understanding surprise is more than simply being capable of sufficiently complex cognition. Additionally, children have to revise their existing theory of surprise. Initially they associate surprise with pleasant events, such as a party or present. These are indeed typical of surprises children experience, but are not defining characteristics. Once children understand the role of mental states in surprise, they have to readjust their theories, which may take some time. In fact, the children in this experiment did not properly understand that surprise was the consequence of a false belief rather than ignorance until they were between seven and nine years old.

This raises the question whether second-order ToM is based on an additional conceptual shift in understanding. At age four children understand that people have mental states about the world. Second-order tasks may need additional understanding that people have mental states about mental states, both beliefs and emotions. It remains an open question whether this requires new conceptual developments concerning the potentially recursive nature of mental states, or simply sufficient information-processing resources.

## Nonmental Perspective Taking

"Theory" theory claims that false belief prediction is based on a new understanding of the representational nature of mental states. If so, children should also begin to understand similar nonmental representational phenomena. This is an interesting test of "theory" theory. Neither simulation nor modularity theory predicts any relationship between mental and nonmental representation. Simulation theory concerns using one's mind to simulate someone else's, so nonmental phenomena fall outside its remit. Modularity theory's claim that ToM reasoning is based on dedicated hardware similarly would claim no natural relationship between mental and nonmental representational understanding.

Zaitchik (1990) tested this prediction with the "false" photograph task. The task was closely analogous to the false belief task. A photograph was taken of a scene: Bert from Sesame Street lying on a mat. While the photograph developed, the scene was changed—Bert leaves and is replaced by Big Bird. At this point, children were asked "In the picture, who is lying on the mat?" Zaitchik found most three-year-olds answered "Big Bird" (incorrect), whereas most four-year-olds answered "Bert" (correct).

Performance on the false belief task was similar. Zaitchik concluded children find mental representations difficult "not because they are mental but because they are *representations*" (Zaitchik, 1990, p. 61).

This initially looked like support for "theory" theory. However, the word "false" in the "false" photograph task is in quotation marks for a reason. The photograph is not false; it is an accurate representation of things when taken. Thus it is closer to a true memory than a false belief. Zaitchik did not report correlations between the false belief and "false" photograph tasks. This was done by Perner, Leekam, Myers, Davis, and Odgers (1998), who replicated the basic findings, but found performance on the two tasks to be unrelated. Furthermore it was straightforward to make the "false" photograph task easier. Simply making sure children were looking at the back of the photograph when the question was asked raised performance from 53 percent to 94 percent (Perner et al., 1998, Expt. 2). It seems children were confused by the question. Similar manipulations, such as making sure children are looking at Maxi when the belief question is asked, make no difference to the false belief task.

The other main form of nonmental representation is language. Doherty and Perner (1998) hypothesized that false belief understanding should develop alongside ability to produce synonyms. This is less than obvious at first glance, but is theoretically well-motivated. Synonyms are words meaning the same thing (e.g., "truck" and "lorry"). Each can represent the same object, just as two different beliefs can represent the same situation. In order to produce a synonym for a given word, one has to understand the relationship between the two words and the object; given the word "truck," one has to produce a word that refers to the same object, but that also differs in form. In the false belief task, one has to infer a belief that refers to the same situation, but also differs from your own belief.

Doherty and Perner used two synonym tasks. In the production task, children were given a word and had to produce its synonym. Poor performance here might result from word-finding difficulties or poor executive function, so in the judgment task, children simply watched while a puppet did the task and had to say whether the puppet was correct. Both tasks were strongly and specifically related to false belief task performance (r = 0.70).

One possible concern is that there are probably no true synonyms (though for preschoolers the words used may be effectively synonymous). There are true homonyms however—words with distinct unrelated meanings, such as "bat" (flying mammal) and "bat" (sports equipment).

Homonyms and synonyms pose similar representational demands, and Doherty (2000) found that the ability to produce synonyms, identify homonyms, and show false belief were all specifically related. Perner, Stummer, Sprung and Doherty (2002) found a similar relationship between hierarchically related word pairs (e.g., "rabbit" and "animal"). The phenomenon is general to any two alternative names, and Perner et al. (2002) explain the relationship between the tasks in terms of requiring a common understanding of *perspective.*

The same logic has been extended to pictures: ambiguous figures like the well-known duck-rabbit are pictorially analogous to homonyms. Doherty and Wimmer (2005), for example, found that children's ability to report both interpretations of an ambiguous figure was closely related to performance on the false belief, homonym, and synonym tasks.

# Conclusion

This chapter has provided a brief overview of research into the development of ToM. In doing so, it has presented substantial empirical evidence that four-year-olds acquire a new understanding of representation which allows them an increasingly sophisticated understanding of mind. The question of how to integrate this claim with infants' implicit abilities remains open, and will be a prime focus of research for the next few years.

# Chapter 6

# How the Self Relates to Others When Perspective Taking Is Impaired

Matthieu Villatte & Roger Vilardaga
*University of Nevada, Reno*

Jean Louis Monestes *CHU d'Amiens and*
*Hôpital Pinel, Amiens, France*

## Introduction

Among the different implications of a relational frame analysis of perspective taking, the understanding of how mental-states attribution operates is crucial, in particular if we consider impairments in this respect seen in certain clinical populations. In this chapter, we will present an overview of the literature on deficits in mental-state attribution and then show how studies conducted in the field of RFT have shed new light on this topic.

## Deficits in Mental-State Attribution in Psychosis

In the past three decades, interest in impairments in PT has grown exponentially in the clinical literature. Most of this work has been conducted on mental-state attribution (or ToM[1]) in schizophrenia and autism spectrum disorder (ASD; for reviews, see Yirmiya, Erel, Shaked, & Salomonica-Levi, 1998; Brüne, 2005a & b). The first major study conducted in this area showed that children with ASD have difficulty adopting the point of view of another (Baron-Cohen, Leslie, & Frith, 1985). This study used the now famous "Sally and Anne" false belief task. For this task, participants were first told a story about a doll (Sally), who puts a marble in a basket and then leaves the room. While she is away, another doll (Anne) moves the marble from the basket to a box. Children were then asked "Where will Sally look for her marble?" Providing the correct answer to this question requires the child to adopt Sally's perspective. Results showed that typically developing children can respond to this task correctly by age four; however, children with ASD continue to fail, even long after this age. Since then, this apparent deficiency in PT in ASD has been confirmed in numerous additional studies using a variety of different types of tasks and indeed it is now considered a core feature of ASD and a key reason that children with ASD have difficulties in social interaction (see Yirmiya et al., 1998).

A decade after the first evidence of impairments in PT in ASD, some researchers began to study a similar phenomenon in psychosis. One study explored the ability of individuals with schizophrenia to attribute intentions to characters involved in social interactions (Corcoran, Mercer, & Frith, 1995) using problems such as the "hinting task." For instance, the participant had to identify the intention of Paul, who is running late for an interview and says to his wife: "I want to wear that blue shirt, but it's very creased." Other studies employed cartoon stories that participants had to sort by guessing the intention of the characters involved in the vignettes (e.g., Sarfati, Hardy-Baylé, Nadel, Chevalier, & Widlöcher, 1997).

---

1    The term Theory of Mind refers the capacity to infer the beliefs, intentions and emotions of others in order to explain and predict their behavior (Premack & Woodruff, 1978).

In each of these studies, there were significant deficits in performance in individuals with schizophrenia.

The studies reviewed thus far suggest deficits in intention attribution but that does not necessarily mean deficits in PT since it cannot be assumed that the latter are required for the former. In fact, the majority of the early theory of mind (ToM) literature on schizophrenia was divided into two main theoretical models that did not refer explicitly to PT. Frith (1992) proposed that people with schizophrenia suffer from a dysfunction in the meta-representational system that normally allows a person to attribute intentions, to self as well as others. While individuals with negative symptoms (e.g., anhedonia) would be totally incapable of attributing an intention, those with positive symptoms (e.g., hallucinations, delusions) would still be able to do so but their attributions would be inaccurate, leading to delusions of reference or persecution, for example. The alternative model (Hardy-Bayle, 1994) argued that only people with disorganized thought demonstrate impairments in mental state attribution. In this model, attribution of another's mental-state relies on cues that can be interpreted in different ways and thus to accurately determine a given mental state, supplemental information is needed. For example, a smile can be interpreted as kindness or as mockery and thus it is useful to consider if it appears in the context of an argument or a friendly interaction. According to Hardy-Bayle, thought disorganization leads to difficulties in taking contextual information into account, one of the results of which is impairments in mental-state attribution.

However, some authors have approached ToM impairments in schizophrenia more directly through PT skills. For example, Langdon, Coltheart, Ward, and Catts (2001) observed that participants with schizophrenia demonstrate poorer performance than controls in visual PT when they have to imagine how an object would look if they had to observe it from another point of view. In addition, their performance on this task was correlated with that on a false-belief task, indicating a link between PT and mental-state attribution. Schiffman et al. (2004) observed that children who later developed a schizophrenia spectrum disorder performed significantly less accurately than typically developing children on a task requiring them to take the perspective of a character in a story.

Mental-state attribution deficits have been seen not only in schizophrenia but also in individuals with schizotypy, a subclinical personality pattern presenting similarities with the pathological syndrome. Schizotypy comprises a cluster of dimensions corresponding to the main characteristics of schizophrenia, including impulsive nonconformity, perceptual aberration, magical ideation, and physical and social anhedonia (J. P. Chapman, Chapman, & Kwapil, 1995) and vulnerability to the development of psychosis increases in people with a high score on these dimensions (L. J. Chapman, Chapman, Kwapil, Eckblad, & Zinser, 1994; Gooding, Tallent, & Matts, 2005). The results of studies examining mental-state attribution ability in individuals with a profile of schizotypy showed that even when no actual symptom is present, slight difficulties in mental state attribution can be observed. For example, Langdon and Coltheart (1999) reported that schizotypal participants were less accurate than controls on a false-belief task. Pickup (2006) observed a correlation between the score on a subscale of the O-LIFE schizotypal personality scale (Mason, Claridge, & Jackson, 1995) and performance on a ToM task requiring inference of the mental states of characters in a short story. Platek, Critton, Myers and Gallup (2003) obtained similar results with another schizotypy scale (the Schizotypal Personality Questionnaire; [SPQ]; Raine, 1991) and a faux-pas task (similar to false-belief attribution tasks); while Langdon and Coltheart (2001) observed visual PT impairments analogous to those reported in schizophrenic patients by Langdon et al. (2001). Together, these results suggest that, just as psychosis itself seems to develop along a continuum, so too might ToM impairment as a characteristic of the condition.

---

# A Relational Frame Approach to Theory of Mind

One empirically based approach to understanding mental-state attribution that might prove useful in understanding deficits of the latter in psychosis is in terms of PT skills. A significant quantity of data already suggests that PT skills might be at the core of ToM skills and indeed PT has already been used to understand mental-state attribution in several developmental or neuroscientific accounts.

As regards developmental studies, M. Taylor and Carlson (1997) reported that the accuracy of four-year-old preschoolers on a ToM task was positively correlated with having an imaginary companion and impersonating. In the same sample assessed three years later, understanding of emotion was correlated with impersonating (M. Taylor, Carlson, Maring, Gerow, & Charley, 2004). According to the authors, children experiment with role-taking when they impersonate and play with their imaginary companion. Other research showed that role-play constitutes a social experience that is linked with ToM development. For example, Youngblade and Dunn (1995) reported that playing roles at thirty-three months was linked to higher performance on false-belief tasks seven months later.

Neuroscience data supports the view that one needs to take the perspective of others to accurately identify one's own mental states. For example, Goldman and Sripada (2005) reviewed studies showing that deficits in faced-based emotion recognition (often categorized as a form of ToM ability) were paired with deficits in the production of the same emotion (for fear, disgust and anger specifically). According to these authors, this supports the idea that one needs to reproduce an observed facial expression to recognize it. Furthermore, reproduction of the facial expression need only appear at the neural level based on research into the activity of mirror neurons, showing that this specific category of neurons is activated during the execution as well as during the observation of a given action (Gallese & Goldman, 1998).

## Relational Frame Theory

The behavior analytic approach to language and cognition offered by relational frame theory (RFT, Hayes, Barnes-Holmes, & Roche, 2001) postulates that PT is the core skill involved in mental-state attribution. In what follows we will briefly outline the RFT approach to language and cognition, as well as the first RFT studies conducted in relation to ToM specifically. These will be explored only briefly, as they are already described elsewhere in this book. After doing so, we will show how this approach sheds new light on mental-state attribution impairments in clinical disorders as well as pointing to possible remediation.

Relational frame theory analyzes language and cognition as the activity of relating events based on contextual cues that determine the appropriate relational pattern to apply. In this account, humans and many other species can learn to relate objects based on their intrinsic physical features, but humans seem unique in that they can also relate events on the basis of social contextual cues. For example, a person can respond to a nickel as bigger than a dime based on intrinsic physical characteristics of the two coins (i.e., a nickel is physically larger than a dime), but can also respond to a nickel as smaller than a dime based on socially established contextual cues that appear in our language (e.g., being taught that a nickel can buy less than a dime). In this way the contextually controlled relational activity allowed by language can change the psychological functions of a given event completely independently of the actual physical characteristics of that event. In addition, RFT has shown that relations do not have to be directly trained to be established. For example, if we are told that a dime has the same value as a given foreign coin, then without any supplemental information, we can derive that the foreign coin has a greater value than a nickel. The arbitrary applicability (under social contextual control) of relational activity as well as its derivational properties allow the generation of an infinity of new relations, among which there are not only relations of comparison, but a multitude of others including sameness (equivalence), difference, condition, analogy, hierarchy and perspective.

## Perspective Taking as Deictic Framing

In the current context, we are obviously most interested in relations of perspective, including I-YOU, HERE-THERE and NOW-THEN, which allow the speaker to differentiate between his or her own perspective and that of someone else. The unique feature of relations of this type, referred to in RFT as deictic relations, is that they have no formal counterpart. That is, these relations can be established only under social contextual control. Thus, a relation of comparison, for example, can be established both according to intrinsic physical characteristics (e.g., a dime is physically larger than a nickel) and under social contextual control (e.g., a dime and a nickel both have a monetary value). In contrast, deictic relational responding can be established only on the basis of countless examples that differentiate the perspective associated with I versus YOU (interpersonal perspective), HERE versus THERE (spatial perspective) and NOW versus THEN (temporal perspective). Training in PT occurs through answering and asking questions such as "What are you doing now?", "Where did you go then?", "Where will I go tomorrow?", and "When did I say that?" Appropriate responding to such questions requires appropriate discrimination of perspective.

## Preliminary Empirical Work

For relational frame theory, perspective is understood as deictic relational framing and empirical studies based on RFT have provided evidence that PT as deictic relational framing is at the core of mental state attribution or ToM. One of the first such studies was provided by McHugh, Barnes-Holmes and Barnes-Holmes (2004), who showed that deictic relational responding follows a developmental trend similar to ToM abilities. In this study, three levels of deictic relational responding complexity were employed: simple, reversed and double reversed. At the simple level, participants had to respond according to the three different types of perspective (interpersonal, spatial and temporal) without having to change their point of view. For example, given the question *"If I have a green brick and you have a red brick, which brick do you have? Which brick do I have?,"* the participant had to answer "red" and "green," respectively. At the reversed level, questions such as *"I have a green brick and you have a red brick. If I were you and you were me, which brick would you have? Which brick would I have?"* required changing perspective to adopt another's point of view (for example, "I" now have the red brick). At a double reversed level, questions involved two types of perspective at the same time (e.g., interpersonal and spatial) and required changing perspective twice. An example of such a question was *"I am sitting on the blue chair here and you are sitting on the black chair there. If I were you and you were me and if here was there and there was here, where would you be sitting? Where would I be sitting?"* Results showed a marked difference in the performance of four and five-year-olds similar to what has been shown for ToM skills in most developmental studies (Wellman, Cross, & Watson, 2001).

McHugh, Barnes-Holmes, Barnes-Holmes and Stewart (2006) brought the RFT approach to PT to bear on the assessment of false belief responding by adapting a task that had previously been used in another study to examine false belief. In the original task, the participant was shown a candy box and asked *"What do you think is inside the box?"* Of course, the participant usually answered *"candy."* Then, the box was opened, and was seen to contain pencils. The participant was then asked *"Before we opened the box, what did you think was inside?"* This second question is critical because it assesses a person's ability to distinguish between what they thought was true before and what they know to be true now. Various studies have used this task since it was first developed and by now the pattern of failures on the task by particular groups (i.e., children below the age of 5, people with ASD and people with schizophrenia) has been shown to be similar to that for the Sally and Anne task which coheres with the idea that, as with the latter, this task assesses mental-state attribution.

From an RFT perspective, the original task assessed responding in accordance with NOW-THEN relations. McHugh et al. (2006) extended this original task by including I-YOU relations. More specifically, the adapted McHugh protocol examined the attribution of both true and false beliefs both to oneself as well as to another person. An example of false belief attribution to another was as follows: *"If I put pencils in the candy box and you are not here, what will you think is inside the box?"* In this case, "You" should be attributed a false belief, that is, *"You will think the box contains candy."* In this study, as in McHugh, Barnes-Holmes, & Barnes-Holmes (2004a), results showed a marked difference in the performance of four- and five-year olds. The combination of data from both studies suggested the utility of the RFT account of PT, conceptualized as deictic relational framing, as being key to ToM / mental-state attribution. One logical next direction for research then was to examine the possibility that this analysis might be effectively applied with respect to ToM impairments in clinical disorders such as autism and psychosis.

## RFT-Based Investigations of Theory of Mind Impairments

### AUTISM SPECTRUM DISORDER

The first RFT-based study to assess PT in a population linked with deficits in mental-state attribution was conducted by Rehfeldt, Dillen, Ziomek, and Kowalchuk (2007). In this study, nine children diagnosed with high-functioning autism spectrum disorder and nine controls (i.e., a total of eighteen children) completed an experimental protocol composed of the same suite of deictic relational tasks (and thus including the same three levels of deictic complexity) as employed in McHugh, Barnes-Holmes, & Barnes-Holmes (2004a). The results showed that participants with ASD demonstrated poorer performance than control participants when they had to reverse deictic relations. In addition, a correlation appeared between performance on reversed NOW-THEN relations and the dimension of daily social skills of the Vineland Adaptive Behavior Scales (Sparrow, Balla, & Cicchetti, 1984). These results thus provided further support for the theoretical link between deictic relational responding and ToM performance. In addition, the association between deictic relational responding and social functioning suggested the relevance of this type of relational activity in more ecological contexts.

## SCHIZOPHRENIA

More recently, Villatte, Monestes, McHugh, Freixa i Baque, & Loas (2010b) used the same deictic relational frame analysis to examine PT in schizophrenia and to compare levels of this ability with levels of mental-state attribution. To assess the latter, this research used an adapted and slightly longer (i.e., 20 item) version of the Hinting task (Corcoran et al., 1995), while to examine the former, it employed the (computer-based) deictic protocol employed by McHugh, Barnes-Holmes, & Barnes-Holmes (2004a).

Let us examine how a Hinting task problem might be conceptualized by RFT in terms of deictic relational responding. For example, take the task: *"John has been on the phone with his friend for over an hour. John says: 'My mother ought to call me in a few minutes'"* (Question: *"What does John really mean when he says this?"*) According to RFT, in order to infer the intention of the character, the participant must change perspective and thus derive deictic relations as follows: *"If I were John (I—You / Other) in that particular place—talking on the phone (Here—There)—and at that moment—a few minutes before my mother ought to call me (Now— Then)—I would intend to..."*[2]. Thus, performance in complex deictic relational responding (i.e., changing perspective) should be correlated with scores obtained on the Hinting task. Results observed by Villatte et al. (2010b) confirmed this. First, patients diagnosed with schizophrenia who participated in the study demonstrated poorer performance than controls on all reversed and double-reversed deictic relations, but not on simple deictic relations, thus indicating a specific deficit in ability to change perspective. Although co-variance analyses showed that the effect of IQ on deictic performance did approach significance, the difference between the two groups remained significant. Response time was also measured and the absence of differences for this variable indicated that errors produced by participants with schizophrenia were not due to impulsivity. In addition, aspects of the presentational format whereby the items were retained on the screen until the participant responded also made it possible to rule out attention or memory deficits as possible causes of the difference between the groups.

---

2    It is likely that other types of relational responding (e.g., conditional relational responding) are also involved in such a task. For example, one might learn to interpret social cues through rules such as "if a person says x, then s/he means y." A deficit in this type of relational responding could thus also lead to impairments in mental-states attribution.

Apart from the difference in levels of deictic relational responding between the two groups however, this study also found a significant correlation between deictic relational responding and ToM performance as measured using the Hinting task. This link was observed not only in patients with schizophrenia (44 percent of ToM performance was predicted by accuracy in reversing deictic relations) but also in healthy participants (41 percent). Although it might yet be argued that deficits in deictic relational framing as demonstrated by patients are only an instance of an impairment in relational framing more generally (that is, an impairment that might also be measured for other frames such as comparison, hierarchy etc.), the clear link between these two tasks in control participants strongly supports the view that deictic relational framing/PT lies at the core of intention attribution.

Another study was conducted to examine deictic relational responding involved in false-belief attribution to the self and to another with the same sample of patients with schizophrenia as in the study reported above[3] (Villatte et al., 2010a). The task employed was a computerized version of that developed by McHugh, Barnes-Holmes, & Barnes-Holmes (2004a) allowing the measurement of response latencies. Results revealed poorer performance of patients in comparison with controls on items requiring (i) taking the perspective of another and thus correctly attributing a belief (whether true or false) to that person; for example *"If I were you, I would not know that you had put pencils in the candy box"*; and (ii) the attribution of a false belief to the self. In RFT terms, these items involve respectively (i) reversal of the I-YOU relation and (ii) responding in accordance with "logical not" (i.e., for false belief). While both these types of items led participants with schizophrenia to produce more errors, there was no difference between the groups when no change of perspective was required to attribute a true belief. For this task (sum score), the effect of IQ was not significant, suggesting once again the independence of mental-state attribution ability and intellectual competency in the context of schizophrenia. Latency data showed that the two groups were equally fast on all patterns of deictic responding but that both responded faster when attributing a belief to the self than to another, which is similar to a pattern seen in exclusively nonclinical participants by McHugh, Barnes-Holmes, Barnes-Holmes, Whelan and Stewart (2007) and is consistent with the idea that an additional process (i.e., change in perspective) is required for the latter task.

---

3    However, the order of the two deictic protocols was counterbalanced to avoid any effect of learning in deictic relational responding.

Hence, results from a number of recent RFT studies suggest that deictic relational framing is impaired in ASD and schizophrenia. These findings cohere with the RFT account of PT and the involvement of the latter in mental-state attribution and provide an RFT interpretation of deficits in mental-state attribution in these conditions. This not only contributes to better understanding of the role of PT in mental-states attribution, but also points the way to possible treatment of these deficits. As will be seen later in this chapter, RFT-based procedures are likely to be particularly relevant in this regard.

## SOCIAL ANHEDONIA

Among the dimensions of schizotypy, social anhedonia, which is characterized by social disinterest, withdrawal and a lack of pleasure from social contact (Eckblad, Chapman, Chapman, & Mishlove, 1982), constitutes a major predictor of development of psychosis (Kwapil, 1998; Gooding et al., 2005), even when it appears in the context of low scores on other subscales of schizotypy (Horan, Brown, & Blanchard, 2007). Considering that mental-state attribution is likely learned through social interactions (see Bartsch, 2002), Villatte, Monestes, McHugh, Freixa i Baque, and Loas (2008) argued that social anhedonia might lead to ToM deficits because fewer social interactions are experienced by people scoring highly on this dimension.

To test their hypothesis, Villatte et al. (2008) conducted a study involving 30 nonclinical participants with a high level of social anhedonia using a longer version of the Hinting task (as in Villatte et al., 2010b). The results showed slightly lower levels of performance by these participants than by controls, in accordance with previous literature reporting slight deficits in ToM in subclinical populations. In addition, Villatte et al. (2008) used the McHugh, Barnes-Holmes, & Barnes-Holmes (2004a) protocol and observed that participants high in social anhedonia were less accurate than controls on tasks involving the highest level of relational complexity that included an interpersonal perspective (i.e., tasks involving I-YOU and HERE-THERE relations). The authors also observed a significant correlation between scores for ToM and deictic relational responding, again suggesting a link between these skills. Villatte, Monestes, McHugh, Freixa i Baque, and Loas (2010a) conducted a belief-attribution deictic protocol with the same sample of participants with high social anhedonia and observed a specific impairment for attribution of belief to another (which requires inversion of the I-YOU relation).

All together, these data suggest that nonclinical people with high levels of social anhedonia have more difficulty than controls in adopting the perspective of another. Social anhedonia is associated with low levels of interpersonal interaction and it is possible that this deficit in interpersonal deictic responding is an effect of lack of social interaction. The more severe ToM deficits observed in schizophrenia might thus result from a developmental history that predates the start of the diagnosable condition.

# Training Deictic Relational Responding To Improve Theory of Mind Ability

Perhaps the most important potential contribution of the RFT conceptualization of ToM is that it might facilitate the identification of contextual variables controlling ToM skills and lead to the elaboration of training procedure that can remediate deficits observed in certain populations. Although the first studies conducted on deictic relational responding have mainly consisted of assessments of particular skills isolated from the learning history of the individual, the data obtained have by now provided considerable support to the RFT conceptualization of mental-state attribution. With regard to the deficits observed in certain populations, the next logical step is to test training procedures developed in accordance with this same conceptualization. Such studies have begun to be carried out on typically developing children who have not acquired a complete repertoire of deictic relational responding.

## Initial Findings

For example, the McHugh et al. (2004a) protocol has been used to train children by including corrective feedback after each trial (Y. Barnes-Holmes, 2001; Y. Barnes-Holmes, McHugh, & Barnes-Holmes, 2004). A seven-year-old child who initially failed trials of reversed and double reversed relations was trained and reached learning criterion in these skills and then succeeded also in generalization tests (which involved a similar protocol but different items). A three-year-old boy was similarly trained with success and, when he reached the age of five, received further training, this time in deictic relations involved in belief attribution to the self and to another. Once again, the procedure proved effective. The authors of this series of training experiments even employed higher levels of deictic complexity, that is, deception tasks in which the participant had to identify where they should put a given object so that it would not be found. In this also, the RFT protocols successfully trained the children to criterion.

While the results from these first studies appeared promising, the generalization tests employed were still relatively far from real social interactions requiring sophisticated PT skills. In order to provide more ecologically valid generalization tests, Heagle and Rehfeldt (2006) conducted a training study with three children using the McHugh et al. (2004a) protocol and generalization tests that were presented as conversations, and referred to situations relevant to the children's daily life (for example, *"I am in the classroom and you are in the yard. Where are you? Where am I?"*). The results of this study showed that the three children reached the learning criterion and succeeded in the generalization test. However, the link with ToM skills was not clearly established since no generalization test based on traditional ToM tasks had been employed. Recently, Weil, Hayes, and Capurro (2011) attempted to address this issue. They trained three 4- to 5-year-old children in simple, reversed and double reversed deictic relations and then used traditional belief attribution tasks to test generalization. All children showed improvement on these tasks in comparison with their performance before deictic training. Hence, whereas the first RFT studies on ToM only demonstrated a correlation between mental-state attribution and deictic relational responding, the work of Weil et al. suggests that deictic skills operate at the core of ToM.

## Future Directions

Thus far, no deictic relational training has been conducted with psychotic individuals. However, some studies based on alternative paradigms have started to examine the possibility that people with schizophrenia might benefit from training in mental-state attribution. For example, Sarfati, Passerieux and Hardy-Baylé (2000) added verbal cues to the cartoon sorting task they had employed in a previous study and showed that half the patients in the study demonstrated normal performance with this new version. Kayser, Sarfati, Besche-Richard and Hardy-Baylé (2006) conducted training sessions based on video sequences showing an interaction among several characters. Results showed an amelioration of the patients' performance in attributing an intention. In Combs et al. (2007) 18 patients suffering from schizophrenia spectrum disorders received a training program on cognition and social interactions lasting several weeks. At the end of the program, their performance on the Hinting task significantly improved. These examples of ToM training in psychosis suggest that the mental-state attribution abilities of people with this condition can be improved. Assuming that deictic relational responding is key to the skills involved, then training in deictic relations might be expected to be at least as effective as the procedures just cited. Targeting deictic relational responding when only subclinical features of schizophrenia are apparent (as in social anhedonia) might also prevent the development of more severe impairments. Future research will determine whether and to what extent RFT procedures might prove useful in the context of these clinical and subclinical conditions.

# Part 3

# The Self: Content and Processes

# Chapter 7

# The Role of Self in Acceptance & Commitment Therapy

Mairead Foody, Yvonne Barnes-Holmes & Dermot
Barnes-Holmes *National University of Ireland, Maynooth*

## Introduction

The concept of self has had a pivotal role in psychological knowledge and
theorizing from their earliest beginnings (e.g., James, 1910). This prominent position has continued in spite of a long-standing lack of consensus
on the concept's core definition and a diversity of emphases on specific
proposed features. For example, Skinner (1974) emphasized self-
awareness as produced by social contingencies that reinforce discrimination of a human or animal's own behavior (see also Dymond & Barnes,
1997). Alternatively, Erikson (1968) proposed the emergence of a conscious sense of self in childhood. Even these approaches, however, are not
necessarily contradictory because both a conscious self and self-awareness

refer to self-knowledge that has an essential quality of being *ongoing* that facilitates a more stable knowledge base about who we are (James, 1890).

The emergence of a sense of self is a core strand in human development and an assumed prerequisite for sound mental health and human functioning (Dymond & Barnes, 1997; Hayes, 1984). By contrast, clinical researchers have often argued that dysfunctional (rather than underdeveloped) aspects of self are associated with, and contribute to, poor mental health. For instance, in the dialectical model of personality disorder, Linehan (1993) proposed that sufferers demonstrate deficiencies in taking the perspective of others and in emotional self-regulation. This presents a picture of mental distress as imbalances in the functioning of a sense of self that have both cognitive and emotional ramifications.

The current chapter has four key aims. First, we summarize the core processes that comprise the functional, behavioral model of human suffering and its treatment known as acceptance and commitment therapy (ACT). Second, we return to the tripartite concept of the *three selves* from original ACT writings and suggest that these still constitute a sound analysis of self within a contemporary ACT model. Third, in doing so, we propose that the concept of *self-as-process* should be located at the center of the ACT process-based hexaflex. Fourth, we suggest that self-as-process might offer an alternative to the more contemporary, but arguably less well-defined, process known as contact with the present moment.

---

# Acceptance and Commitment Therapy (ACT)

Acceptance and commitment therapy is one of the third-wave behavior therapies that have been applied across the full range of mental health problems. Indeed, its breadth of benefits is now well established in the clinical literature with positive outcomes reported in numerous areas, including depression (Zettle & Hayes, 2002) and psychosis (Bach & Hayes, 2002). The breadth of application, and perhaps success, of ACT stems from the fact that the approach is based on a set of generic principles regarding human verbal behavior that may be summarized as: emotional acceptance vs. avoidance; cognitive and emotional fusion vs. defusion; values-directed action; and the importance of a flexible sense of self.

## ACT Model of Processes

ACT is distinct from other behavior therapies because of an underlying heuristic model (referred to as the "hexaflex") that articulates conceptually specified and testable mid-level processes (see Figure 1; see also Hayes, Luoma, Bond, Masuda, & Lillis, 2006). Such a model with operationally definable behavioral processes that have the potential for individual sources of empirical support (e.g., in componential analyses) would be the ideal bridge between basic science and clinical practice. Ideally, models should be dynamic in order to permit ongoing adjustments to both science and clinical practice (i.e., the therapy poses questions for the science and the science validates therapeutic techniques or dictates technical adjustments). There should also be synergy among individual components, and all processes should be consistent with the model's underlying theoretical and philosophical assumptions. In the case of ACT, the model must be contextual, functional, and behavioral. Each of the model's component processes in their current hexaflex form is discussed briefly below.

*Figure 1.* A hexaflex model of the psychological processes ACT seeks to strengthen.

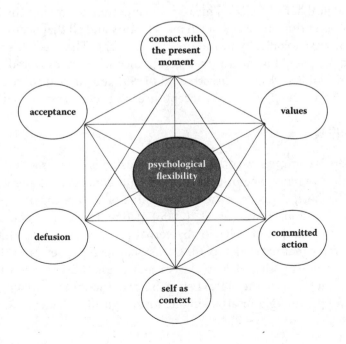

## PSYCHOLOGICAL FLEXIBILITY

There is empirical evidence to support the view that behavioral inflexibility is associated with many forms of mental distress (e.g., Bond & Flaxman, 2006). Hence, it is not surprising that psychological flexibility rests at the center of a behavioral hexaflex of mental health. From an ACT perspective, psychological flexibility is in principle both a process and an outcome. In practice, however, it is more likely the former because you are unlikely to ever reach a point at which you have acquired maximum flexibility in any skill. According to Hayes et al. (2006), psychological inflexibility is the "...inability to persist in or change behavior in the service of long-term valued ends" (p. 6), which results from verbal behavior interacting with, and often overriding, direct contingencies.

## ACCEPTANCE

A focus on acceptance is not unique to ACT and is a central tenet of numerous contemporary treatment approaches (e.g., dialectical behavior therapy, DBT; Linehan, 1993). According to Levin and Hayes (2009), the ACT definition of acceptance is: "the active and aware embrace of those private events occasioned by one's history without unnecessary attempts to change their frequency or form, especially when doing so would cause psychological harm" (p. 15). This particular definition implies the importance of accepting all that exists in one's history and all that occurs physically and psychologically in the present moment. There is considerable empirical support for the utility of acceptance when investigated in both experimental (e.g., Hayes, Bissett, et al., 1999) and clinical contexts (e.g., Bach & Hayes, 2002). For ACT, acceptance is a process, not an outcome.

## DEFUSION

There is community consensus that defusion is a key process in ACT, although it remains one of the most difficult concepts to operationally define. In short, defusion is the undermining or unraveling of cognitive/emotional fusion. Hayes et al. (2006) define fusion as excessive or improper regulation of behavior by verbal processes, such as rules and derived relational networks (p. 6). Defusion, therefore, refers to the creation of contexts "that reduce the stimulus functions transformed by thought" and "reduce the literal believability of thought without ever getting rid of the thought or attacking its form logically" (Fletcher & Hayes,

2005, p. 319). Many ACT outcome studies that have shown positive results include defusion along with other processes in the ACT model (e.g., Bach & Hayes, 2002; Hayes, Bissett, et al., 1999). In addition, there are preliminary RFT analyses of different types of defusion intervention (Luciano, Ruiz, Vizcaino, et al. 2011). For ACT, defusion is a process, not an outcome.

## VALUES

For ACT, values are almost entirely conceptualized as process (rather than outcome) variables, because an individual cannot readily reach a point at which a value is fully achieved (e.g., being a good partner; see Blackledge & Barnes-Holmes, 2009). Values are also highly personalized. According to Hayes, Strosahl, and Wilson (1999), values are defined as: "verbally constructed, global, desired and chosen life directions" (p. 206) and verbally constructed future reinforcers. Values, therefore, provide an alternative source of behavior regulation than fusion and avoidance (Fletcher & Hayes, 2005). Numerous studies support the efficacy of values clarification in both experimental (e.g., Paez-Blarrina et al., 2008) and clinical contexts (e.g., McCracken & Yang, 2006).

## COMMITTED ACTION

Committed action is necessary for the attainment of values. That is, you can move in the direction of your values only if you achieve the short-term, medium-term, and long-term goals in which your values are manifested through specified committed actions (Fletcher & Hayes, 2005). For ACT, committed action is a process and cannot be an outcome.

## CONTACT WITH THE PRESENT MOMENT

According to Fletcher and Hayes (2005), contact with the present moment involves shifting attention to what is happening in the here-and-now and "contacting both internal stimuli, such as bodily sensations, thoughts and feelings and external stimuli, such as sounds, sights, smells and touch" (pp. 320–21). Hayes et al. (2006) have suggested that an important benefit of making contact with the present moment is that it actively encourages ongoing self-awareness. For ACT, contact with the present moment is a process, not an outcome.

## SELF AS CONTEXT

The concept of self as context is unique to ACT and was initially one of the three selves (along with *self as content* and *self as process*, see Hayes 1995). Self as context involves adopting a perspective from which a coherent sense of self is greater than, and distinguishable from, one's thoughts, feelings, and emotions (Flaxman & Bond, 2006). In short, self as context refers to the absence of categorizing and evaluating one's content as oneself. As a result, it may be difficult to separate self as context from defusion. We will return to this issue later.

There is limited empirical evidence to support self as context as an individual component. However, one notable study by L. M. Williams (2006) reported lower scores on a post-traumatic stress disorder (PTSD) scale for war veterans who received all phases of ACT, relative to those exposed to an ACT protocol in which the self as context component was absent.

# ACT Definitions of the Self: The Three Selves

Although the concept of self is not used in ACT as a technical term (Hayes, 1995), it has played a central role in both ACT and RFT since their inception. For example, Hayes (1995) proposed that "a significant role for therapy... [is] an attempt to redefine who the client takes himself or herself to be" (p. 964). Similarly, the PT or deictic relations (i.e., I-YOU, HERE-THERE, and NOW-THEN) are among those that have received considerable empirical attention in RFT research (e.g., McHugh, Barnes-Holmes, & Barnes-Holmes, 2004a & b).

From an ACT perspective, self was initially conceptualized in terms of the three selves—self as content, self as process, and self as context. Collectively, these have also been referred to as: three *levels* of self, three *senses* of the concept of self, and three *knowing* selves. All were believed to be natural by-products of verbal behavior (Hayes, 1995). Our preferred means of describing the three selves is in terms of three *senses of self*.

Figure 2 provides an overview of an RFT conceptualization of the three selves. There are two key points we would like to emphasize. 1. There are two constant aspects to the self—your perspective which is always HERE-NOW *and* your psychological content, which can be located HERE-NOW or THERE-THEN, depending upon which sense of self you are operating in at any point. Hayes (1995) referred to these two aspects (self and content) as the dual functions of self in terms of "functioning both as a doer and as an observer of the doing" (p. 94). So, there is, in general, no change in perspective (*observer*), just changes in the location of content (*doer*). 2. Switching content always occurs in a partly bidirectional manner. Specifically, you can switch bidirectionally between self as process and self as content, and this happens readily because in both your content is located HERE-NOW. Similarly, you can switch between self as process and self as context, but this will involve switching content from HERE-NOW to THERE-THEN. However, you cannot switch between self as content and self as context because you would have to be engaging in self as process in order to do so. In this way, self as process mediates all changes in the location of your content. Each of the three selves is described below.

*Figure 2.* Conceptualization of the three selves as perspective taking relations.

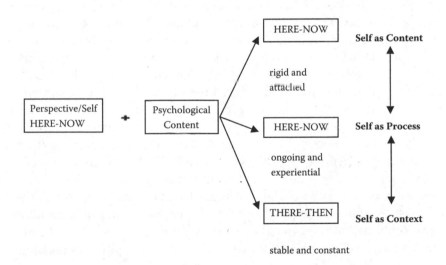

SELF AS CONTENT

Put simply, self as content involves describing and/or evaluating oneself (i.e., creating verbal statements about the self and evaluating these statements). In the conceptualized self, your individual world is structured by the literal meaning of your psychological content, such that who you are is interpreted in terms of what your mind tells you at various times. This literality is problematic (Hayes et al., 2006). To illustrate this point, let's simplify this behavior into several steps. First, there is nothing inherently wrong with describing and/or evaluating yourself, whether these evaluations are positive or negative. Second, a problem begins to emerge when any aspect of your content becomes coordinated with who you are. This coordination relation (between content and YOU/self/observer) is often referred to as *attachment* because the piece of content in question is attached to YOU, as a human being. Attached content automatically becomes part of the conceptualized self.

According to Torneke (2010), self as content "is, by necessity, an extreme simplification. This is its very point and at the same time a limitation" (p. 110). In other words, self as content is an extreme simplification of all that the self is in the sense that there should be much more to the self than what the self as content suggests at any particular point in time.

We can think of all this in more technical RFT terms (see Figure 2, top right). In self as content, your psychological content (descriptions, evaluations, etc.) is coordinated with (i.e., same as) the self because both are located HERE-NOW. In other words, there are coordination relations between who you are and what you think. The self is always HERE-NOW, that is the place from which the whole human being observes. Your content may be HERE-NOW, but only if it is ongoing and experiential (that would be self as process; see below). The instant your content is HERE-NOW and this is not ongoing and experiential, then the content is rigid and conceptualized. As a result, these functions of the content transform to the coordinated self and this in turn becomes rigid and conceptualized (i.e., you are attached). This level of cognitive fusion makes it very likely that your content will exert some control over overt behavior, especially because the self is in relational networks with many other types of content and so on. The only alternative is to keep your content as ongoing and experiential (i.e., stay in self as process).

In our developmental histories, we are trained from a young age to adopt our perspectives from HERE-NOW in terms of discriminating and evaluating everything that we do. This is likely the way in which our perspective-taking skills develop and for the most part early on, that is a good thing. So, even for verbally sophisticated individuals, there will always be a certain amount of content that is coordinated with HERE-NOW, in a manner that is consistent with your history.

The more verbally sophisticated we become the more solid the self becomes and the more fluent we should be in operating in self as process (or even self as context) with regard to our psychological content. Ideally, there should be only a minimal amount of content that is rigid and conceptualized because your detailed experience and constancy of the self should indicate that content is only content and not who you are. However, given that our developmental histories are full of discriminating and evaluating everything that we do, we would need special training in order to continue to operate in self as process. Indeed, we would also need special training to transform the coordination relations between content and self as HERE-NOW to relations of distinction or hierarchy in which the self is HERE-NOW but our content is THERE-THEN (self as context).

**Self as Content in Therapy.** Clients often come to therapy with a conceptualized self, which they want to change or swap for another (more, better, different) conceptualized self (Hayes, Strosahl, et al., 1999). As such, they are open to change on specific features of their self and their content, but unfortunately are often wedded or attached to the construction of the conceptualized self as a generic strategy. Indeed, this strategy and the conceptualized self as a whole are often ardently defended by clients early on. In ACT terms, they struggle with this relationship between self and content and struggle with conceptualizing the self as a strategy. It is in respect of this struggle and with reference to the ossified conceptualized self that the koan-like phrase "Kill yourself every day" has been used (Hayes, 2002).

## SELF AS PROCESS

At one level of analysis, self as process (see Figure 2, center right) is the simplest of the three selves to define. In short, it involves ongoing experiencing and describing of your thoughts, behaviors, etc. The word "ongoing" is important here because that which is described in self as process is fluid and must be perceived as HERE-NOW (see Torneke, 2010). Although perceptions of your content as HERE-NOW are problematic when operating in self as content, in self as process your content as HERE-NOW is simply the way we learn to talk about our behavior, feelings, etc., and facilitates communication (Hayes, 1995). The main distinction between self as content and self as process in this regard is the lack of fusion in the latter between the self and the content.

The fluid nature of self as process and its inevitable emergence in our developmental histories capture the endless changeability of what we experience, feel, etc., and what is by definition the lack of constancy therein. Indeed, Hayes (2002) highlighted this quality when drawing parallels among self as process, mindfulness, and Buddhism. Lack of constancy is not problematic in this context because it allows for maximal behavioral flexibility. That is, if my ongoing experience is ever-changing, then I have as broad an array as possible of behavioral options. Indeed, it is only when the content of self as process feeds into self as content, that the need for coherence in the conceptualized self shuts some of these options down and reduces behavioral flexibility (and reinforces the conceptualized self, thereby reducing flexibility at a later stage).

**Self as Process in Therapy.** Learning to experience what is happening to us on an ongoing basis is a critical feature of our developmental histories, but there are many examples of how difficulties can emerge when this training history is problematic. In short, our experiences must be coordinated with descriptors that are consistent with the verbal world around us and problems emerge when they are not. For example, a client may not have appropriate breadth in using emotional terms to describe current feelings (D. Barnes-Holmes, Hayes, & Dymond, 2001). Hence, a core feature of ACT is to establish self as process skills and facilitate maximum coordination between the descriptors the client employs and those used by the verbal community. Doing so also allows the therapist to gain better insight into how clients actually feel and what is happening for them in the moment. This, in turn, will permit a better understanding of how these descriptors feed self as content and how the conceptualized self has been constructed by an individual. Furthermore, facilitating self as process allows greater flexibility in shifting between self as process and self as context, thus making self as content less likely.

## SELF AS CONTEXT

Operating in self as context involves detachment (defusion) from your psychological content (evaluations, etc.). Specifically, unlike both self as content and self as process, your content, when in self as context, is THERE-THEN (see Figure 2, bottom right). The following quotation from Hayes (1995) offers a nice definition of self as context: "*I* in some meaningful sense is the location that is left behind when all of the content differences are subtracted out" (p. 96). In other words, in self as context all that is left in HERE-NOW is I.

Just as our developmental histories require (for communicative and social reasons) that our content is HERE-NOW in terms of both self as content and self as process, it is equally important that our histories establish the skills required to switch content from HERE-NOW to THERE-THEN (Blackledge & Barnes-Holmes, 2009).

**The relationship between transcendence and self as context.** It seems plausible that highly competent meditative practices may allow you to access a place that feels nonverbal, and it is thus tempting to consider that self-as-context is nonverbal. D. Barnes-Holmes, Hayes, and Gregg (2001) have summarized this position across the following two excerpts:

> Spirituality is an experience of "transcendence" or "oneness" that comes when literal, analytic, and evaluative functions of relational framing are massively reduced, and the relational functions of I, HERE and NOW are thereby allowed to predominate. (p. 243)

> A sense of transcendence results, in large part, from a situation in which the evaluative functions attached to HERE and NOW repeatedly transfer to THERE and THEN in these two relational frames. More specifically, when an evaluation (located I, HERE and NOW) is discriminated as just an evaluation, it immediately acquires the relational functions of I, THERE and THEN. If this form of shifting within the frames keeps repeating itself, a person's "normal" perception of reality may be undermined, leading to a sense of transcendence. From an RFT perspective this is exactly what happens during some forms of meditation. For example, dispassionate observation of spontaneous thoughts and feelings is encouraged in Buddhist forms of meditation, and with sufficient practice, feelings of tranquility and transcendence often emerge (see Hayes, 1984). For RFT, the "experience" of transcendence occurs because each evaluative function that occurs during meditation immediately loses most of its psychological functions when it shifts from I, HERE and NOW to I, THERE and THEN. (p. 244)

Hence, the ongoing defusion that comes with self as context, in terms of the massive reductions in the transformations of evaluative and other functions through the relations of HERE-NOW would indeed feel like transcendence. However, this behavior is ultimately verbal because it continues to require that you observe from the perspective of I-HERE-NOW. It is important to emphasize, therefore, that self as context is unique in terms of the content being located THERE-THEN and this, in turn, provides a more stable perspective of I-HERE-NOW.

The transcendent experience has another quality that is unique. This is best illustrated through examples. Imagine a musician working on a score or an artist working on a canvas. In both cases, these individuals are highly absorbed in a single focus. But this focus is always *in addition to* the observer. The focus feels almost entirely automatic in the sense that these highly practiced and competent individuals have learned to focus on only that endeavor and nothing else. After many years of practice, this focus would become highly automatic. However, the individual is always observing at the same time. In short, there is always the observer and the doer and they always remain distinct.

Now consider a Vipassana meditation master. What this individual is focusing intensely on is herself (not a canvas or a score, just herself). This is an extremely rare situation in which she is focusing solely and entirely on herself and nothing else. In addition, across many years of training, she learns to do this with high automaticity, so that she can quickly reach a place of almost no content for extended periods of time. In this context, it would feel like the observer and the doer had collapsed into one because there is little doing (i.e., no transformations of stimulus functions either HERE-NOW or THERE-THEN) and all observing. In short, there is nothing HERE-NOW, but I on an ongoing basis. However, this very fact would suggest that even this type of behavior is verbal because you are still operating from the PT frames.

Although possible, accessing such a place would require vast practice and would last a considerable length of time only if you had developed high levels of automaticity in this regard in order for the transformations of stimulus functions to remain at such a low level. Hence, the two great challenges to a highly verbal organism attempting to reach such a height are: 1. Getting there and 2. Staying there. This would present enormous challenges for anyone, let alone an individual who has a history of fusion and experiential avoidance.

**Self as Context in Therapy.** In a therapeutic context, ACT attempts to increase the extent to which clients engage in self as context, largely through experiential exercises (e.g., the Observer Exercise). Doing so, in turn, weakens the control of thoughts and feelings over behavior (Barnes-Holmes, Hayes, & Dymond, 2001).

## Psychological Flexibility: Switching Between Self as Process and Self as Context

The primary goal of ACT is to increase psychological flexibility, and flexibility with regard to the self is pivotal in this regard. Specifically, this would involve an individual being able to switch readily between self as process and self as context. Self as process is a largely experiential sense of self in which your psychological content is ongoing and experiential, although it is HERE-NOW. However, this latter fact means that you can very easily become attached to aspects of content and thus you would quickly find yourself in self as content. Hence, Figure 2 illustrates a bidi rectionality between self as content and self as process and ACT would suggest that you learn to switch readily from self as content to self as process in order to minimize fusion. In short, when operating in self as process you can easily get sucked into self as content and when operating in self as content you need to switch quickly to self as process.

Figure 2 also highlights the importance of switching flexibly between self as process and self as context. It seems unlikely that you could operate to a great extent in self as context because you would quickly find yourself operating in self as process (because new experiences are happening all the time). Hence, these ongoing experiences would quickly draw you from self as context to self as process. In the other direction, there will be occasions in which the risk of slipping from self as process to self as content is great and in this situation (involving what we can think of as *sticky* content) it would be beneficial to switch from self as process to self as context. In this way, self as context is the safest place to operate with regard to your content and essential in dealing with content with which you have a history of being fused. But, as noted above, it is highly improbable that you will stay long in self as context and thus it is likely you will return quickly to self as process.

## The Importance of Self in ACT

The current ACT hexaflex incorporates self as context as one of the six essential and interrelated processes and self as context holds a central place at the heart of the model. Indeed Hayes, Strosahl, and Wilson (1999) asserted that "this sense of observing self is critical to acceptance work." However, before suggesting below what we see as a possibly useful minor revision to the hexaflex, it seems important to be clear about what we are trying to do. The hexaflex is a heuristic model of processes which to date have not been subject to functional analyses. If one was to start with a bottom-up analysis, there would be no hexaflex because such a model is top-down. If we start with a top-down model, then the aim becomes about searching for functional analytic terms that might map onto those already present within the model. But this may be neither possible nor useful. For example, if existing processes turn out not to be functionally identifiable, then they would have to be abandoned. That is difficult to do once a model gets established in a verbal community, especially when this occurred in the absence of functional evidence. So, in a sense what we are trying to do in integrating RFT concepts into a top-down heuristic model is the mixing of two types of analyses. However, if the hexaflex model is widely adhered to and understood by a specific verbal community, then perhaps the type of integration we present here is a good place to start.

In the current analysis, if one argues that a high level of flexibility is required between self as process and self as context, then one might reasonably assume that both senses of self should at least be present, if not central, to the model. Indeed, it follows that if self as context is central, and it is strongly related in flexibility to self as process, then self as process should also lie at the heart of the ACT process model. We have depicted this potential adjustment to the ACT hexaflex in Figure 3. Furthermore, excluding self as process from the ACT model is potentially problematic. Specifically, it implies that we should operate from a self as context perspective all the time for maximum mental well-being. Yet self as process is an important and beneficial sense of self and it would be impossible to reach self as context without gaining important self knowledge through self as process.

*Figure 3.* Proposed new ACT process hexaflex.

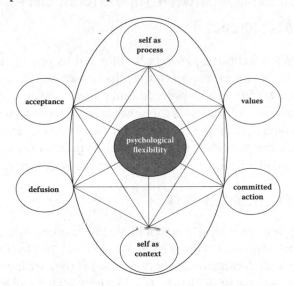

## IS CONTACT WITH THE PRESENT MOMENT SYNONYMOUS WITH SELF AS PROCESS?

If we are arguing currently that self as process should be central to the hexaflex and self as process is your ongoing experiential awareness of self, then it might follow that contact with the present moment *is synonymous with* self as process. Indeed, Hayes et al. (2006) appear to have suggested exactly this when talking about contact with the present moment: "A sense of self called 'self as process' is actively encouraged: the defused, non-judgmental ongoing description of thoughts, feelings, and other private events" (p. 9).

There are conceptual advantages to using the concept of self as process over contact with the present moment. Specifically, the latter is not a technical term and has many unhelpful colloquial connotations. Self as process is more succinct and connotation free, especially when one is trying to specify processes which should be susceptible to scientific and experimental scrutiny. Furthermore, contact with the present moment implies a specific technique, although the hexaflex is a model of psychological *processes*, not techniques. In summary, we have no specific ax to grind with the concept of contact with the present moment, but the concept of self as process appears to be more useful and indeed consistent with earlier ACT descriptions.

# The Relationships between Self as Process and Other ACT Processes

In order to establish a central place for self as process in the ACT model, it is necessary to reproduce the relations among the existing processes with regard to self as process. Since there already appears to be consensus that self as process is the sense of self encouraged when characterizing contact with the present moment (Hayes et al., 2006), one might assume that the relations between self as process and the other five processes remain unchanged. These relations are briefly presented below.

## SELF AS PROCESS AND ACCEPTANCE

Self as process and acceptance facilitate one another. This sense of self *is* experiential awareness of the present moment and thus facilitates acceptance of thoughts, feelings, and emotions as what they are in that moment and nothing else (in past or future, etc.). Indeed, Fletcher and Hayes (2005) clarify the relationship between self as process and acceptance as follows: "ACT teaches clients to repeatedly return to their experience in the present moment without judgment and with acceptance" (p. 323).

## SELF AS PROCESS AND DEFUSION

In self as process, we argued previously that your psychological content is HERE-NOW, but that the transformations of stimulus functions (evaluative, etc.) are massively reduced. If they were not, you would quickly find yourself in self as content. Again, the difference with self as context is that in this case your psychological content is experienced as THERE-THEN. But this raises the difficult question about defusion and its relationship with the three selves.

**Are you only engaging in defusion when in self as context?** Both fusion and defusion are difficult concepts to define and our distinction between self as process and self as context forces us to ask whether one is engaging in defusion in both or either sense of self. Let us consider the relationship between self as context and defusion first because that seems the most straightforward. When your psychological content is THERE-THEN, it is easy to define that as defusion because relationally your content is distinct from I (the term itself "de-fusion" even supports this view). Therefore, if we take a very narrow definition of defusion to mean that your psychological content must be THERE-THEN, we have to assume that defusion is possible only when operating in self as context.

Consider instead a broader definition of defusion that incorporates one's psychological content even when HERE-NOW as in self as process (hence defusion not strictly defined by THERE-THEN). In this case, defusion is defined more broadly as a massive reduction in the transformations of functions regarding your content (but the content is not *necessarily* THERE-THEN). Of course, one might then ask whether this level of defusion is distinct from the defusion in self as context. The point is that the definition of defusion is not based on the content being THERE-THEN; rather self as process is ongoing and experiential and this facilitates defusion. The content is HERE-NOW, but it is not rigid and attached because one's experience is ongoing. According to this view, the answer to the question above is that there is defusion at both self as process and self as context, but not of course at self as content (that is fusion). Parenthetically, a preliminary analysis has differentiated several types of defusion trial according to the transformation of functions that might be involved and presents potentially relevant data in this regard (Luciano, Ruiz, Vizcaino et al., 2011).

## SELF AS PROCESS AND VALUES

Operating in self as process by making ongoing experiential contact with your psychological content and not permitting it to slide you into self as content maximizes your potential for value-consistent behavior. Indeed, values are highly personalized and self-related and thus can only come about by self as process. In contrast, domination by self as content makes it more likely that nonpersonalized values will be abstracted and followed and these will be less consistent with one's perspective on oneself. As a result, self as process and values facilitate one another. One example of the very strong overlap between self as process and contact with the present moment is illustrated by Hayes et al.'s (2006) description of the relation between contact with the present moment and values: "The goal is to have clients experience the world more directly so that their behavior is more flexible and thus their actions more consistent with the values they hold" (p. 9).

## SELF AS PROCESS AND COMMITTED ACTION

Self as process enhances committed action and commitments to pursue stated values involve commitments to self as process. For example, self as process permits you to work toward your values because your behavior is no longer controlled by your psychological content, avoidance, etc.

## SELF AS PROCESS AND SELF AS CONTEXT

Self as process and self as context are two coordinated senses of self across which we must learn to switch with flexibility, as appropriate. Self as process facilitates self as context by permitting pure observation of your content without allowing this to become coordinated with who you are. Once this type of coordination (fusion) happens, then you are in self as content. As long as your content in self as process is ongoing and experiential, then the possibility of fusion is greatly reduced and you will stay away from self as content. But, as noted above, there will be many circumstances in which self as process experiences become coordinated with self and fusion happens. Switching from self as process to self as context largely precludes this happening because problematic content can become THERE-THEN and the possibility for fusion is reduced further.

---

# Concluding Comments

This current chapter set out to articulate an RFT account of self and to examine the overlap between this and the current hexaflex as employed in ACT. In simple terms, our account reiterates what has been said in early ACT writings about the three selves and the thesis here proposes that these continue to constitute a succinct functional RFT account of self. Although it may be impossible to build purely functional bridges between RFT and the current ACT hexaflex, this chapter's account of self is a possible step in this direction. For ACT clinicians, this may serve only to illustrate the utility of RFT for understanding human verbal behavior.

# Chapter 8

# The Self as the Context for Rule-Governed Behavior

Carmen Luciano *University of Almería, Spain*

Sonsoles Valdivia-Salas *University of Saragossa, Spain*

Francisco Ruiz *University of Almería, Spain*

## Introduction

After being diagnosed with diabetes, 21-year-old Maria has thoughts such as "Now I need to change my daily routine," "This is terrible," "I don't know what to do with this," etc. She relates the diagnosis to her self in the future (e.g., "I will not be able to have children"), and in the past (e.g., "I should have taken better care of myself"), and sadness and anger show up. Sometimes, she gets "fused" with her negative thoughts and feelings and, instead of going to college and hanging out with her friends as before, she stays home crying, complaining about her bad fortune and blaming herself. At other times, she can see herself as separate from her thoughts and notice what is really important for her (i.e., her studies and her friends). At these times, she can see that if she gets in the habit of not going to college and not spending time with her friends she may lose contact with what she values (e.g., education, relationships) and thus in spite of being angry and sad, she goes to college and meets her friends.

This example shows us a person having thoughts about herself and reacting to them in two different ways. The first, more problematic way, is reacting in accordance with the content of her private events (i.e., thoughts and emotions), blind to what is important for her in the long run. The second, healthier, way is reacting to her private events as transitory responses in the overarching context of her life and of what matters in the long run. These alternative reactions may both be conceptualized in terms of self-relevant rule-governed behavior, which is the subject of the current chapter. We will discuss alternative types of behavior regulation in the context of the self, how certain patterns of rule-governed behavior can lead to problematic forms of experiential avoidance and how other patterns may be more psychologically beneficial.

## Behavior Regulation and the Self

From a functional analytic perspective, the development of self depends on the existence of a verbal community formulating questions and shaping answers so that the person learns to report her own behavior. From a relational frame theory (RFT; see, e.g., Törneke, 2010) perspective, asking and answering such questions requires relational framing. The latter refers to the relating of two or more events based on arbitrarily established contextual cues that specify the relational pattern or frame (Hayes et al., 2001; Rehfeldt & Barnes-Holmes, 2009). It is based on a history of interactions with one's verbal community that establishes contextual control over a variety of different frames, is generalized across situations and produces the alteration of the functions of related stimuli without necessitating direct conditioning. Examples of frames include coordinate (e.g., same as), comparative (e.g., more than, less than), hierarchical (e.g., belongs to), temporal (e.g., before, after), causal (e.g., if...then...) and deictic (I-you, here-there, now-then) (see also chapter 1, present volume).

The framing of thoughts, emotions, memories, and other experiences of oneself occurs automatically as someone gains fluency in relational framing. RFT suggests that three senses of self develop on this basis (see chapters 1 and 7 and Luciano, Valdivia-Salas, & Ruiz, 2011, for more detail). Thoughts, feelings, reasons and "rule-like" descriptions of oneself that one derives (e.g., "I am an anxious person, what can I do?") are referred to as *self-as-content*. The verbal community also provides conditions for the discrimination of one's ongoing behaviors and this is referred to as *self-as-process*. In addition, as one experiences these self-relevant events over time one also comes to discriminate a consistent locus for them all (I-here-now); this provides the basis for *self-as-context*. RFT suggests that getting caught up in (behaving "fused with") self-as-content may lead to psychological problems by blocking us from acting in accordance with long-term values. Conversely, getting fluency in self-as-process and (in particular) self-as-context are the means by which such ineffective behavior regulation may be overcome by allowing the person to choose in accordance with rules specifying what is important in one's life (i.e., values) (for a detailed analysis see Luciano, Valdivia-Salas, & Ruiz, 2011). The purpose of the current chapter is to provide a functional analysis of the patterns of rule-following that underlie both bad and good.

In the example of Maria given above, after the diagnosis of diabetes, Maria frames herself as different from others, compares her past with her present and future, derives causes for her disease etc. (e.g., "I shouldn't have eaten so many sweets," "Others can eat chocolate but I can't from now on," "How am I going to deal with this?" "I might go blind," "This is too much to bear," and so on). This kind of relational framing (evaluative thoughts, reasons to do or not do certain things, etc.) is based on her personal learning history and is inevitable and not a problem in and of itself (for more comprehensive detail see the dimensions of the self as described in D. Barnes-Holmes, Hayes, & Dymond, 2001; Luciano, Valdivia-Salas, Cabello-Luque, & Hernández, 2009; Luciano, Valdivia-Salas, & Ruiz, 2011). However, derived thought and emotions may come to function as self-rules that automatically control other behaviors in problematic ways.

Maria's reaction to her self-content might be automatic, based on fusion with some of that content, or it might involve simply noticing her self-content and acting under the control of what she values. One way or the other, her reaction will be in the service of something; it will have a personal meaning. The personal meaning of her actions will depend to an important extent on what her interactions with her community in connection with the occurrence of particular self-content have taught her over the years. The community teaches the child through multiple interactions to discriminate her ongoing thoughts and feelings. Furthermore, based on these interactions, a perspective of self (or self-as-context) will emerge and be given a discriminative function to control other behavior. The community provides formulae (i.e., rules to be followed) and sets up contingencies to teach a person how to react to others' words as well as her own (i.e., her thoughts and feelings). Based on this teaching, a person may learn to react in a problematic way (i.e., automatically, based on fusion) or in a psychologically healthier way (by discriminating the ongoing occurrence of thoughts and emotions and choosing in accordance with personal values). The specific social contingencies that the community provides relating rules to actions define the culture in which the person is immersed.

The repertoire of responding to thoughts, sensations or memories about oneself has been called different things in the behavior analytic literature, including rule-following, rule-governed behavior, instructional behavior and verbal regulation. In part, this variation has to do with the lack of consensus concerning the very concept of "rule" (see O'Hora & Barnes-Holmes, 2004; Parrot, 1987; Schlinger, 1990; Skinner, 1969; Törneke, Luciano, & Valdivia, 2008, for details). For the present purposes, and in accordance with relational frame theory (RFT; Hayes, Barnes-Holmes, & Roche, 2001) we understand a rule as a stimulus that alters or establishes psychological functions of events based on transformation of functions through relational frames and typically involving coordinate, comparative, temporal and/or causal relational cues (see e.g., D. Barnes-Holmes, Hayes, & Dymond, 2001). Understanding a rule (i.e., relationally framing appropriately in accordance with the cues involved) is necessary for rule- following to occur; however, understanding a rule does not necessarily lead to rule-following (see Hayes & Hayes, 1989; Luciano et al., 2009; Törneke, 2010).

In behavioral terms, the effect of the rule on behavior is the key when addressing rule-understanding and rule-following. Analogous to talking about stimuli independent of stimulus functions, talking about a rule independent of its function (i.e., its behavior-regulatory effect) may be misleading. The function of the rule will determine the particular type of behavior regulation seen. For example, effective (defused) behavior regulation involves choosing from self-as-perspective (or self-as-context). Problematic (fused) behavior regulation occurs when the person behaves according to the literality of self-as-content. The same rule, topographically speaking, might have either of these two very different functions, depending on the individual's history.

In this chapter we discuss the self as a context for behavior regulation. We start with the most basic forms of behavior regulation and proceed to the most complex and we discuss the problems that can arise from both. In the final part of the chapter we discuss the importance of ongoing discrimination of one's own behavior which enables regulation of behavior from self-as-perspective.

## Types of Rule-Governed Behavior (RGB)

In 1982, when there was little knowledge about derived relational responding and transformation of functions, Zettle and Hayes (see also Hayes, Zettle, & Rosenfarb, 1989) described three types of RGB: pliance, tracking, and augmenting. Later, these three types were analyzed in terms of RFT concepts and this has led to some adjustment and refinement of the labels used to describe the behaviors involved (e.g., instructional behavior, verbal regulation, relational/nonrelational instructional control) (see Barnes-Holmes, O'Hora, Roche, Hayes, Bissett, & Lyddy, 2001; Luciano et al., 2009; Tarbox, Tarbox, & O'Hora, 2009; Törneke, Luciano, & Valdivia, 2008). In this chapter we will mostly use the old term RGB although other terms will also be used. In what follows, the three types of RGB will be described with an emphasis on the way in which they may become problematic.

### Pliance: Rule-Following Controlled by Socially-Mediated Contingencies

The functional class referred to as pliance is rule-governed behavior that results from a history of multiple examples in which a speaker provides the listener with reinforcement contingent on the correspondence between the rule and the listener's behavior. The shaping of pliance starts by providing the listener with direct contingencies of reinforcement for rule-following. For instance, a mother may start allowing her child Tommy access to his favorite meal only upon a correspondence between her rule (e.g., "go wash your hands") and Tommy's behavior (i.e., washing his hands). As the child acquires fluency in relational framing, both as listener and as speaker, and in the application of temporal and causality relational cues, and comes to frame an increasing number of words and referents through coordination, he is able to understand and follow more complex rules. For example, "If you wash your hands before eating, I will give you CLO which is the same as the chocolate cookies you like." The child has never eaten CLO before and his mother has never previously asked him to wash his hands before eating CLO. However, the child has experience with chocolate cookies and he likes them very much. In addition, he can frame through coordination (for example, "CLO" = chocolate cookies; "eating" = actual eating). Furthermore, he can frame through temporal relations. Thus, when it is time to eat, the rule given by the mother transforms the behavior of hand washing into a condition (i.e., causal or conditional framing) for access to CLO. This is also supported by the fact that the mother has acquired credibility based on a history of properly reinforcing the child's rule-following. Given sufficient practice in derived relations, the child might even derive a rule, as self-content, such as "If I want my mom to let me eat CLO, I better go now and wash my hands first." If he follows this rule, then this is quite different from simply following a rule provided by someone else since this is derived pliance.

As relational framing gains complexity in the child's repertoire, he will also understand and produce additional content about himself (i.e., self-as-content), such as "I am less intelligent than my brother, so I will...," "my friends do not like me, so I...," etc. Without taking perspective from this content (see self-as-process and self-as-perspective in other chapters), the child will automatically react to the function of the rule provided by the type of behavioral regulation that is predominant in his repertoire. If it is pliance, then he will react in line with the history of contingencies that others have provided for the correspondence between the rule and the action.

There are as many types of pliance as histories of contingencies mediated by others. For example, pliance will differ depending on whether primarily controlled by positive or negative, or immediate or delayed consequences; whether contextualized to a particular person or life domain, or generalized across situations; whether imposed (e.g., "do this") or open to choice (e.g., "you may or may not do this, but only by doing so will you be allowed to play video games later"). Of particular importance, pliance will differ depending on whether or not a proper transition to tracking occurs.

Appropriate development of rule-following involves making the child more sensitive to the natural consequences of following rules. For instance, after the child follows a rule such as "let's put these toys away before we play with the train," the parents should make explicit the natural consequences of doing so (e.g., "now we have room"; see next section on tracking for more examples). Usually, parents should fade out the arbitrary consequences involved in pliance and ensure replacement by natural ones to facilitate the emergence of tracking (as explained later). A history of contingencies in which natural consequences of rule-following are not made relevant will lead to generalized pliance. For instance, parents who want to shape behaviors in their child may start by providing contrived social praise and access to toys when the child follows the rule of tidying the toys. If the parents do not progressively promote natural consequences for tidying her toys, then after several instances and a sufficient framing repertoire, the child will probably tidy (only) to get approval and something from them. In other words, her tidying will be in a relation of coordination or in a frame of causality (if...then) with getting others' approval or something else. If "others loving me" is established as the reinforcer across life domains, then the child will generate and/or follow rules about tidying (or helping, studying etc.) that are controlled only by the consequences mediated by others that she expects in return.

Following the explicit or implicit rule "you ought to comply with what others think is good for you so that they are happy with you," or a functionally equivalent one, as a core life-rule may lead the person to put her life in others' hands, with the problematic outcome that the result of her behavior might not be what she is looking for because the consequences provided by others are not as predictable and controllable as other sources of reinforcement. Consequently, she might be trapped in needing others' approval, behaving to get it, not obtaining it, and then more of the same all over again. The likely result is a restricted life and poor contact with many other potentially reinforcing consequences that need tracking to be contacted (Hayes, Strosahl, & Wilson, 1999; Törneke et al., 2008).

To understand in sufficient detail how this way of behaving becomes a problem, we need to understand the interaction between generalized pliance and augmenting. The latter can contribute to the perpetuation and extension of the former by adding control by abstract, verbally constructed consequences (e.g., when feeling good is connected to others' approval and feeling good is established as a necessary state to do other things in life). This will be further elaborated upon when addressing problems with augmenting.

## Tracking: Rule-Following Controlled by Natural Consequences

The functional class known as tracking is rule-governed behavior that results from a history of multiple interactions in which doing what is stated in the rule is followed by natural as opposed to arbitrary consequences. In other words, tracking is rule-following under the control of the apparent correspondence between rules and the way the world is arranged (e.g., Hayes et al., 1989; Hayes et al., 2001; Zettle & Hayes, 1982).

The simplest form of tracking involves a track specifying a direct contingency, that is, a behavior and a natural (i.e., non-arbitrary) consequence. The behavior is performed and the consequence is contacted (e.g., if you wash your hands with soap, they will feel smooth). Tracking may also involve long-term consequences such as seeing flowers after taking regular care of plants or knowing more for the exam after regular studying. These long-term consequences augment the reinforcing value of the immediate consequences, such as, in the last example, submitting assignments on time, attending classes regularly, etc. This is an example of how augmenting interacts with tracking, which will be elaborated upon later.

Tracking usually follows some practice with pliance. For instance, while the child is brushing his teeth as an instance of pliance, the parents might progressively fade contrived consequences such as "you are such a good boy" or "now you can sit and watch TV," etc., and introduce descriptions that make explicit the natural consequences of what the child is doing. In this case: "now your teeth are smooth and your mouth is fresh!" Later, once the child acquires fluency in relational framing, he may derive and follow his own rules. For example, the child who brushed his teeth to make them smoother may learn what cavities are and relate them as opposite to smooth teeth. Based on this, he may derive and follow the rule "I should brush my teeth so that I don't get cavities."

According to the personal history of tracking regulation, tracking may become controlled by immediate natural consequences (e.g., smoking reduces my stress) instead of delayed natural consequences (e.g., smoking is destroying my lungs). Tracking may also be controlled by magical formulas (e.g., "red is the lucky color, wear it to the test") that would lead to superstitious behavior whether provided by others or self-derived. As with pliance, tracking may be controlled primarily by negative or by positive reinforcement. It might also be contextualized to particular circumstances, such as rules provided by others but not derived. When conditions such as just listed are coupled with a lack of PT abilities (i.e., self-as-process abilities) that might otherwise promote the function in self-as-perspective of choosing, then regulation of behavior becomes problematic.

## PROBLEMS WITH TRACKING

More specifically, tracking becomes problematic in several circum-stances (Hayes, Strosahl, & Wilson, 1999). One is when it is applied to contexts where it cannot work. For example, consider the rule "Things that do not serve a function should be disposed of." This track may be helpful when dealing with objects such as a broken appliance. However, following this track with private events (e.g., thoughts, feelings) is futile because of the way language works. Imagine a person for whom this rule has been effective with things in the outside world but who now comes to evaluate certain thoughts and feelings as barriers that keep him from enjoying others' company (e.g., "while I'm this anxious I cannot say a word," "this anxiety is jeopardizing my social life"). He may follow the above rule by attempting to banish these thoughts, which are experienced as barriers to valued action; however, as suggested, language processes do not work that way and thus his efforts will likely be futile. The ironic likely results of his rule-following (i.e., less company) will cohere with his self-content (i.e., being socially anxious and needing to figure out how to deal with it) but not with what he would choose for himself in the long term.

Tracking can also lead to problems when the track is inaccurate. Consider, for example, the rule "in order to get rid of this anxiety, I will stay home while I recover my confidence." There are two sources of rein-forcement that will strengthen rule-following. First, not feeling a lack of confidence will serve as a potent negative reinforcer for tracking the short-term contingencies specified in the rule. Second and closely related to the former, reinforcement for tracking the short-term consequences implies positive reinforcement for "being right" according to the rela-tional network that has established recuperating self-confidence as a nec-essary step for getting rid of anxiety.

However, tracking mostly for short-term consequences does not allow the person to experience that the short- and long-term conse-quences (feeling confident now and getting rid of anxiety later) are not coordinately related as suggested by the rule, and that in fact the result will be more and not less anxiety in the long term. This paradoxical effect is a very central process in many clinical problems. As another example, take a man addicted to alcohol. Tracking the rule "I will feel better after drinking" is effective in the short run. In the longer term, however, the man continues drinking, his problems worsen and thoughts and feelings about his poor abilities to manage his life strengthen. Thus, short-term tracking of self-consequences results in long-term self-destructive consequences; he is trapped by his poor repertoire and fails to develop alternative repertoires.

The example of tracking just presented involved negative reinforcement but that was not the whole story. Just as in the case of pliance, augmenting also plays a critical role in the maintenance of ineffective patterns of tracking by perpetuating a pattern that is mistakenly believed to be in the service of valued and personal trajectories.

## Augmenting: The Most Advanced Form of Rule-Following Behavior

Augmenting is "rule-governed behavior due to relational networks that alter the degree to which events function as consequences" (Hayes, Barnes-Holmes, & Roche, 2001). A relational network may establish new events as effective consequences, leading to formative augmenting (e.g., after learning that *danke* means "thank you" in German, the probability of the behavior followed by *danke* increases) or alter the consequential properties of previously effective events, as in motivative augmenting (see more details in Hayes et al., 2001; Luciano et al., 2009; Törneke, 2010). For example, suppose a child has always refused to eat vegetables. One day, however, his mom, who is a credibility context for the child, tells him, "If you eat vegetables, you will be a big, strong boy!" Later, the child starts eating vegetables. The reinforcing properties of becoming big and strong transform the previously aversive properties of eating vegetables, so that now, eating vegetables (the texture, the smell, the taste) means getting closer to the reinforcer, in this case, becoming big and strong.

In brief, augmenting is behaving in accordance with the transformation of reinforcing or aversive functions. As with other rules, just because an augmental is understood does not mean it will definitely come to control behavior. This will depend on the establishing operations in place related to the augmental in each particular moment and the relevant type of rule-following for the person in particular. In the example above, although the child understood the relation between eating vegetables and becoming big and strong, if this consequence was not relevant for him, then the aversive taste of vegetables would not be transformed as discriminative for eating vegetables. However, the transformation might occur later in his life if big and strong were connected to something he values (e.g., dating).

## AUGMENTING AND OTHER TYPES OF RULE-FOLLOWING

As mentioned, augmenting occurs connected to either pliance or tracking. For example, consider a rule stating a causal relation between recycling and receiving the approval of others at some point afterwards. For a person with a strong history of pliance based on immediate contingencies, this rule might not function as discriminative for recycling when necessary. However, it might function as an effective augmental for learners with a history of pliance that was based on delayed or intermittent consequences.

Imagine now that the rule states that recycling is needed for a healthier planet decades from now. This augmental will not have any impact on the previous person, but only on those with well-established tracking based on delayed and probabilistic consequences in which case the person will begin to recycle based on the verbally established consequences (Hayes, et al., 1989; Luciano et al., 2009; Törneke, 2010). This example shows the importance of analyzing rules based not on their topography but on their function.

Augmenting gives flexibility to rule-following because it allows current immediate consequences to be transformed by relating them to abstract and desirable values. In the example above, augmenting makes the current consequences of eating vegetables (i e., unfamiliar taste and texture) less aversive (e.g., because of their relation with growing big and strong). We do not mean, however, that augmenting always involves behaving according to what is important. Contrarily, augmenting may lead to problems when it establishes the reinforcing properties of events that interfere with effective (valued) actions. Before describing how augmenting may lead to problematic forms of experiential avoidance, we briefly address the relation between effective augmenting and values.

## AUGMENTING AND VALUES

Values are based on a conjunction of explicit contingencies and transformation of reinforcing or aversive functions. During this process, lots of actions are hierarchically related to goals and, likewise, those goals are related to values (e.g., Y. Barnes-Holmes, Barnes-Holmes, McHugh, & Hayes, 2004; Dahl, Plumb, Stewart, & Lundgren, 2009). The hierarchy established for values (values contain goals, goals contain actions) is coordinated with the experiential locus we have learned to tact as I or ME and the function established to control behavior when, for example, the child was taught to respond to what she wants and why she wants it, as well as to choose what to do, and to realize the consequences of her choices. When values have been successfully constructed and contacted from self-as-context, or the perspective of the self, the person is in a better position to deal with aversive or appetitive functions (i.e., whatever self-content may show up). More technically, values establish the conditions for successful augmenting regulation because they transform the aversive or appetitive properties of present conditions as well as of consequences of actions (Luciano et al., 2009, 2011; Törneke et al., 2008).

Contrarily, a person who has not successfully constructed her values (e.g., connections between actions, goals and values have not been properly established) or has not developed proper self-as-process or self-as-context, and derives self-rules related to the (un)satisfactory evaluation of her life, will most likely behave fused with such rules and be trapped in suffering. We will address this in more detail next.

# Destructive Experiential Avoidance as a Form of Ineffective Augmenting

Problematic forms of augmenting lead to Destructive Experiential Avoidance (DEA; Hayes, Wilson, Gifford, Follette, & Strosahl, 1996). Experiential avoidance is a type of rule-following in which the person behaves deliberately so as to either avoid or escape from discomfiting private events (thoughts, memories, sensations, and so on), or to retain pleasant ones. The effect of such deliberate actions is, however, paradoxical. Though in the short run, it can work to reduce discomfort and increase the feeling that one is doing what one is supposed to do, in the long run it often leads to problematic consequences: mainly, discomfiting private events increase and strengthen while one's personal life becomes entangled and one's satisfaction is reduced. This context serves an establishing function that will set the conditions for lots of self-rules to emerge about the person himself, his possibilities, his future, etc. Without the fluency in perspective taking needed to be able to choose otherwise, the person will automatically avoid and the pattern will be perpetuated. Thus his life will continue to be characterized by very restricted behavior regulation and failure to contact psychologically important events and experiences. Destructive experiential avoidance as described here has been proven to be central in a wide range of psychological disorders (Hayes et al., 1996, 2006).

As previously mentioned, augmenting can interact with pliance and tracking by connecting them with abstract consequences (Törneke et al., 2008). The more abstract the desired consequences are, the harder it is for direct consequences to affect behavior. For example, as indicated in the preceding section, generalized pliance is problematic because this inflexible repertoire prevents the person from taking steps that will result in positive reinforcement. Instead, he keeps trying to get something (others' love and help or any other consequence that others might mediate) that is highly uncontrollable and unpredictable (i.e., specific reciprocation from others even when his behavior is not felt by others as having such a function) in order to feel good about himself. However, this pattern of regulation becomes worse when feeling good most of the time is established as a primary goal for achieving other goals in life (e.g., being a good coworker). Complex relational framing is involved here. On the one hand, certain feelings or thoughts about oneself (e.g., "I want to be a normal person") are framed in coordination (rather than in hierarchical relations) with ME and are also framed in coordination with acting toward particular goals coordinated with feeling good. On the other hand, "feeling good" is established as a necessary component (i.e., causal or conditional framing) for reaching what a person really values in his life (Hayes et al., 1998; Luciano et al., 2009; Törneke, 2010; Törneke, et al., 2008). This relational network will be defended in order to maintain coherence, the sense that one is doing the correct thing in order to achieve a good life. This coherence is the context for the person becoming trapped in destructive regulation in which he needs to feel well most of the time before he can live a valued life and he only feels well depending on others' behaviors.

A similar phenomenon occurs when augmenting interacts with ineffective tracking. For example, take a depressed person who ruminates over past and future events. She justifies "thinking over" as a way to find a solution to her problems. It is not helping her to solve them and thus, ultimately it is ineffective; however, in the short term, it is negatively reinforced in that it blocks other negative thoughts or feelings (e.g., 'I am a failure'). In addition, her efforts are boosted by several logically connected rules such as the following: "Feeling good is necessary in order to be normal, which is itself necessary before I can live a valued life," and "I feel better when I think things over" so therefore "I am right to continue to think things over." Her deliberate effort to get rid of discomfiting thoughts and feelings (i.e., ineffective tracking) is potentiated by the connection of this track to augmental rules about feeling well and being normal as key goals for having a fulfilling life. In addition, the coherence of this relational network sustains the feeling of doing right when she ruminates and this effect may itself be boosted by rules such as "I am right to continue to think things over." Ultimately, however, the person is trapped in a cycle of problematic regulation that is sustained, as long as she cannot readily differentiate her self-rules from the person who is having them, and as long as she is unable to see the connection between the short- and long-term effects of her actions in an accumulative temporal stage, which necessarily involves fluency in deictic and hierarchical framing (Luciano, Ruiz, Vizcaíno, Sánchez, Gutiérrez, & López, 2011).

To sum up, fears and unwanted thoughts show up, get attached (or coordinated) to the self, as conceptualized self, and become the target for avoidance as if this was essential in order to live. This type of rule-governed behavior will not pay off in the long run because it is under the control of being right, or the coherence of the relational network, as opposed to efficacy and it blocks the occurrence of those behaviors oriented toward gaining positive reinforcement as part of a meaningful life. Said another way, destructive experiential avoidance is *ineffective augmenting* regulation because it is mostly fused (automatic) actions as opposed to behavior in freely chosen directions controlled by abstract consequences (i.e., values).

## Overcoming Destructive Experiential Avoidance

When this repertoire is present, the person may be diagnosed, sooner or later, with one or more psychiatric disorders. Depending on the explanation given for his/her problem, the person may be submitted to forms of treatment that might make things worse as, for example, when treatment is oriented to the control of thoughts, memories, or sensations in order to live (a strategy that involves sophisticated rules that potentiate problematic augmenting with which the person is already familiar). In contrast, the theoretical approach advocated in this chapter encourages the person to take responsibility for his human condition. This means learning to behave in accordance with the empirically observed laws that govern human behavior, including especially verbal behavior, in order that behavior regulation might be effective. Informally stated, these laws suggest that: (a) humans learn to behave on the basis of abstract, long-term consequences, as personal values that will direct their life; (b) humans learn that thoughts, sensations, and memories (which may be considered self-rules) can show up unexpectedly. The source of these private events, as self-rules, is related to the formation of the self-as-content; (c) humans inevitably react to such events when they show up; the reaction might be an action either fused to self-as-content or defused from it. In the former case, the literality of self-as-content is in charge, while in the latter case, the self-as-context is in charge; that is, ongoing self-as-content is discriminated through self-as-process and the context of values becomes available via self-as-perspective and the person chooses. Finally (d) these actions will be subject to further transformations of function as they have consequences that will be evaluated by the behaving person as being either more or less in accord with the type of life that he wants.

Given our current knowledge of laws of behavior and relational framing, we are now in a better position to implement successful clinical procedures and, most importantly, to understand why they work on the basis of the transformation of functions involved. We will just mention that the first key issue in undermining problematic rule-following behavior is experiencing the result of a spiral of unsuccessful efforts in relation to personal values such as has been described in previous examples used in this chapter. This opens the door to the clarification of valued trajectories that will set the stage for acceptance of private events (self-as-content that is evaluated as a barrier) This will only be possible by learning to verbally discriminate between myself and the thoughts and feelings I am experiencing, and by learning to make choices from the self-as-perspective. This perspective involves experiencing the "I" located HERE and NOW while any thought/feeling experienced is located THERE and THEN, which enhances the hierarchical and controlling functions of the self. From this perspective one can contact personal values and the transformed consequences of behaving in one way or another. This is the context for choosing according to personal values because it is this perspective from which values become present. As already mentioned, experiencing what is important for oneself is the context for effective augmenting and, consequently, valued actions become transformed as satisfactory even when aversive functions are present (e.g., pain or discomfort when doing whatever). This way, the avoidance function of self-as-content (e.g., 'I am too weak to cope with pain—I cannot do it') will be altered and behavior change will occur on the basis of alternative present sources of stimulus control connected with what is important for the person. All these verbal discriminations are established by multiple experiential opportunities that will set up the conditions for effective augmenting with accurate long-term tracking. That is, rule-following in which private contents, as self-as-content, are no longer something to fight against (if aversive) or to cling on to (if appetitive), but are simply part of the process on the way to effective long-term and abstract reinforcing consequences (Hayes, Strosahl, & Wilson, 1999; Törneke, et al., 2008).

To sum up, the development of abilities for detaching from the self-as-content and, consequently, achieving or re-acquiring self-as-perspective, is possible through ongoing discrimination of whatever private events show up (self-as-process). However, it is the hierarchical and perspective relationships achieved in a particular moment with respect to self-as-content that allows choosing behaving (between the literal function of self-as-content or its transformation in the context of present stimulus functions connected with values). In recent work (see Luciano, Ruiz, Vizcaíno, Sánchez, Gutiérrez, & López, 2011; Luciano, Valdivia-Salas, & Ruiz, 2011) we have started to empirically explore some of these key processes. More specifically, we have provided an empirical RFT-based analysis of several varieties of defusion intervention employed in acceptance and commitment therapy (ACT; Hayes, Strosahl, et al., 1999). For example, one type of intervention (labelled defusion-type 1) involved deictic multiple exemplar training to differentiate the ongoing process of having thoughts ("I + my thoughts and emotions - HERE & NOW" to "I - HERE & NOW *while* my thoughts and emotions - THERE & THEN). A second type of intervention (defusion-type 2) aimed to make explicit the hierarchical relation between me and my private content (I - HERE and all my thoughts, emotions and actions - THERE *and also* PART of ME) that was implicit in the previous intervention. A third intervention (defusion-type 3) aimed to make explicit the perspective-taking function implicit in the two previous interventions or relational contexts, that is, the choosing function possible through self-as-perspective. Findings of this preliminary work point to the superior effect of the administration of the combination of all three types of intervention as compared with administration of type 1 alone. Much further investigation of these processes will be required, but this is an illustration at least of how RFT research is exploring the processes discussed in this chapter. All of the interventions described seem essential in ACT; however, a deeper description of these issues is out of the present scope.

# Summary

Humans uniquely can frame and derive rules about their own behavior. Natural language establishes the conditions for a child to become verbally competent from early in development. This facilitates the transition from basic rule-following (i.e., pliance and tracking) to the most advanced type, augmenting. In the absence of particular interactions needed to establish fluency in one's ability to discriminate self-as-content (rules concerning oneself and one's behavior that may become rigid and ineffective) from self-as-process (i.e., the moment-to-moment experience of thoughts, memories, feelings and sensations as they happen) and self-as-context (i.e., the abstraction of the common perspective to all these actions that establishes the function for behavior regulation) problems can arise as one can behave "stuck" in self-as-content. Fortunately, the enhancement of self-as-process and self-as-context are the means by which such ineffective behavior regulation may be overcome.

# Chapter 9

# The Self in Cognitive Behavior Therapy

Hamish J. McLeod & Joseph Ciarrochi
*University of Wollongong, Australia*

## Introduction

Approaches within traditional cognitive behavior therapy share certain assumptions concerning human psychology. They assume that the content of one's cognitions concerning the self or otherwise has a direct effect on emotion and observable behavior, that it is sometimes possible for cognitions to be incorrect or distorted in relation to "objective" truth, and that incorrect or distorted cognition may produce emotional and behavioral problems (see e.g., Abramson, Seligman, & Teasdale, 1978; Beck, Rush, Shaw, & Emery, 1979; Bentall, Corcoran, Howard, Blackwood, & Kinderman, 2001). Given these assumptions, the challenging of incorrect or unhelpful cognitions is taken as a central aim of traditional CBT treatment strategies. This emphasis on cognitive change assumes that emotion regulation is achieved through changing thoughts, attitudes, or beliefs (Hofmann & Asmundson, 2008). This has been referred to as a mechanistic model of human cognition that can be contrasted with the functional contextualist conception that underlies contextual behavioral science (Hayes, Strosahl, & Wilson, 1999). Therapies based on the latter, such as acceptance and commitment therapy (ACT), eschew a focus on cognitive content in favor of achieving change through the alteration of the context in which thoughts are experienced.

Granted, there are important differences between traditional CBT and contextual behavioral approaches such as ACT. Nevertheless, the recognition within the traditional CBT model of the potential effects of cognitive content, particularly those concerning the self, and the analysis of those effects on behavior under certain circumstances (referred to within ACT as "cognitive fusion") makes a contribution to the understanding of human psychology and in particular psychopathology that offers insight even for proponents of alternative conceptions such as contextual behavioral science.

Although the contemporary CBT literature refers to various self-related concepts such as self-esteem, self-focused attention (e.g., rumination), and negative self-talk, it would be an error to treat the self as a unitary "thing" that is prodded and molded into better shape by CBT. Instead, there are multiple aspects of the self that can be described in relation to their content (e.g., critical thoughts directed at the self) and the processes that operate on that content (e.g., biases in automatic attentional or memory processes for self-referent information). In this chapter we will describe the evolution of the self in the CBT literature from its largely descriptive early formulations to the more multifaceted and multilevel contemporary conceptualizations. This includes consideration of how the distinction between conscious and unconscious information processing has influenced cognitive models of distorted self-representation such as that seen in disorders such as schizophrenia. We will also examine the points of agreement and departure between the clinical conceptualizations of the self as it is described in CBT treatment guidelines and the findings from social-cognitive psychology research on the self. We will suggest that a somewhat unitary view of the self in CBT born out of clinical observation has been replaced with a multidimensional set of cognitive processes and structures that span multiple aspects of memory and levels of conscious awareness.

In addition, as the second half of this chapter in particular may indicate, despite differences in assumptions, in some respects CBT theory and research on the self are showing a degree of convergence with current contextual behavioral scientific concepts. For example, there appears to be increasing recognition from within traditional CBT of several concepts important in contextual behavioral science, including psychological flexibility, meta-cognition, the observer perspective, and the effects of implicit or "unconscious" processes. Each of these is discussed in this chapter also.

---

# Content-Based Views of the Self in CBT

CBT approaches give the content of cognition a privileged position in the chain of causality between a stimulus and an emotional or behavioral response. The content of cognitions, appraisals, and beliefs about the self are implicated in numerous broad cognitive models of psychopathology (e.g., self-discrepancy theory; Higgins, 1987) and specific models of circumscribed clinical disorders (e.g., Clark's model of panic disorder; Clark, 1996). The general cognitive therapy model (A. T. Beck, 1976; A. T. Beck et al., 1979; J. S. Beck, 1995) distinguishes three main types of mental event that are implicated in psychopathology and are targeted in treatment. These are automatic thoughts, intermediate beliefs, and core beliefs.

## Automatic Thoughts

Automatic thoughts are the ubiquitous, reflexive, often fragmentary ideas and images that occur for all humans as a part of everyday mental experience. They cannot be "switched off" or subjected to the same degree of cognitive control as more reflective deliberate forms of thinking. However, one of the tasks in CBT is to help the patient become more explicitly aware of negative automatic thoughts (NATs; A. T. Beck, 1976). The association between these thoughts and negative emotional and behavioral responses is explicitly taught to the patient as part of the rationale for challenging the accuracy or utility of the thought content (J. S. Beck, 1995). This is consistent with the mechanistic assumption that helping the client to change their thought content will lead to a change in emotions or observable behaviors.

Although the range of automatic thought content is potentially vast, this diversity is often simplified by referring to common co-occurring patterns of thinking. The cognitive (or depressive) triad of negative thoughts about the self, the world, and the future is one of the most widely used examples of this (A. T. Beck et al., 1979). The impact of negative thoughts on the self is that patients may exhibit a habitual pattern of self-criticism that is treated as an objectively true representation of the status of the self and contributes to the maintenance of low mood (Dozois, 2007). However, as there is considerable individual variation in the specific content of this negative self-talk, CBT theorists posit a role for more enduring cognitive structures from which these negative automatic thoughts emanate. This leads to the specification of various forms of belief, broadly separated into intermediate and core beliefs.

## Intermediate Beliefs

Intermediate beliefs are classified into subtypes of *rules* (e.g., "I should always be self-reliant"), *attitudes* (e.g., "It is terrible to have to ask for help"), and conditional *assumptions* (e.g., "If I ask for help, it means I am incompetent"). Intermediate beliefs sit on the midpoint of malleability between automatic thoughts (the most amenable to modification) and core beliefs (rigidly held unconditional beliefs that are resistant to modification).

These beliefs will be directly relevant to the dysfunction of the self when they codify an unworkable standard (e.g., "I must never upset another person") or arbitrarily impose catastrophic, exaggerated, or otherwise distorted expectations on the self (e.g., "It would be *unbearable* if another person does not like me"). CBT theorists posit that beliefs will exert an effect on affect and behavior in the abstract (e.g., the use of safety behaviors in anxiety disorders; Helbig-Lang & Petermann, 2010) as well as influencing the response to actual stressors (e.g., triggering a strong depressive response following the violation of a self-imposed rule; Showers, Limke, & Zeigler-Hill, 2004).

It is proposed that the form of intermediate beliefs affects their modifiability (J. S. Beck, 1995). Specifically, rules and attitudes are claimed to be less amenable to evaluation than conditional assumptions even though they are permutations of each other. The argument is that becoming aware of a conditional assumption (e.g., "If I ask for help, it means I am incompetent") promotes more cognitive dissonance (i.e., discomfort caused by the presence of conflicting content) than awareness of the rule from which the assumption is derived (e.g., "I shouldn't ask for help") (J. S. Beck, 1995), which in turn is amenable to reduction by rejecting distorted or "irrational" thoughts with more evidence-based functional alternatives. Indeed, the latter is one of the mechanisms by which psychological treatments are argued to work (Tryon & Misurell, 2008)[1].

## Core Beliefs

Although core beliefs are sometimes referred to as being synonymous with schemas, it has been proposed that it is more accurate to view them as the *content* of schemas (A. T. Beck, 1964)[2]. This content consists of global and overgeneralized propositions that are inflexible and relatively impervious to change. The specific content of core beliefs is often asserted to be self-focused and organized around the main themes of helplessness, unlovability, or both (J. S. Beck, 1995). These themes are generally ascribed to the self as reflected by "I" statements such as "I am inadequate," "I am incompetent," "I am defective." But, the content of core beliefs can also reflect propositions about other people (e.g., "Other people are devious"; (Fowler et al., 2006). The functional implications of core beliefs for understanding the onset and maintenance of psychopathology is most easily understood when they are examined in relation to the concept of schema, addressed next.

## Structural Views of the Self in CBT

### Schemas

The schema concept in CBT has been co-opted from cognitive psychology in an attempt to explain the origin of negative thoughts about the

---

1    But it should be noted that the response to cognitive dissonance may be to defend the rigidly held dysfunctional rule even more vigorously despite the presence of contradictory evidence. This problem is dealt with in motivational interviewing treatment by explicitly using strategies such as "rolling with resistance."

2    Unfortunately, this lack of conceptual clarity about the nature of schemas is reflected in substantial variability in the way that the concept is defined by practicing clinicians (James, Todd, & Reichelt, 2009).

self that are characteristic of diagnoses such as major depression and various personality disorders (A. T. Beck, 1964; A. T. Beck et al., 1979). J. M. G. Williams, Watts, MacLeod, and Mathews (1997) identify several features of the schema. It is a stored body of knowledge with a consistent internal structure that provides a template for organizing and making associations between new information. These structures are abstracted from experience and reflect prototypical representations of regularities between stimuli. The learned relatedness between stimuli results in the spreading of activation between schema elements such that exposure to one stimulus (e.g., "Joe complained about the service") will prime likely interpretations of the situation (e.g., that Joe feels he has waited too long for his restaurant meal). In most situations these "top down" processes act as useful heuristic models of the world that conserve cognitive resources and allow rapid responding to change. However, these predictions can be prone to bias and error when the activated schema is not appropriate to the actual situation.

Schemas are often central to the sense of self. They are models of how the self relates to the world, and especially to other people. There is extensive evidence that self-referent information is encoded and recalled more readily than non-self-referent information (Wisco, 2009) and this can have a detrimental effect on psychological functioning when self-schema content is dominated by themes of being weak, unlovable, or defective (Young, Klosko, & Weishaar, 2003).

## Dysfunctional Self-Schemas

Adverse early experiences are assumed to shape self-representation schemas that can lie latent and unrecognized for years until activated by current life stressors. Once activated, this dysfunctional schema (or schemas) biases the processing of ongoing experience and provides the substrate for negative thoughts about the self, the world, and the future. In understanding depression, the proposition is that dysfunctional schemas are a form of psychological diathesis that exert minimal impact on processing during times of normal mood but may be irrationally maintained during symptom exacerbation.

> [The patient] seriously believes and is quite consistent in his beliefs that he is deprived, defective, useless, unlovable, etc. In fact, this internal consistency is often maintained in the face of repeated and dramatic external evidence contradictory to these

beliefs. The beliefs are generally organized into a system similar to that Kuhn (1962) described as a scientific "paradigm." The patient's observations and interpretations of reality are molded by this conceptual framework. As in the case of scientific beliefs, a personal paradigm may be shaken and modified when the individual is prepared to recognize an anomaly that the existing paradigm cannot accommodate or evidence that disconfirms the paradigm. (At. T. Beck et al., 1979, p. 61)

Two critical elements about the self can be drawn from this description. First, negative labels are applied to the self (e.g., "I am unlovable") and maintained in the face of contradictory experiences. This reflects an emphasis on the *content* of the self-schema and reflects the idea that they are "...a form of semantic memory that describes the qualities associated with the self" (Brewin, 2006, p. 769). Like other forms of semantic memory, global self-propositions are abstracted from experience and are accessible independently from the time and place when the knowledge was acquired. Hence, a person may be consciously aware of a proposition about themselves (e.g., "I am helpless") independently of the original encoding experience(s) that contributed to the acquisition of that proposition. Like other semantic knowledge, these propositions are treated as facts that are applied to understanding the nature of the self and the interpretation of the meaning of events. The second feature of self-schemas is that they are organized in a structure of multiple elements that are internally consistent to the individual but that can be "shaken and modified" when the individual is exposed to disconfirmatory evidence.

Segal (1988) delineates three possible relationships between self-schema and depression. First, *availability* models suggest that depressed people hold a greater number of negative constructs about the self relative to non-depressed individuals and these predominate during a depressed episode and are changed by successful treatment. Second, *accessibility* accounts reflect a greater ease of access to negative self-constructs and these are preferentially accessed during a depressive episode. This accessibility account is consistent with mood congruency effects that demonstrate preferential access to memory information that is consistent with the mood state during retrieval (Blaney, 1986). Furthermore, accessibility accounts do not require any asymmetry in the ratio of negative to positive constructs available for attribution to the self, only that the negative ones are accessed more readily (Segal & Muran, 1993). The third, *negative self-schema* model proposes that depressed individuals differ from non-depressed because of a different structural relationship or interconnectedness between constructs relating to the self. For example, the depressed person may have a high degree of inter-relatedness between negative elements of knowledge about the self. Thus, activating one element of an elaborated network of negative information about the self triggers a spread of activation to related constructs (Wisco, 2009).

Only the negative self-schema model predicts that negative conceptions of the self will remain available following the remission of a depressive episode. Without an enduring negative self-schema, mood congruency effects alone will be sufficient to explain the presence of negative self-referent thoughts and beliefs during a depressive episode. Segal's (1988) review reflects many of the difficulties encountered when the structural or descriptive cognitive models used in therapy are subjected to closer empirical scrutiny. As more empirical investigations of the cognitive therapy model of self-schemas have emerged, it has become clear that emotional processes are as important as cognitive processes in shaping the course of mental illness (David & Szentagotai, 2006). It has also become apparent that simple dichotomies of positive versus negative self-schemas and singular notions of the self-concept are inadequate to explain the existing data.

## Singular vs. Multiple Selves

Although there is reliable evidence that information stored in memory contributes to the subjective sense of a continuous "self" across time (Conway & Pleydell-Pearce, 2000), this is not synonymous with the existence of a unitary self-schema. Instead, there is more support for the existence of multiple self-schemas that are differentially activated depending on situational cues (Dalgleish & Power, 2004; Markus, 1990; Power, 2007; Showers, Abramson, & Hogan, 1998; J. M. G. Williams et al., 1997). This leads to the proposal that the phenomenological experience of a singular "I" is an artifice and instead that the self is composed of multiple subsystems (Dimaggio, Hermans, & Lysaker, 2010; Klein, 2010; Power, 2007). For CBT, the existence of multiple possible selves presents both propositions about the psychological substrate of emotional disorders and a target of treatment. For example, if a depressive self-schema is dominating information processing and impeding the operation of more adaptive self-schemas, then treatment could entail attempts to develop or enhance the functioning of more adaptive self-schemas.

At this point, it is necessary to make a distinction between the concepts of self-knowledge as a dissociable form of information represented in the brain (Klein, Cosmides, Costabile, & Mei, 2002) and subcomponents such as "self-aspects" (Showers et al., 1998) that exist within that pool of self-referent information. The basic principle is that we can represent information about the self (e.g., "I once got a speeding ticket") without it being integrated within a more elaborated self-schema (e.g., a "bad me" schema that comprises multiple behavioral exemplars, self-attitudes, and beliefs about failing to live up to acceptable standards). This issue is addressed by postulating that networks of self-referent information that are frequently co-activated acquire the properties of an idiosyncratic self-schema within the broader pool of self-referent information. This has been referred to as compartmentalization (Showers, 1992) or modularization (Power, 2007).

## Compartmentalization

Compartmentalization refers to the "splitting off" (Dalgleish & Power, 2004) of a set of concerns about aspects of the self such that they have a high degree of interconnectedness to each other and weaker unity with other aspects of the self (Power, 2007). The affective valence of these compartmentalized self-schemas can be positive or negative and they can be related to domains of self-functioning role (e.g., "me as a parent"), contexts (e.g. "my interactions with my boss") and idiosyncratic aspects of the self (e.g., "me as an optimistic person") (Power, de Jong, & Lloyd, 2002; Showers et al., 1998; Showers et al., 2004). By definition, activation of one aspect of a compartmentalized self-schema will facilitate the activation of related elements with the same affective tone. In a negative self-schema example, activating "me with my boss" might make available negative self-evaluations such as being unassertive, liable to be criticized, and underperforming. In contrast a positive compartmentalized self-schema such as "me with my spouse" might activate self-features such as being loved and being dependable. These compartmentalized schemata can be contrasted with an "integrative" self-schema structure where positive and negative features co-activate (Showers et al., 2004).

Schema compartmentalization is typically assessed using a self-descriptive card-sorting task (Linville, 1985, 1987). Participants are asked to generate as many self-aspects as needed to describe themselves. They are then given cards with 20 different positive (e.g., outgoing, capable) and 20 negative (e.g., weary, disorganized) adjectives and are asked to allocate those that they see as relevant to each idiosyncratic self-aspect. The descriptors can be allocated to more than one self-aspect and once the sorting is completed each self-aspect is rated on a 7-point Likert scale along dimensions of subjective importance, positivity, and negativity. The degree of compartmentalization can be statistically assessed, with perfect compartmentalization occurring when a self-aspect is ascribed entirely positive *or* negative descriptors. Other values derived from the self-concept task reflect subjective judgments about the importance of aspects of the self, self-complexity, and the proportion of negative items used across all self-aspects. Self-complexity scores reflect a combination of the total number of self-aspects generated and the degree of overlap of adjectives across those self-aspects. Hence, individuals with higher self-complexity will generate more self-aspects and show a lower degree of overlap between groups of descriptors ascribed to those self-aspects.

These ways of measuring self-representation and appraisal of aspects of the self have shed some light on the role of self-concept in clinical disorders such as depression and bipolar affective disorder. Showers et al. (1998) conducted a two-year longitudinal study of 132 university students identified at baseline as showing high or low vulnerability to developing depression. Their results indicated that self-structure and content interact to protect *against* low mood. Both the content and structure of self-concept changed in response to stressful life events and the reported amount of negative features of the self was greater when stress was higher. But, although participants who displayed a low vulnerability to depression ascribed more negative content to the self-aspects during the period of higher stress, they rated these negative self-aspects as less important and showed a greater degree of compartmentalization. Showers et al. suggest that "… [r]elegating negative beliefs to distinct or narrowly defined aspects of the self may help one perceive those beliefs as less important" (p. 491).

In summary, it appears that the flexibility of the self-concept in the face of stress (e.g., being able to compartmentalize positive and negative aspects of the self) combined with a change in the appraisal of self-aspects (e.g., viewing negative aspects of the self as less important when stressed) is associated with lower depression and dysphoria. By extension, being unable to flexibly adjust the organization of one's self-concept (i.e., high rigidity) combined with a tendency to view negative self-aspects as highly important increases the negative impact of stress on mood[3].

---

3    This is consistent with the emphasis within ACT and similar therapies on the important role of psychological inflexibility including rigid self-concept.

While Showers et al.'s (1998) results suggest that compartmentalizing the self may be an effective short-term coping response, studies of self-structure in patients with unipolar and bipolar affective disorders indicate that high negative compartmentalization is associated with diagnostic status even during times of clinical remission. For example, Alatiq and colleagues found higher proportions of negative self-attributes and greater compartmentalization in bipolar patients compared to controls (Alatiq, Crane, Williams, & Goodwin, 2010). The participants with a history of unipolar depression returned scores that were in between the other two groups. Power et al. (2002) reported similar findings but they observed a high degree of positive *and* negative compartmentalization in remitted bipolar patients. Their study also included a non-psychiatric comparison group of people with chronic diabetes to control for the effects of chronic illness on sense of self. The diabetes patients showed significantly lower levels of compartmentalization, thereby demonstrating that the tendency to split off self-aspects and view them as entirely negative or positive is not simply a response to having a chronic disabling condition.

Overall, these results provide partial support for aspects of cognitive therapy models of the role of the self in the origin of affective disorders. Showers et al.'s (1998) results suggest that inflexibility in the way that the self-concept is constructed in the face of stress is associated with greater emotional distress. This fits with the proposal that negative self-schemas are rigidly applied across situations (Beck et al., 1979). Also, the finding that remitted patients with bipolar and unipolar affective disorders show higher negative compartmentalization than controls suggests that problematic self-organization can persist beyond acute phases of illness. However, in addition to examining how the self is structurally organized in clinical disorders, there is a clear need to determine how appraisals of the information contained within self-structures affects the expression of psychopathology.

# Perceptions and Appraisals of the Self

A well-known aphorism in CBT is that *interpretations* or *appraisals* of events cause emotional distress, not the events themselves. This goes some way to explaining why the same stressor will provoke different consequences in different individuals. This principle can also be applied within individuals; the same class of external stressor may provoke different reactions in the same individual over time. The activation of different self-schemas across time helps explain this effect but as described above, the appraisal of the available self-concepts (e.g., how important they are) also exerts an effect on affective reactions to stressors (Showers et al., 1998). Therefore, understanding how the self affects psychopathology requires more than the specification of its structural features.

One of the functional features of schema-driven information processing is that prior beliefs and memory for regularities in the environment bias the allocation of attentional resources in new situations and affect what is remembered of an event. Allocation of attention to the self at the expense of awareness of the external world has been implicated in the pathogenesis of various disorders ranging from depression (Pyszczynski & Greenberg, 1987) to social phobia (Moscovitch, 2009). For example, Moscovitch (2009) proposes that the driving force behind many social phobia problems is not the fear of social situations per se but perceived flaws in the self such as skill deficits, character flaws, problems with physical appearance, or deficits in the ability to conceal anxious feelings. Hence, in this formulation, the phobic stimulus is not public speaking or going to a party; it is deficient features of the self that the individual attempts to conceal by deploying safety behaviors. An implication is that cognitive-behavioral treatments should involve exposure to the feared aspects of the self, as well as the feared external trigger situations (Moscovitch, 2009).

The general information-processing view assumes that the moment-to-moment experience of the self reflects the activation of particular self-schemata, termed the *working self-concept* (Markus & Nurius, 1986), *the working self* (Conway, 2005; Conway & Pleydell-Pearce, 2000), and *the experiencing self* (Dalgleish & Power, 2004). It is generally asserted that only one experiencing self is available to consciousness at a time (Power, 2007) and this constrains and "grounds" the available self-views (Conway, 2005; Conway & Pleydell-Pearce, 2000). However, it has been necessary to pose the additional concept of the *reflective self* or *observing self* (Power, 2007) to explain the phenomenological experience of being able to observe the operation of the experiencing self (e.g., noticing that one is having negative thoughts about the self) and the loss of sense of self that can occur in certain states (e.g., dissociative experiences during panic) or in disorders of self such as dissociative identity disorder and schizophrenia (Berrios & Markova, 2003; Power, 2007)[4]. For some patients, the enhancement of reflective self capacity may be necessary to enhance

---

4    Similar distinctions have been made in the ACT literature with the explicit separation of "self as content" from "self as context" and "self as process" (Hayes et al., 1999).

awareness of alternative functional dimensions of the self or to reduce negative compartmentalization and an overly restricted self-structure (Dimaggio et al., 2010).

Specifically targeting the adaptive functioning of the reflective self has been addressed in the CBT literature only relatively recently (e.g., Fannon et al., 2009; Segal & Muran, 1993). This reflects a shift in emphasis from attempting to change the content of self-schemas and their products (e.g., conditional beliefs and negative automatic thoughts) onto metacognitive strategies that promote a greater awareness of one's thinking processes (often with the aim of encouraging a nonjudgmental perspective on the products of those processes). However, given that low self-reflection may have developed as a simplistic but partly effective strategy for reducing awareness of feared aspects of the self (Showers et al., 1998), it is likely that promoting self-awareness may be threatening for some patients (e.g., those with greatly elevated interpersonal sensitivity such as paranoid or borderline personality disorder patients). Hence, therapy conducted in an atmosphere of collaboration, safety, and compassion may be needed in order to promote the self-exploration necessary for developing greater self-acceptance (Gilbert, 2009).

The fact that some people experience considerable difficulty with consciously reflecting on aspects of the self has meant that CBT theory and clinical practice has had to account for the impact of conscious and unconscious processes on psychopathology. This issue is exemplified by the proposition that some forms of psychopathology such as mania and persecutory delusions are defenses against experiencing *conscious* thoughts relating to low self-worth (Bentall et al., 2001).

## Conscious vs. Unconscious Self-Processes

The standard CBT approach includes promoting awareness of mental events such as negative automatic thoughts, unhelpful rules and conditional assumptions (A. T. Beck et al., 1979; J. S. Beck, 1995). The basic CBT model emphasizes that these stimuli will have a deleterious effect on emotional state and behavior even if the patient does not fully recognize their operation. Self-monitoring homework tasks such as keeping a thought record and questioning strategies such as the "downward arrow" technique (J. S. Beck, 1995) are deployed in order to explicitly bring these mental events into conscious awareness so that they can be systematically evaluated. So, these mental events are "preconscious" in that they can operate outside of conscious awareness but are potentially available to introspection.

But some self-processes that are implicated in cognitive models of psychopathology are thought to operate entirely outside of awareness because their function is to prevent the confrontation of negative views of the self. This type of explanation is typically invoked where a distorted self-view develops to protect fragile self-esteem (Bentall et al., 2001). An example is the proposal that persecutory delusions form a defense against implicit (unconscious) low self-esteem that allows maintenance of positive explicit self-esteem by ascribing the source of negative experiences to the malign actions of others (Kinderman & Bentall, 1996).

## The Self Esteem—Implicit Association Test (SE-IAT)

Empirical findings thus far collected from a self-esteem variant of the Implicit Association Test (SE-IAT; Greenwald, McGhee, & Schwartz, 1998) demonstrate that investigating unconscious processes can provide a more comprehensive understanding of the multiple processes that contribute to the experience of the self. The SE-IAT is a reaction time task that uses speed of responding as an index of the degree of association between concepts (Greenwald & Farnham, 2000). The stimuli are manipulated along self-other and positive-negative dimensions. Response times are faster when the target word and attribute matches the implicit association held by the participant (e.g., self-clever) than when they fail to match it (e.g., self-stupid). Unlike explicit assessments of self-concept, the SE-IAT has the advantage of being a more direct index of the spreading activation property of semantic networks where exemplars of a particular category that are more closely associated produce faster responding (e.g., "bird-canary" vs. "bird-ostrich") (Collins & Quillian, 1969). When assessing self-esteem, response latencies are interpreted as an index of how much the self-concept is associated with positive versus negative material. MacKinnon and others (MacKinnon, Newman-Taylor, & Stopa, 2011) used this measure to test the hypothesis that people with persecutory delusions would display the paradoxical combination of high explicit but low implicit self-esteem (Bentall et al., 2001). Patients with persecutory delusions actually showed similar levels of implicit self-esteem to healthy control subjects but lower explicit self-esteem. This directly opposes the "delusions as defense" model.

Although MacKinnon et al.'s (2010) results demonstrate a need for refinement of self-concept-based theories of persecutory delusions, the methods used reflect progress toward more convincing measures of schemata and related unconscious processes.

# Summary Comparison of Social-Cognitive & CBT Concepts of the Self

The literature reviewed in this chapter suggests that the conception of the self in clinical CBT and related areas of empirical research is evolving. Unitary notions of a single "self" have been replaced by multifaceted ways of describing how self-referent information is organized, stored, accessed, and reorganized in the mind. Furthermore, content-based models of the self have been significantly extended by incorporating conscious and unconscious cognitive processes that affect self-construction. These extensions of the original cognitive models reflect the greater emphasis on the importance of metacognitive processes in understanding psychopathology (e.g., Janeck, Calamari, Riemann, & Heffelfinger, 2003). Figure 1 presents a possible formulation of the ways that multiple self-referent concepts from clinical models of CBT correspond to those derived from social-cognitive research.

Three levels of conscious processing are invoked in the descriptions of self-constructs in CBT and related social-cognitive research. These are depicted in Figure 1 with the preconscious level shaded to highlight a degree of permeability between fully conscious and unconscious levels. Although psychological therapy may help a patient to identify and verbally label core beliefs that underpin much of their distressing thoughts and emotions, these beliefs are abstractions derived from a myriad of learning experiences, most of which will have occurred without full conscious awareness. This differentiation of conscious from preconscious processing is particularly important when trying to quantify the operation of processes such as "schema activation" (Segal, 1988) that fall within the unconscious or barely preconscious realm. Because schema activation is not fully reportable using verbal means, it has become necessary to utilize research methods that rely on behavioral response times (e.g., the Self-Esteem IAT and variants of the Emotional Stroop tasks) rather than answers to questionnaire.

By definition, self-referent schemata are summaries of experience, not a veridical record of all of the details of all of the specific learning events that shaped any given schema. Hence, Figure 1 places the examples of depressogenic schemata and early experiences within the class of unconscious phenomena. The related constructs and processes in the social-cognitive literature include notions of implicit association between stimuli (that influence response times independent of explicitly expressed beliefs and attitudes), spreading activation between conceptually or semantically related information, and priming effects. All of these phenomena exert a measurable effect on behavioral functioning but are independent of the types of controlled information processing usually assessed with questionnaires or other explicit assessment procedures. Furthermore, we argue that this underlying information is not accessible in any complete way but that it is possible to become aware of the derivatives of this information (e.g., core beliefs, self schemas).

*Figure 1:* A comparison of social-cognitive and CBT constructs relating to the self

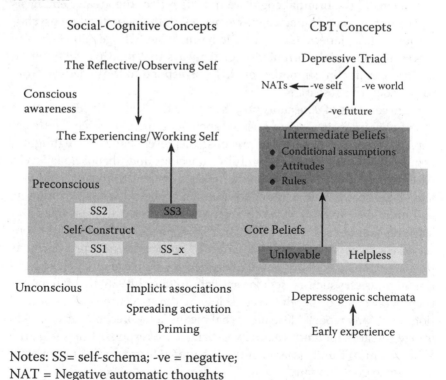

Notes: SS= self-schema; -ve = negative;
NAT = Negative automatic thoughts

The constructs specified at the preconscious level in Figure 1 are potentially responsive to introspection but may operate largely without conscious awareness for most people. Social-cognitive models use constructs such as the self-concept or self-schema to convey these ideas (Dalgleish & Power, 2004; Showers, 1992). The subfields of SS1, SS2 etc. in Figure 1 are presented to convey that the self-concept may be compartmentalized into subunits that are differentially activated. In CBT these ideas correspond to the notion of Core Beliefs, which may be distilled down to fundamental concerns about lovability or helplessness (J. S. Beck, 1995). This reduction of core beliefs to only two main themes is not universally endorsed. For example, Young's Schema therapy model postulates up to 13 maladaptive unconditional schemas about the self and others that include themes of fear of abandonment, defectiveness, and entitlement (Young et al., 2003)[5]. However, at the functional level, most CBT models propose that self-schemas can exert an influence on thoughts, feelings, and behavior even if they are outside of conscious awareness. One implication of this is that CBT treatment frequently involves helping the patient become aware of negative attitudes toward the self, conditional assumptions about self-worth, and dysfunctional rules that they impose on themselves. This potential for conscious scrutiny is depicted in Figure 1 by situating "Intermediate Beliefs" across the boundary of preconscious and conscious processes.

The final point of comparison in Figure 1 addresses the concepts and processes that are most readily subject to full conscious awareness. In CBT, emphasis is placed on the impact of the cognitive (or depressive) triad on emotional state and behavior. The self-referent subtype of these (negative views of the self) are expressed in Negative Automatic Thoughts (NATs) that arise briefly in consciousness and dissipate quickly but exert an effect on emotions and behavior. Clinical models of traditional CBT are less clear in specifying the mechanisms by which these thoughts are "read" or appraised by the individual. There is a tacit assumption that NATs are judged to be "true," but the observer that makes this judgment is not a focus of much therapeutic attention. This partly avoids the messy problem of infinite regress to unsatisfactory structural concepts such as a homunculus or "true self "that observes and judges thoughts and feelings but it leaves an important gap in the clinical models. However, social-cognitive conceptions of the self have achieved some clarity by specifying

---

5     Young et al. (2003) also differentiate unconditional maladaptive schemas that are learned early in life from conditional maladaptive schemas that are shaped by later experience and are modified over time.

modes of processing as an alternative to a unitary and static observer of the self. Figure 1 shows that there is a distinction drawn between the working or experiencing self and the observing or reflective self. Ultimately, these are still descriptive concepts that serve to more accurately portray phenomenological experience but do not explain how these experiences arise. But they do provide a more nuanced way of separating the experience of a thought (e.g., "I am a failure") from the capacity to observe, judge, or appraise that thought. The development of "third wave" mindfulness-based variants of CBT reflects a move towards incorporating these distinctions more completely into therapy (e.g., Hayes, Strosahl, & Wilson, 1999).

# Conclusion

Despite a pedigree stretching back to early Greek philosophy, the concept of self infiltrated psychiatric and psychological writing only in the nineteenth century with the conceptualization of "disorders of the self" such as schizophrenia (Berrios & Markova, 2003). CBT as a theoretical and therapeutic endeavor has embraced the proposition that self-belief, self-criticism, self-esteem, and related concepts are central to the understanding of a range of psychopathological conditions. However, there is considerable variation in the way that the self is invoked both as a basis for suffering and as a focus of change efforts such as "schema modification." This partly reflects the problem of treating the self as a unitary concept. As Berrios and Markova note: *"The self was never meant to be a solid object like a stone, a horse, or a weed, nor even a concept to be considered as semantically tantamount to changes in blood flow or test scores" (p. 10).* The evidence presented above indicates that progress is being made toward developing a more multifaceted and dynamic view of the self. Furthermore, as regards the relationship between traditional CBT and the alternative contextual behavioral approach to therapy represented by ACT, as indicated, in some respects CBT theory and research on the self are showing a degree of convergence with current contextual behavioral scientific understandings. This convergence will hopefully benefit both traditions, especially with respect to the conceptualization of the self and the use of this concept in the psychological treatments of the future.

# Part 4

# The Self: Mindfulness and Transcendence

# Chapter 10

# The Self and Mindfulness

Kelly G. Wilson, Michael Bordieri & Kerry Whiteman
*University of Mississippi*

## Introduction

This chapter relies on a behavioral conceptualization of self as a starting point for an exploration of the relationship between self and mindfulness. After considering both self and mindfulness individually, they will be considered together using the psychological flexibility model as an organizing framework for exploring the connections these domains share. Finally, potential research implications and applied applications will be presented as an invitation for future research in this area.

## Understanding Self

Intellectual battles have been fought over the nuances, origins, formation, and "true" nature of self. Yet for most, there is general agreement that self is a noun. Self is an "it," though its precise location does not get a great deal clearer than pointing one's finger at oneself and saying, "right here." Even in its noncorporeal form, "self" seems to have edges: it is a thing. It is a noun. It is distinct, at least to the extent that I can tell yours from mine. The behaviorist view of self is often difficult to grasp for those outside the behavioral tradition. The difficulty lies in the fact that, unlike virtually all other uses of the word, when used by the behaviorist, "self" is a verb. This differs from typical usage in the scientific community and also from the native ways we learn to speak of self.

For the behaviorist, self is an integrated set of behavioral repertoires, and these repertoires serve an important function within a social-verbal community. We learn to speak about self through many of the same processes through which we learn to speak of other events in our world (cf. Skinner, 1945). We are not born able to answer questions about our "self." The nature of the repertoires from a behavioral viewpoint is described in detail in this volume (see chapters 1 and 2, for example). However, for the sake of a self-contained chapter we will examine self briefly. We learn to speak about self as a noun because it is useful in our social interactions to characterize our "self" as a relatively static, individual entity. Doing so makes it possible for us to predict and sometimes influence the behavior of others and for others to do the same with respect to us. If I say, "I feel ill," you are not likely to ask me to go jogging. If I say, "I feel sleepy," you can predict that I will respond favorably to an offer to take a nap. According to Skinner's analysis, we learned to say things like "I feel X" or "I think X" because we have a history where answering those sorts of questions in a way that allowed others to predict and influence our behavior were reinforced.

Young children are not good at talking about themselves. The repertoire is underdeveloped. We ask them at the dinner table, "Are you still hungry?" They say "No." Ten minutes after all of the food has been put away, they proclaim, "I am hungry!" This leads to negative social consequences. Mom and Dad say, "Well, you should have eaten more. You will be good and hungry for breakfast though." Eventually these consequences produce accurate reporting (where accurate reporting is equivalent to reporting that allows for good prediction of behavior). The questions asked that require reports are myriad and have to do with what they did before, what they would like to do later, what they see and hear and smell, think, feel, and are inclined to do. They share one common feature—all ask for responses from a particular perspective.

For our purposes, we can think of this unique perspective as being the sum of a person's history brought to bear in the moment of the question being asked. Learning to answer from this unique perspective and learning that others have their own perspective occurs through a process of multiple exemplar training. We ask children no end of questions about themselves, and we reinforce or punish according to their answers. Later, we begin asking them questions that require them to answer about the perspective of others. Initially, they are bad at this. When we ask them about what someone else sees, feels, or hears, they are likely to answer from their own perspective, not the other person's perspective.

Teaching flexibility with respect to perspective taking (PT) involves asking numerous questions that require the listener to see from alternate perspectives (often accompanied by supplementary instructions that facilitate this) in order to produce reinforcement:

1. From another's perspective ("How do you think your sister felt when you took her toy?")

2. From your future perspective ("Are you sure you want to eat all your candy now, rather than saving some for later?")

3. From the future perspective of others ("Is that going to make your father happy?")

4. From your own past perspective ("What were you thinking when you drew on the wall?")

5. From the past perspective of others ("Is that what your teacher wanted you to do?")

Nonresponsiveness or unconventional responses are not likely to be met with positive consequences. We learn to answer in conventional ways that lead to an ability, shared within the community, to predict and sometimes influence one another's patterns of activity. The process is somewhat imprecise, but functional. In the midst of this repertoire building, senses of "I" and "you" emerge that seem every bit as substantial as the distinctness of physical objects such as tables and chairs. In a way, "I" and "you" are distinct—but not as entities. They are distinct, rather, as bundled behavioral repertoires. Just as we learn to walk, speak, and play the guitar, we learn to take perspective. Thus, the question "Where is the self?" is analogous to asking "Where is the 'play guitar'?" There is no play but in the playing; there is no self but in the *selfing*.

There is one terribly interesting difference between selfing and playing guitar, though. The difference is that we need a guitar to play the guitar. When we start to learn, we need a guitar to play. After mastering the guitar, we need a guitar to play. Selfing is different. In order to learn to self, we need to be asked questions about self. Once we master selfing, however, we no longer require those questions; we can generate our own. This does not mean that the questions are never needed or never influential. It just means that in addition to the questions asked by the community around us, we are capable of questioning ourselves. Sometimes the questions we ask ourselves are quite useful: What kind of person do I want to be? What can I do now to grow into being that person?

We learn to relationally frame events in the world to one another and to relate ourselves to those events (see Hayes, Barnes-Holmes, & Roche, 2001 and Törneke, 2010). Some of these relations depend on perspective for meaning. We will focus on three of what are called, in relational frame theory, *deictic relations*: 1) I-you, 2) here-there, and 3) now-then (for more in depth coverage see chapter 3 of this volume). I-you, here-there and now-then, depend on perspective for their meaning. For example, there is no here or there in the world except in relation to someone's perspective. I am here-now writing and you are there-then (later) reading—from my perspective. But from your perspective, I am there-then (before) writing and you are here-now reading. That simple shift in perspective changes my "now" into your "before" and my "here" into your "there. These three relational frames enable many benefits including planning, delayed gratification, predicting the motivations of others, empathy, and creating rules for behavior based on past problems, for example. Unfortunately, these frames in combination with evaluative frames such as better-worse, good-bad, worthy-unworthy can also sometimes create verbal traps that consume people's lives.

While the PT repertoire is enormously helpful in some respects, it almost invariably turns to questions involving self-evaluation and personal worth. Am I a good person? Will I ever succeed in life? Am I lovable? Am I smart enough, pretty enough, strong enough, kind enough? Am I too anxious, depressed, damaged, or incompetent? Am I normal? Why am I not like others? Will I ever feel normal? Everyone asks themselves these sorts of questions; however, becoming preoccupied with them can have disabling consequences.

People can become attached to these sorts of questions with such tenacity that they miss out on sources of reinforcement that lie all around them. Ruminating about one's past mistakes or future failures in the domain of friendship can lead a person to be less psychologically available to actual activities involved in being a friend. Time spent worrying about one's worthiness as a friend is time spent disengaged from friends and potential friends. This is not to say that reflection on past and future events is bad. In fact, it is essential in living one's values. However, flexibility is key. Inflexible attachment to questions such as the above is what produces problems.

Even a glance at psychiatric diagnostic categories reveals the prevalence of PT frames inflexibly held. For someone with anorexia: *I* am 110 pounds *now*. And that is *bad*. *I* look at pictures of *myself before*. *I was* so much more in control of *myself* then than I am *now*. If I could lose this weight (*later* is implied) *I* could be like *I was* (*before*). The anxiety disorders are littered with imperatives about what must be done *now* to avert disaster *later*, about what *others* will think about *me* if they find out what a mess *I* am. Mood disorders are likewise filled with frames connected to bleak futures and mournful pasts.

A major difficulty that arises for humans is that this ability to verbally construct I-you, here-there, now-then, good-bad means that no matter where we are, we can construct a later or a before that is better (see K. G. Wilson, Hayes, Gregg, & Zettle, 2001). Alternatively, if the current situation is perfect, watch out, because it might not last! Becoming lost in comparisons between what one is and should be, between pasts and futures both imagined and real, can disconnect people from possibilities for living that exist in the present moment. The same repertoires that are extremely helpful in negotiating the social environment trap us. Freeing people from verbal traps and helping them to become engaged in the moment-by-moment richness of their lives is a central focus of mindfulness interventions. Said simply, mindfulness appears to provide release from these verbal traps that humans seem so good at constructing for themselves.

## Understanding Mindfulness

Mindfulness is oftentimes considered to be synonymous with the practice of meditation. However, mindfulness is actually one of two major traditional approaches that guide meditation practice: *concentration* and *mindfulness meditation* (Kabat-Zinn, 1982). Concentration meditation involves an individual's narrowed focus on a single object for an extended period of time to the exclusion of any other "distracting" mental activity. Mindfulness meditation, on the other hand, entails a more flexible approach that begins with attending to a specific object or sensation, but then expands to encompass any individual observation of the present moment.

Within the mindfulness tradition, extraneous thoughts, feelings or sensations are not considered to be distractions, but additional observations of the present moment that should be treated with equanimity (Kabat-Zinn, 1982). More formally, mindfulness can be conceptualized as the "nonjudgmental observation of the ongoing stream of internal and external stimuli as they arise" (Baer, 2003, p. 125). It is this particular mindfulness tradition that has been incorporated most frequently into Western psychological interventions.

A variety of interventions have been developed that are comprised almost entirely of teaching mindfulness. Mindfulness-based stress reduction (MBSR) was one of the first interventions to fully incorporate mindfulness into the therapeutic process in Western medicine (Baer, 2003; Kabat-Zinn, 1982). The techniques found to be effective in MBSR have been the basis for various subsequent interventions including mindfulness-based cognitive therapy for depression (Segal, Williams, & Teasdale, 2002) and mindfulness-based relapse prevention for substance dependence (Bowen et al., 2009).

Emerging literature suggests that mindfulness processes can also be enhanced using less structured and shorter therapeutic interventions that can be integrated within existing treatments. For example, Hazlett-Stevens and Borkovec (2001) found that speaking-anxious participants given progressive muscle relaxation prior to a public speaking task reported less subjective distress during the exposure task and overall better outcomes from the exposure. This finding is suggestive of the role mindfulness might play in enhancing therapeutic interactions as relaxation techniques such as progressive muscle relaxation encourage deliberate and focused engagement with the present moment as one moves attention from one body part to the next.

McHugh, Simpson, and Reed (2010) recently demonstrated that a ten-minute mindfulness exercise was effective in reducing over-selectivity (i.e., situations when only a limited set of available stimuli control behavior) among older adults. Older adults given the ten-minute breathing induction were less likely to rely on intuitive "rules of thumb" and displayed greater adaptation to and flexibility with task demands. These basic experimental preparations demonstrate that brief mindfulness exercises can yield meaningful outcomes and enhance the efficacy of other treatment components.

Many interventions have been developed that include mindfulness exercises and processes as components of larger interventions packages. For instance, acceptance-based behavior therapies (ABBTs) have emerged in recent years as an extension of traditional behavioral and cognitive behavioral treatments (see Roemer & Orsillo, 2009, for a review). ABBTs have integrated mindfulness and acceptance-based components within existing empirically supported treatment technologies and have focused treatment development efforts primarily in the alleviation of anxiety disorders (Mennin, 2005). Dialectical behavior therapy (DBT), another contemporary behavioral treatment, is a program that addresses mindfulness skills as well as distress tolerance, emotion regulation, and interpersonal effectiveness skills (Linehan, 1993). The mindfulness skills training component in DBT promotes an individual's ability to observe, describe, and participate in the present moment using a nonjudgmental, focused perspective toward all aspects of experience (Baer, 2003). Acceptance and commitment therapy (ACT) is another contemporary behavioral model that uses mindfulness processes to facilitate contact with avoided experiences in the service of enabling individuals to live a richer and more vital life (see Hayes, Strosahl, & Wilson, 1999; Hayes, Strosahl, & Wilson, 2011). ACT treatment protocols include eyes-closed exercises that target present-moment awareness such as the leaves floating on a stream exercise that encourages individuals to observe their thoughts as an ongoing process the same way one would watch leaves floating down a stream (Hayes, Strosahl, & Wilson, 1999).

# Mindfulness, Self, and the Psychological Flexibility Model

Mindfulness and self could potentially be understood through a myriad of conceptual lenses, including theoretical, philosophical, and psychological. Our analysis will rely on a contemporary contextual behavioral perspective in general orientation and on the *psychological flexibility model* as a more specific organizing framework for contextual behavioral thinking. The psychological flexibility model provides a theoretical account for the change processes in acceptance and commitment therapy (ACT). However, the model is much broader than ACT, in the same sense that behavior analysis, as a theoretical framework, is larger than any single application of behavioral principles. The psychological flexibility model is a unified model of human functioning and adaptability (Hayes, Strosahl, & Wilson, 2011). It involves a set of six macro-processes that are themselves based on basic behavior analysis in combination with *relational frame theory*, a contemporary contextual account of human language and cognition (Hayes, Barnes-Holmes, & Roche, 2001; Torneke, 2010). The six processes are contact with the present moment, acceptance, defusion, self, values, and committed action.

From a psychological flexibility perspective, mindfulness is seen primarily as the interface of four of these six core processes: contact with the present moment, acceptance, defusion, and self (Hayes & Plumb, 2007; K. G. Wilson & DuFrene, 2008). We will use the psychological flexibility model in order to examine mindfulness in terms of both its potential relationship to problems with self and its potential ability to enhance repertoires involved in PT.

## Self, Mindfulness, and Applied Challenges

Self is the psychological flexibility model process most central to the purposes of this chapter. It is also a central process in mindfulness. As described at the outset of this chapter, from a behavioral view, self is cultivated in a crucible of questions that share one common feature: they all involve the person asked to take the perspective of "I." The answers to all of the questions, implicitly or explicitly, begin with the word "I." "Did you dream last night?" "What book would you like to read?" "Are you sad?" "What do you see?" "What do you want?"

From a behavioral view, self is repertoire, and two potential problems with self-as-repertoire predominate: First is the underdevelopment of PT repertoires. We would expect to see the underdevelopment of PT in environments in which the relevant questioning is impoverished or narrow. Institutionalization might produce a reduced set of such questions and developmental problems might also precipitate deficits in the questioning environment. If a child is unresponsive to questions, as seen among some developmental disabilities, questioning will be attenuated—not entirely, but almost certainly reduced. If we consider the PT repertoire as one that exists in a dynamic relation to the questioning environment, we can predict other sources of difficulties besides underdevelopment. Sometimes the unresponsiveness of the individual, as described above, is not the driving force behind fewer PT questions. Instead, the structural elements of institutions may inhibit questioning and therefore development. We should expect impoverishment of questioning where institutions are understaffed and where there is a premium on orderly functioning of the institution over development of repertoires.

The second potential problem with self-as-repertoire is fusion with verbal rules about self. There is a risk in psychological and other health problems that individuals may become excessively identified with their difficulties. In some regards the problem is in the structure of self-description. "I am obese." "I am depressed." "I am an alcoholic." If such identity relations are mixed with many identity relations, there is likely little risk. For example, the alcoholic client who identifies this way at Alcoholics Anonymous meetings would be unlikely to be harmed by such identification if it were one of many: "My name is Bob and I am an alcoholic." "I am recovering." "I am getting in shape." "I am working on my relationships." "I am a big science fiction fan." If the identifications are varied, there is a smaller likelihood that any single one will exclusively organize behavior. Also, the more varied the identifications, the more likely that an individual will experience a sense of self that is independent of any particular content.

Consider the impact of chronic serious mental illness on the questioning environment. The more distressed the client, the more likely the clinician is to ask about difficulties. Difficulties get our attention and in so doing increase the likelihood that questions about safety ("have you had any thoughts of harming yourself?"), symptoms ("have you been hearing any voices?"), and compliance ("have you been taking your meds?") dominate the conversation. It is not that such questions are bad; however, a focus only on such questions could lead the client to experience a narrowing of self as only a "distressed" or "troubled" individual (Wilson & DuFrene, 2008). One of the potential impacts of mindfulness work is to expand the range of questions we ask our clients. Noticing different physical sensations and thoughts, and letting each go requires PT across multiple contents. This may be particularly important with our most distressed clients. Moving deliberately and flexibly between pleasant and challenging experiences should broaden the repertoire and foster a richer experience of self.

In its most generic implications, this suggests that mindfulness, which contains the cultivation of self and PT processes, ought to be beneficial in virtually any chronic or institutionalized population capable of participating in a mindfulness practice. Mindfulness practice should assist in cultivating self-repertoires among individuals whose repertoires are markedly underdeveloped, such as those with intellectual disabilities. Under such circumstances, we might expect massed training in PT to be a central precursor to mindfulness practice, since training in PT is done with physical objects where appropriate responses can be shaped

(McHugh, Barnes-Holmes, & Barnes-Holmes, 2009). Mindfulness should likewise be beneficial to individuals who have reasonable self-repertoires, but whose debilitating psychological or other health problems or institutionalization have narrowed the repertoire.

Mindfulness exercises have the potential to generate a great deal of PT that is not focused solely on difficulties. Taking perspective on breath, noticing psychological content, and returning to the present moment should, theoretically speaking, have salutary effects on fusion with self-as-content. While acceptance, defusion, and present-moment processes may have independent salutary effects, within this process, we expect to see specific enhancement since "I" am accepting, "I" am letting go of tightly held rules about me, and "I" am making contact with my breath in this moment. "I-ing" across diverse contents creates precisely the conditions that should allow the individual to abstract a sense of self that is not identical with the contents of consciousness, since the only constant is the unique perspective. What arises is a transcendent sense of self with wholly naturalistic causes (see Hayes, 1984, and chapter 11 of this volume for more in-depth coverage of self, transcendence, and spirituality).

In the subsequent sections, we will address the potential benefits of the other three mindfulness processes (i.e., contact with the present moment, acceptance, and defusion) and then reflect back on the implication of those processes for our central topic: self.

# Contact with the Present Moment, Mindfulness, and Applied Challenges

Contact with the present moment is the most recognizable psychological flexibility process involved in mindfulness. This process focuses on our ability to bring attention to bear in a deliberate, focused, yet flexible fashion. However, the aspect that is of primary interest within this model is present-moment attending as skillful behavioral pattern. Use of mindfulness to engender greater contact with the present moment may be particularly useful with individuals showing deficits of present-moment processes.

## WORRY AND RUMINATION

Worry and rumination can be thought of as examples of highly inflexible I-Then PT. Intensive engagement in the remembered past or imagined future leaves individuals less responsive to contingencies present in the current environment (Friman, Hayes, & Wilson, 1998). Although the precise mechanisms of change have yet to be demonstrated empirically, individuals presenting with worry and rumination ought to be responsive to practice at moment-by-moment attending, which is a central component of mindfulness (cf. Hazlett-Stevens & Borkovec, 2001).

As described in the previous section on self, there is a danger that individuals become excessively identified with their own worries. Mindfulness interventions ought to work on two fronts. First, they should build PT by directing attention in a moment-by-moment way. Second, they should disrupt the highly rigid and repetitive patterns of PT inherent in worry and rumination.

## POOR ATTENTION

Other potential problems with present-moment processes might be found among clients presenting with difficulties such as attention deficit/hyperactivity disorder (ADHD). The deliberate slow pacing of mindfulness interventions should build attentional skills and also pacing skills. Child behavior problems may also involve attentional problems that could benefit from skillful allocation of attention found in mindfulness interventions. In addition, difficulties with attention are part of the diagnostic criteria for some anxiety and mood disorders, potentially compounding the usefulness of present-moment skill building.

## IMPACT OF PRESENT MOMENT ON SELF

The indirect impact of present-moment processes on self should result from the disruption of patterns of fusion and avoidance as seen, for example, in worry and rumination. Present-moment processes ought to also impact self processes directly. Practice at noticing and deliberately bringing attention to bear inherently involves PT. Such PT lays the foundation for noticing the "I" that notices. Metaphorically, psychological contents are the furniture in the house. The "I" that notices is the house itself (Zettle & Hayes, 2002). The most likely circumstances in which one is likely to notice that there is an observing "I" that is distinct from the content of consciousness are circumstances where the content changes repeatedly, but where the "I" noticing remains. Mindfulness becomes part of the pattern of multiple exemplar training that is seen as shaping PT repertoires and for the emergence of a sense of self.

# Acceptance, Mindfulness, and Applied Challenges

A third core process in the psychological flexibility model analysis of mindfulness is acceptance and its counterpart *experiential avoidance*. Experiential avoidance has a long history of attention in clinical problems and many diagnostic categories can be understood as disorders of avoidance (Hayes, Wilson, Gifford, Follette, & Strosahl, 1996). Some difficulties are easily understood in this way. For example, panic disorder has been characterized as the fear of fear. When anxiety is something to get anxious about there is a potential compounding effect of anxiety plus anxiety about anxiety. Similarly, if depression is something to get depressed about, depression will be compounded. A recent meta-analysis by Ruiz (2010) has found that experiential avoidance is associated with greater general psychological distress as well as greater depression and anxiety.

## PRACTICE AT ACCEPTANCE

Within formal mindfulness practices, equanimity with respect to mental content is explicitly instructed (Kabat-Zinn, 1982). For example, in a breathing meditation, it is common to be distracted from the practice by physical sensations, such as discomfort in the legs or back, or by distracting thoughts. Mindfulness practices are fairly uniform in suggesting that one ought not suppress or fight against these thoughts and feelings, but instead notice and acknowledge them and then gently return to the practice (Baer, 2003). Formal meditation practices offer many, many opportunities to practice acceptance.

The human ability to reason, judge, evaluate and plan is an extraordinary adaptation. However, it can also be an extraordinary burden. One need not venture into the realm of clinical diagnoses to find people who become so preoccupied with problem solving that they lose contact with the reinforcers that are directly available in their lives. This is a quite natural state of affairs. When our mental capacities were evolving on the savanna, problems were often lethal (e.g., lions, starvation). Our evolutionary trajectory favored attention to problems and systematic avoidance of those problems (Wilson & DuFrene, 2008). All of these mindfulness practices, while not discounting the reality or importance of the problems of day-to-day living, are an invitation to practice small intentional breaks from that problem-solving repertoire.

## IMPACT OF ACCEPTANCE ON SELF

In terms of direct and indirect impacts of the acceptance component of mindfulness on problems of self, we should expect that the major benefits would accrue where problem solving and avoidance themselves become a sort of identity. Letting go of avoidant problem-solving repertoires and taking an open posture with respect to difficult psychological content should alter the individual's relationship with the difficult content. If clients can begin to notice differences in their relationship with content, there is inherently a distinction being made between "I" and content. Moving from persistent struggle to noticing that "I am a person who has struggled and in this moment I am a person who is letting go of struggle" involves a dislocation of self processes from struggle and the opportunity for more flexible PT.

# Defusion, Mindfulness, and Applied Challenges

The fourth process relevant to mindfulness is defusion. Fusion refers to the ability of verbal rules to overwhelm the effects of directly experienced contingencies (see Shimoff, Catania, & Matthews, 1981). Fusion, in commonsense terms, is the capacity of verbally competent humans to be trapped by a "storied up" version of the world. Mindfulness sets a context in which verbal rules are to be noticed and acknowledged, but not acted upon. Being able to defuse from the control exerted by these self- and other-generated rules is a skill that can be learned. This process has deeper and more technical meaning than is captured by this thumbnail description. For more detailed treatment, Torneke (2010) provides a clinically connected analysis and both Blackledge (2007) and Hayes and colleagues (2001) provide a denser and more technical analysis including analyses outside the clinical realm.

## PRACTICE AT DEFUSING FROM DIFFICULT PSYCHOLOGICAL CONTENT

If we were to personify difficult psychological content we might say that it has a "demanding" quality. Pain, embarrassment, anxiety, and depression clamor for solutions and they also clamor for attention. Formal mindfulness offers many opportunities to notice these demanding, difficult psychological experiences and to let go of attempts to suppress (i.e., acceptance) as well as to interact with the difficult material in a variety of different ways. For example, some meditations ask that the client treat difficult material with compassion (Gilbert, 2009) while others ask clients to simply notice thoughts as they pass, treating them as if they were leaves on a stream (Hayes, Strosahl, et al., 1999). By encouraging a greater breath of flexibility within interactions with cognitive content, these mindfulness interventions lessen the stimulus control exerted by this content and place a greater emphasis on the functional properties of cognitions (i.e., defusion).

## IMPACT OF DEFUSION ON SELF

Defusion has strong implications for self processes. One of the key difficulties in the domain of self, for some presenting problems, is fusion with problematic rules about self (see chapter 8, present volume). Whether the self-relevant rules are about the client's future, past, personal integrity, vulnerability, or capacities, those rules can narrow one's repertoire. Mindfulness exercises that focus explicitly on holding these rules lightly and on broadening one's repertoire in their presence should both decrease the behavior regulatory functions of those rules and provide direct experience with a sense of self independent of them.

---

# Self, Mindfulness, and Emerging Applied Science

According to our analysis, many applied difficulties, including *DSM*-defined clinical syndromes, arise from or are exacerbated by underdeveloped and/or rigid PT repertoires. Inflexible self repertoires often combine with temporal and causal frames to create verbal traps that limit personal development and quality of life. In popular culture and in much of applied psychology, the most commonly applied solution has been to manage the ways individuals regard themselves. Negative cognitive content has been viewed as the chief culprit. The 1960s gave rise to a large body of work suggesting that positive thoughts about self, including self-efficacy and self-esteem, are necessary and sufficient precursors to effective action and emotional well-being (Bandura, 1982; Coopersmith, 1967). In clinical psychology, the 1970s and '80s and '90s witnessed the ascendancy of the complementary view that negative patterns of thinking about self played a causal role in emotional disorders (e.g., A. T. Beck, 1976; Dozois & Beck, 2011). Beck's cognitive triad extends topographically beyond thoughts about self to thoughts about the future and the world. However, when self is thought of as emergent from PT, it becomes apparent that a negative perspective on the world and future are likewise part of the core PT repertoire.

With over 30,000 peer-reviewed articles on self-esteem and self-concept published in the past fifty years, and over 17,000 books listed by a popular online bookseller, this content-oriented view of self has fully permeated scientific study as well as popular culture. Despite this popularity, a recent meta-review of self-esteem interventions has concluded that boosting self-esteem does not lead to beneficial outcomes and may in fact lead to undesirable outcomes such as increased narcissism (Baumeister, Campbell, Krueger, & Vohs, 2003). A more recent cross-temporal meta-analysis of self-esteem and academic performance found that while self-esteem has increased considerably among adolescents and young adults in the past twenty years, there was no evidence of increased academic performance or reductions in substance use or mental health problems (Gentile, Twenge, & Campbell, 2010). Our culture-wide attempt to change the contents of thoughts about self appears to be effective, but there is little evidence that these changes produced socially beneficial outcomes.

This finding parallels recent research in cognitive therapy. Jarrett and colleagues measured depressive symptoms and change in negative cognitive content over multiple time points among patients treated with cognitive therapy (Jarrett, Vittengl, Doyle, & Clark, 2007). They found that among some patients, cognitive content did not change even though depression remitted. Also, change in depression tended to precede change in cognitive content when such change did occur. These findings led the authors to conclude that "changes in cognitive content during and following cognitive therapy for recurrent depression [are] substantial and enduring, but not predictive of change in depressive symptoms" (Jarrett et al., 2007, p. 432).

The above analysis does not call into question the efficacy of cognitive therapy, including traditional cognitive behavior therapy, which leans heavily on Beckian cognitive intervention strategies. Cognitive therapy enjoys solid empirical support for its efficacy both in acute treatment and over extended follow-up (Vittengl, Clark, Dunn, & Jarrett, 2007; Hollon et al., 2005). However, teaching clients that they can and should change negative cognition, and that such change is a necessary precursor to clinical improvement appears to be inert at best. Jacobson and colleagues'

(1996) dismantling study of cognitive therapy showed no advantage for the conditions containing cognitive interventions over the condition containing only behavioral activation. These findings held for acute treatment (Jacobson et al., 1996), as well as at two-year follow-up (Gortner, Gollan, Dobson, & Jacobson, 1998), and the general finding was replicated in a subsequent study (Dimidjian et al., 2006).

Further, Dimidjian and colleagues (2006) found that although mild to moderately depressed individuals fared equally well in treatment regardless of whether they received cognitive-change-oriented interventions, severely depressed participants actually did significantly worse in the condition containing these interventions. These data are of particular interest in light of the positive benefits of mindfulness-based interventions with chronically depressed individuals (Teasdale et al., 2000) as well as with individuals with remitted depression, but whose remission is unstable (Segal et al., 2010).

Taken together, the findings described above suggest that change in negative cognitive content is not a necessary precursor to well-being and further that attempts to intervene directly may actually be harmful to some individuals. Evidence suggests that difficult emotional and cognitive content may be quite persistent for many individuals. The emergence of mindfulness approaches offers an alternative approach to clinical problems that so frequently overlap with problems of self. A mindfulness approach takes a different tack from attempts to change negative content. Mindfulness-based interventions instead focus efforts at helping clients to distinguish themselves from negative cognition and emotion. There is some evidence supportive of the potential importance of mindfulness when difficult content is persistent, including DBT for borderline personality disorder (Linehan et al., 2006), ACT for severe substance dependence (Hayes et al., 2004), and MBCT for chronic depression (Teasdale et al., 2000), among others. Although the putative mechanisms of mindfulness interventions have not yet been well established, early results are promising both in terms of outcomes and also because there is an abundance of research looking explicitly at the change processes involved in these treatments. It appears likely that the current crop of mindfulness-based interventions will grow their outcome and process evidence bases simultaneously. Because of the close interconnection between mindfulness processes and self, this emerging evidence has the potential to inform our understanding of both mindfulness and self.

## Conclusion

In order to ensure that mindfulness both produces good outcomes and works by theoretically specified mechanisms, we need solid theoretical guidance and testable hypotheses. In this chapter, we have examined mindfulness and self from a psychological flexibility theoretical perspective. We have presented a large number of theoretically coherent process accounts regarding components of mindfulness and the potential impact they might have on self-relevant repertoires in different populations. These hypotheses go beyond assertions about the general improvements we might expect from mindfulness and extend to the specific processes that could be enhanced in mindfulness protocols to the benefit of specific populations. The advantage of such a theoretical account lies in its testability and in its ability to integrate findings across problem domains and across different mindfulness approaches. Ultimately the robustness of the analysis will be found in its capacity to produce a body of empirical work that is both supportive and expansive.

# Chapter 11

# A Naturalistic Approach to Transcendence: Deictic Framing, Spirituality, and Prosociality

Jennifer Villatte, Matthieu Villatte & Steven C. Hayes
*University of Nevada, Reno*

## Introduction

The purpose of this chapter is to link contemporary contextual behavioral work on the self to the issue of spirituality and its role in prosociality. This is a difficult task for many reasons, including the tendency for behavioral scientists to avoid issues of religion and spirituality, and the obvious difficulties in taking a purely monistic approach to spiritual and religious issues. Nevertheless, it seems worthwhile, both because spirituality is an important human experience, and because it has a known relationship to a wide variety of important psychological and social outcomes.

In what follows we will touch on some of the data on the psychology of religion, and attempt to link these data to the key role of deictic relational framing in a sense of transcendence. We aim to provide a monistic, naturalistic approach to understanding an important human phenomenon with significant impact on psychological well-being for individuals and societies. Finally we will try to show that when linked with evolution science, a contextual behavioral interpretation of transcendence leads to testable ideas about how to foster prosociality itself.

# The Psychology of Religion and Spirituality

Psychological accounts of religion and spirituality can be traced to the very origin of psychology itself. William James's classic text *The Varieties of Religious Experience* (1902) is a good example. Proponents of the Clark School argued that religion is a purely psychological phenomenon and can only be properly examined by the scientific method (cf. Leuba, 1912; Hall, 1917). From the beginning, psychologists have understood that spiritual and religious experiences are of fundamental importance to understanding human psychology and enhancing human flourishing. The psychology of religion and spirituality also provides an important challenge for any psychological perspective that claims to be relatively comprehensive.

## The Importance of Spirituality

Spirituality in particular appears to be of nearly universal importance to human beings. If not linked to theology per se, the vast majority of people will agree that spirituality is an important matter, even in very secular societies (Houtman & Aupers, 2007). Humans seem to have an inherent sense of the importance of experiences of transcendence, oneness, and connection. With verbal consciousness comes the awareness of the potential to transcend the distinctions that separate one from the rest of the world, and that awareness often leads us to seek meaning and value in our actions, and to strive to infuse our lives with purpose and intention.

A steadily growing global movement has begun to seek a path to spirituality outside of religious and theistic contexts. Books like *The Little Book of Atheist Spirituality* (Comte-Sponville, 2007) top best-seller lists and popular magazines like *O* have monthly columns on "Spirit." Strident atheist scholars, like Daniel Dennett, write of being "transported with awe and joy and a sense of peace and wonder" during "moments of spirituality" (2010). Despite declining rates of religious affiliation and service attendance, personal interest in religiosity and spirituality remain high (Berger, 1999). In the 1990s, the proportion of US adults feeling a need to "experience spiritual growth" rose from 54 percent to 82 percent (Myers, 2000). It seems that religion is not being eliminated, but being transformed, resulting in more personal practices that focus on a sense of holism, spirituality and transcendence (Roof, 1993).

## Empirical Investigation of Spirituality

There is a voluminous literature on the psychology of religion and spirituality (e.g., Hood, Hill, & Spilka, 2009) troubled at times by conceptual ambiguity and methodological limitations. It appears that spirituality is not merely an aspect of religiosity, but a distinct phenomenon that can be defined and measured independently of religion or theology. Scientists have examined how religion and spirituality develop, affect behavior, and relate to suffering and well-being and these topics are important in popular science books of the day (e.g., Dawkins, 2006; D. S. Wilson, 2003). Though many persons consider themselves both religious and spiritual, the two follow different courses and are differentially related to psychosocial factors. Religiosity remains stable throughout the lifespan, while spirituality tends to increase with age, especially after age 60 (Dillon & Wink, 2007). Spirituality is negatively correlated with self-righteousness and competitiveness, while religiosity is positively correlated with authoritarianism, self-righteousness, self-sacrifice for others, and interdependence with others (Zinnbauer et al., 1997). Spirituality has a significant influence on thriving beyond the moderating role of religion (Dowling et al., 2004).

## Positive Effects of Spirituality

Spirituality is known to be correlated with well-being, even in childhood. A study of 320 children ages 8–12 found that children's spirituality, but not their religious practices (e.g., attending church services, praying), was strongly linked to their happiness (Holder, Coleman, & Wallace, 2010). While temperament also predicted happiness, spirituality remained a significant predictor even after accounting for temperament. Adolescence is a key time for identity development and a strong spiritual identity is associated with lower levels of psychological distress and higher levels of personal meaning, prosocial behaviors, and community service (Furrow, King, & White, 2004). Results from the *Monitoring the Future study* (Wallace, Forman, Caldwell, & Willis, 2003) suggest that 61 percent of US adolescents rate their faith as "very important" or "pretty important." This figure has held steady from 1976 to 1996, while rates of religious affiliation and religious service attendance have declined during the same time period (C. Smith, Denton, Fans, & Regnerus, 2002), suggesting that a personalized spirituality may be replacing the importance of organized religious practices. Adolescents who rate spirituality or religion as highly personally salient, regardless of religious affiliation, are less likely to engage in risk-taking behaviors and more likely to participate in extracurricular activities, volunteer service, and civic engagement that serves their schools and communities (Kerestes, Youniss, & Metz, 2004; Regnerus, Smith, & Fritsch, 2003).

Spirituality has important effects on coping with serious illness and injury. In a study of 75 people with spinal cord injury, "existential spirituality," defined as a worldview in which individuals search for purpose and meaning in their lives, was positively associated with life satisfaction, general health, and social quality of life, whereas "religious spirituality," defined as a relationship with a higher power, did not predict any outcomes (Matheis, Tulsky, & Matheis, 2006). A study of 136 participants in rehabilitation following serious injury or illness found that spirituality was a significant predictor of overall life satisfaction (Tate & Forchheimer, 2002).

Spirituality appears to buffer people against the harmful effects of stressful life events, such as recovery from breast cancer (Ashing, Padilla, Tejero, & Kagawa-Singer, 2003), coping with the death of a child (Brotherson & Soderquist, 2002), recovering from substance abuse (Brome, Owens, Allen, & Vevaina, 2000), and leaving abusive relationships (Oman, Hedberg, Downs, & Parsons, 2003; Potter, 2007). A study of low-income, rural women in the United States found that spirituality accounted for 39 percent of the variance in total wellness as measured by the Five-Factor Wellness scale (Gill, Barrio Minton, & Myers, 2010). Though total scores of religiosity and spirituality were both positively correlated with wellness, the spirituality subscales (particularly purpose and meaning in life, unifying interconnectedness, and private practices) were the major contributors in this respect.

Spirituality has been linked to indices of prosocial behavior, such as forgiveness, defined as "a suite of prosocial changes in one's motivations toward an interpersonal transgressor such that one becomes less avoidant of and less vengeful toward the transgressor" (McCullough, Bono, & Root, 2007, p. 491). There is empirical evidence that a disposition toward forgiving others is positively related to measures of physical and mental health (A. H. S. Harris & Thoresen, 2005). Leach and Lark (2004) found spiritual well-being and spiritual transcendence were positively correlated with trait forgiveness of others, and this effect held after controlling for Big Five personality traits. Evidence also suggests that spirituality may mediate the relationship between forgiveness and recovery from interpersonal trauma (Schultz, Tallman, & Altmaier, 2010) and substance use disorders (Lyons, Deane, & Kelly, 2010).

# A Science of Spiritual Experience

At a superficial level dualism seems inherent in concepts like "spirit" and therefore monistic scientists have sometimes avoided the study of religious and spiritual practice, particularly in the area of spiritual experience itself. Natural science helps explain why religion exists as a social institution. For example, evolution scientists have provided extensive evidence that spiritual and religious practices often alter the conditions that are known to foster cooperation and prosociality within a group, thus providing competitive between-group advantages (D. S. Wilson, 2003). This is important work but it leaves untouched the issue of how natural science can deal with spiritual experiences themselves. Some natural scientists have argued that human beings cannot be fully understood by looking at human behavior solely from a non-transcendent point of view (Goldsmith, 1994). Contextual behavior science, which rests on the radically pragmatic philosophical assumptions of functional contextualism, offers an alternative approach that both acknowledges the important role of spiritual experience in human well-being and provides a naturalistic account of the phenomenon (Hayes, 1984).

Spirituality can be looked at as a supernatural phenomenon, of course—as a connection with a spirit world or nonmaterial creator god—but naturally science would have nothing to say about such matters other than to analyze the conditions under which such claims are made. Of more interest is to examine spirituality as a natural psychological phenomenon, because this is an approach that can readily be integrated into important areas of scientific research.

Contrary to its original English meaning, the word "spiritual" no longer refers only to the dualistic notion of the nonmaterial, but is now commonly used to describe that which relates to "our search for the transcendent" (Nelson, 2009, p. 8). This aspect in particular can be examined as a naturalistic phenomenon. In the current chapter, we do not address specific spiritual traditions, beliefs, or practices. Instead, we attempt to provide an analysis of the psychological processes that lead to a phenomenal sense of transcendence and refer to certain core definitional aspects that tie the concept to the natural world, including the experience of transcending one's physical and conceptualized selves, a sense of purpose and intention, and a harmonious connection with other conscious beings and with the natural world. This type of analysis of spirituality has important implications for understanding key human experiences and points to psychological processes that can be used in behavioral interventions to reduce human suffering and enhance individual and collective well-being. Further, spirituality seems to be a uniquely human experience, suggesting that it is underpinned by processes that are also uniquely human. Language and cognition are the main candidates, which mean that a scientific account of spirituality must begin with an analysis of verbal behavior.

## The Transcendent Self

Although modern science can link verbal and cognitive activities to a brain that we can observe and touch, humans commonly have the feeling that there is something that exists beyond the body. This may be why any material approaches to psychology are sometimes suspected of reductionism. Conversely, events that are literally outside of the material world are not anything science can address. It seems important not to be left with an incomplete scientific account for what is perhaps one of the most emblematic experiences of being a human, that is the feeling of "being more than a body."

As with our field's founder, William James, our analysis of spirituality begins with consideration of the self. It is our argument that the issues of "self" addressed in this volume provide a strong foundation for understanding the experience of transcendence. Given the extensive descriptions provided earlier here, we will assume a fair amount of technical knowledge about deictic relational framing in describing our analysis.

Verbal organisms do not interact with the world in the same way as nonverbal organisms. Skinner famously noted that "self-knowledge is of social origin" (1974, p. 30) and suggested that the social-verbal community made it possible for humans not just to see, but to see that they see. Indeed, the verbal community establishes contingencies that lead to a kind of self-awareness in which responses are made to one's own responses. This occurs when we are asked questions like "What happened to you yesterday? What did you see? What did you eat?" and so on. "There are no natural contingencies for such behavior. We learn to see that we are seeing only because a verbal community arranges for us to do so" (1988, p. 286). In Skinner's approach this skill is critical because "self knowledge has a special value to the individual himself. A person who has been 'made aware of himself' is in a better position to predict and control his own behavior" (1974, p. 31).

An article written nearly 30 years ago entitled "Making Sense of Spirituality" (Hayes, 1984) attempted to add something to this behavioral approach to self-knowledge: verbal organisms do not just see, or see that they see, they also do so from a consistent locus or point of view. That article was one of the first to describe the core ideas behind both acceptance and commitment therapy (ACT; Hayes, Strosahl, & Wilson, 2011) and relational frame theory (RFT; Hayes, Barnes-Holmes, & Roche, 2001), and explicitly linked what we now term "deictic relational responding" to a transcendent sense of self.

Children are indeed trained to make self-discriminations by answering questions such as, "Where are you? What are you doing over there? What am I doing now?" but one of the invariants that is abstracted from these discriminations is the perspective from which reports are made. Self-awareness is not just responding to responding but also doing so from a particular locus. There is a growing body of evidence that this sense of locus is established by deictic relational frames, in particular those of I versus YOU; HERE versus THERE; and NOW versus THEN (see e.g., chapter 3 in this volume). In laboratory and educational settings it has been shown that these relations emerge through a process of multiple exemplar training (e.g., Weil, Hayes, & Capurro, 2011) but in natural language situations the training is probably much looser. For example, a child answering the question "What did you eat?" has to distinguish that question from "What did your brother eat?" The question "What am I doing now?" needs to be distinguished from "What was I doing yesterday?" As the repertoire of deictic relational framing strengthens through exposure to such questions, an ability to observe and describe events from the point of view of I-HERE-NOW emerges.

Once such a perspective forms, it is possible to integrate content into a strand or storyline of "things I did" or "things I saw" in which the word "I" refers to a particular perspective. In an important sense "I" *becomes* that perspective.

Perspective Taking (PT) is an unusual action because it is embedded in the observation of things. Scientifically it is quite possible to talk of PT as an event, but experientially it cannot be fully seen itself, at least not for the person engaging in this behavior. To see one's perspective, perspective must change. Metaphorically it is like the sense one has of looking from behind one's eyes—to look *at* that sense it is necessary to move aside and to look back, but then perspective has moved to the side, because the place from which one looks is embedded in the very act of looking.

A key argument presented originally in Hayes (1984) and expanded in later writings (e.g., D. Barnes-Holmes, Hayes, & Gregg, 2001) is that PT of this kind leads to the experience of transcendence and provides a naturalistic psychological ground for the distinction between a material and a spiritual self. The argument is a fairly simple one: Continuity of consciousness emerges in part from an I/HERE/NOW perspective, but this perspective itself can never fully be the target of observing behavior. We are sometimes aware of this perspective and thus we have no doubt about its existence. But as we try to describe this perspective, the experience and the description part company: when we are aware of the description of PT we are aware of it from a deictic perspective of I/HERE/NOW and the original act of PT is now THERE and THEN.

If this analysis is correct, PT is embedded in the action of being aware of what is happening in our life and integrating these experiences into a continuous strand; and yet we cannot contact the limits of that action, or at least we cannot do so with verbal awareness. This combination provides a sense of "edgelessness" to PT. Everywhere we go, there we are; everything we know, we were there to know it. In other words, the verbal nature of observing from an I/HERE/NOW perspective in humans is the origin of a sense of transcendence. The apparent immutability of PT together with the changing content of experiences (thoughts, emotions, and bodily sensations) engender a feeling of distinction between the mind and the body, experienced as a spirit/matter duality. Although the premises of these beliefs are literally in contradiction with natural science, the variables that give rise to them are not.

We are not arguing that PT is literally immutable. Our argument is that its embedded nature establishes a sense of continuity that is seemingly immutable. While we experience thousands of thoughts and emotions across our life span, and while both our physical appearance and the external world are constantly transformed by time, our perspective seemingly remains the same. The way we think may change, our senses may decline or disappear, but even these changes are observed from a constant I-HERE-NOW point of view. The latter has no edges that can be consciously known and thus no "features" that can change. At the same time we know that we will die. Experiencing a sense of permanence while knowing the impermanence of the self is often lived as a disturbing contradiction. In this regard, it is interesting to note that most religions refer to an afterlife and that even many nonreligious people leave open the possibility that some part of us, which is usually not an element of our body, will remain in this world or another. Even when death is recognized as the genuine end of the self, it is still extremely difficult to have a representation of the absence of self, because such absence is observed precisely from the perspective of the self, even if it is in imagination. Such feeling of persistence of the self beyond death increases when people attribute a meaning to their actions that transcends their mere existence, which is linked to the sharing of values with a community of individuals.

The apparent continuity of PT thus leads to a transcendent sense of the self that goes beyond time and matter limits. We will call this *intra-transcendence* as it refers to the connection of an individual with his or her own self across time and space. We have argued that such experience is crucial for the development of psychological flexibility (Hayes et al., 2011) because it fosters detachment from psychological experiences and conceptual definitions of the self, through a posture of the self as a context of these experiences. From this point of view, difficult emotions can be accepted and repertoires of actions extended, since the self is then more than transient states of mind and not limited to rigid descriptions.

From the point of view of relational frame theory (Hayes et al. 2001) the same deictic frames that give rise to I/HERE/NOW can give rise to the perspective of YOU/THERE/THEN and all possible combinations. This is because frames are mutual. Just as there can be no UP without DOWN, or IN without OUT, there can be no HERE without THERE, NOW without THEN, or I without YOU. Thus, taking an I/HERE/NOW perspective is based on the same verbal skills that allow a person to imagine themselves being aware as a child, or as an old person near death; or to imagine being in different places; or to imagine looking out of the eyes of another.

Because a sense of perspective emerges from bidirectional relational frames, awareness of an I/HERE/NOW perspective also leads to another kind of transcendence that we call *inter-transcendence* to refer to a sense of interconnection with the perspective of other people, times, and places. This extension of PT is central to another aspect of spirituality—a sense of compassionate connection with others.

When asked about a sense of spirituality, people usually mention a particular way of relating to others that doesn't lean merely on physical exchange (W. R. Miller & Thoresen, 2003). For example, they might describe a moment during which they shared an experience with someone who understood that experience the same way; that is, with similar emotions, feelings, or thoughts. Such sharing might happen among people celebrating a religious event, or between two friends communing over their contemplation of a sunset. Such connection requires a sophisticated repertoire of interpersonal PT because it requires that one be aware not only of one's own psychological experience, but also of that of the other.

Studies conducted in the contextual behavioral science tradition have explored the implications of this deictic framing view of PT. Researchers have found that the ability to adopt the perspective of another codevelops with the capacity to identify what others think or feel (e.g., McHugh et al., 2006). Accuracy in attributing an intention to another is predicted by the ability to change perspective (see chapter 6, this volume). Training children in PT enhances their capacity to identify others' mental states (Weil et al., 2011). In addition, individuals demonstrating impairments in PT linked to mental disorders also tend to experience difficulties in mental-state attribution (chapter 6). There have been debates about the processes operating at the core of mental-states attribution, whether what is critical is the ability to gather and interpret social cues using rules or the ability to change PT (see Carruthers & Smith, 1996). It seems likely that both processes are involved. For example, it is conceivable that one might reach others' emotional states by following rules, such as "If I see a person crying, they must be sad," or through PT by contacting the emotion that one would feel if one was crying oneself. However, we believe that these two paths lead to different experiences and, in particular, that the former leads to *conceptualized* connection while the latter leads to *contextual* connection in which the context is the shared sense of PT. In other words, following rules leads to understanding others through the knowledge of their conceptualized self, while changing perspective (though also requiring verbal relational responding) constitutes a step toward feeling interconnected with others. The deictic basis of PT leads to the sense of knowing what others feel and think without necessarily having (or being able) to describe how that happens, which might be responsible for a feeling of transcendental connection.

Consistent with this view, some empirical findings indicate that having a well-developed deictic repertoire is necessary to demonstrate interest in social contact and to engage in interpersonal interactions. For example, Villatte et al. (2008, 2010b) showed that people who score high on measures of social anhedonia are impaired in higher levels of deictic framing, notably when it requires adopting the point of view of another. However, Vilardaga, Estévez, Levin, and Hayes (2011) showed that higher levels of social anhedonia were predicted not only by lower deictic framing skills, but also by low empathic concerns and high experiential avoidance, indicating that PT alone might be insufficient to achieve interpersonal connection. If one tends to avoid difficult emotions, and if PT puts one in contact with pain from the perspective of others, then PT might be undermined. For example a person might turn away from a person who is suffering in order to avoid feeling discomfort themselves. Alternatively, one might conceptually recognize the suffering of people living in extremely poor conditions through verbal descriptions but meanwhile refuse to experience the emotional results of PT processes. Such examples suggest the need for supplemental processes in order for PT to help go beyond the psychological events constituting the conceptualized self. *Inter-transcendence* requires the same processes of psychological flexibility as the self-as-context posture requires for oneself; that is, detachment from our conceptualization of the other through PT and acceptance of the others' thoughts and emotions, driven by the value of connecting with others. Being in the same place or time isn't required to feel such connection with other persons. Indeed, some people report connecting to a friend living thousands of miles away or even to a long-deceased parent as they are experiencing thoughts or feelings related to some common value. As we will see in the following section, building and sharing values seem to contribute greatly to a sense of spirituality. Verbal processes applied to the self are of central importance in this respect.

# Transcendence and the Evolution of Prosociality

Evolution scientists, including those coming from a behavioral tradition, have defined several features that seem critical to the development of cooperative and prosocial behavior (D. S. Wilson, 2007). These dimensions are worth reviewing because they provide clear guidance from a natural science perspective for the possible role of transcendence and PT in pro-sociality. Individual adaptations such as stronger muscles or bigger teeth promote the success of the individual, whether or not others benefit. Altruistic behavior, conversely, is often disadvantageous to the individual. A prairie dog that emits a cry on seeing a predator protects others but is more salient to the predator as a result of the cry and thus more likely to be the victim of predation. How would such behavior evolve? There is a growing consensus in evolution science that altruistic behavior of this kind is primarily due to multilevel selection (between and within group) (e.g., D. S. Wilson & Wilson, 2007). Behavior of this kind provides competitive advantages to the group in their competition with other groups. If a niche establishes between-group selection linked to important and retained consequences, a base condition for the evolution of cooperation exists.

The relation of between-group rather than within-group selection to prosociality is not merely a mathematical extension of evolution theory: Experimental science has shown it to be sound (see Wade, Bijma, Ellen, & Muir, 2010 for a review on research with domesticated animals). For example, suppose commonly caged chickens are allowed to breed on the basis of individual success in egg laying. Alternately, an entire cage of several birds is allowed to breed if they are successful as compared to other entire cages in egg production. After just six generations the "between group" criterion will lead both to far more eggs and to more living chickens (Muir, 1996) because those selected on the basis of individual success fight constantly (even to the point of cannibalization) while those selected on the basis of group success cooperate. In other words, if "we" is not the unit of selection, individuals will seek to claim the resources of the group for their selfish ends. The second key feature is that selfish adaptations need to be confronted. If individual "bad actors" can easily get away with selfish adaptations, cooperative behavior is disadvantaged (Ostrom, 2009).

These findings are relevant to deictic relations and PT in two major ways. First, it is worth noting that relational framing abilities themselves probably evolved in the context of a cooperative species. Converging lines of evidence indicate that our ancestors experienced a shift in the balance between within-group and between-group levels of selection that suppressed fitness differences within groups and caused groups to become more potent units of selection (D. S. Wilson, 2007). If this occurred, human evolution can be thought of as an example of a "major transition" similar to what happened in the evolution of eukaryotic cells, multicellular organisms, and eusocial insect colonies. In all of these cases, groups became functionally organized enough that they qualified as higher-level organisms in their own right. To some degree human groups appear to qualify at least crudely as so-called "super-organisms" (Reeve & Hölldobler, 2007).

In the context of a cooperative species, the bidirectionality characteristic of relational framing can be trained in the context of mutual speaker and listener roles. This seems possible, as some have claimed (Tomasello, 2008) that "cooperation came first." Consider the simple frames of coordination found in naming. In a common stimulus equivalence paradigm, there might be training of object → oral name, and testing of the derived relation of oral name → object. This simple act of symmetry requires the integration of speaker and listener roles. In natural language situations speakers and listeners are both involved in a social system in which symbolic relations are understood to be equivalent regardless of role—precisely what has not been shown in nonhuman communication systems (Clark, 1996, 1997).

Although likely established in the context of cooperation, deictic relational framing enormously increases the potential for prosocial behavior and further cooperation. The logical link between PT and cooperation led Tomasello to claim that PT was itself a foundation of human language (2003), but further research showing that nonhuman species show some degree of PT skills (based on what RFT theorists would consider to be nonverbal processes) led him to revert to the "cooperation first" hypothesis (Tomasello, 2008).

Deictic framing is relevant to multilevel selection fostering a collective "we" sense of humanity and indeed of the self. Furthermore, a transcendent sense of self fosters the development of other processes that restrain bad actors that undermine group formation and multilevel selection intrapsychically and interpersonally. Finally, these cognitive skills foster prosocial selection criteria that are part of the evolution of cooperative behavior. Thus, deictic framing fosters the very evolutionary processes that are known to be key to cooperation: group selection; suppression of within-group adaptation; and selective retention of successful outcomes at the level of the group.

## Transcendence and the Internal and External "We"

Human language and cognition from an RFT point of view can lead to behavioral divisions: ways of being and behaving that function as relatively integrated behavioral repertoires. For space reasons, this argument can be presented only in outline form (but see Hayes et al., 2011).

Behavioral psychology has long held that there are discrete response patterns that function in a relatively independent fashion—almost as separate "selves" (Skinner, 1974). For example, a person can adopt a persona as a highly rational person who can solve all problems; or a person who will never be hurt; or a person who is better than everyone else; or one with a loving heart. These response patterns compete within—almost as if each is threatened by the other. A thought such as "I am a good person" will tend to pull its polar opposite "No you are not, because..." Relational frames tend to organize these responses and response repertoires in such a way that they seemingly must compete with each other because rules of combinatorial entailment in relational framing lead toward consistent ("logical") networks. For example, "I am a good person" and "I am a bad person" seemingly cannot both be true and thus effort is often expended trying to strengthen one thought at the cost of the other. This situation is the exact opposite of between-group selection—it is an instance of "within repertoire" competition similar to the competitive caged-chicken example mentioned earlier.

This same pattern of competition can occur in larger repertoires. For example, a person may begin an intense but loving relationship, only to find that the "person who will never be hurt" repertoire demands escape from the vulnerability of intimacy, while "the person who can solve all problems" provides myriad solutions such as "don't escape but don't let her get too close." The person with these various reactions can be thought of as a "we"—a collection of many response repertoires—but in some contexts the individual reactions and various discrete response repertoires each seek outcomes that undermine those sought by others.

A transcendent sense of self is a repertoire as well, but it is one in which none of these various reactions and "selves" needs to leave or change for the other reactions to have a place. From the point of view of I/HERE/NOW, all of these reactions are merely reactions to be observed, not logical entities that must live or die on the basis of rules of combinatorial entailment. They can coexist even if they are logically contradictory because it is possible simply to be consciously aware of them from a perspective of I/HERE/NOW without attachment to judgment. Thus a transcendent sense of self increases the sense of the whole person as a collective—as a "we"—and helps remove the consequences that feed selfish adaptations linked to only certain reactions (e.g., the escape from the relationship that feeds the "person who will never be hurt" repertoire). In other words, the processes of acceptance and defusion that are commonly sought in acceptance and commitment therapy (ACT; Hayes et al., 2011) and other mindfulness-based therapies can be seen as a kind of declaration of peace or internal cooperation among aspects of one's repertoire; and a transcendent sense of self facilitates those processes. This is similar to the previous example of chickens for whom success is defined for the entire cage, rather than individuals. The impact of deictic relations has two distinguishable aspects, both of which are supported by evolution science as conditions that foster cooperation: creation of a collective (the sense of a whole person despite the many competing reactions within) and withdrawal of the selfish benefits of individual adaptations.

That same collection of effects occurs when a transcendent sense of self is given its natural social extension (natural in the sense that the deictic relations themselves are extended across time, place, and person). If I am aware of another person in pain, pain will arise in me. Some of this is due to nonverbal processes. Signs of pain in others will elicit aversive reactions in a wide variety of organisms. Deictic framing establishes a socially interconnected sense of self that fosters amplification of this effect—to be aware from the point of view called "I" is part of the same relational process that permits being aware from the point of view called "YOU." The same applies to HERE and THERE and to NOW and THEN.

## Promotion of Prosociality

The openness to one's own reactions that is necessary for integration of seemingly incompatible reactions is inhibited if feelings generated by others are treated differently than feelings arising from one's own direct history. For example, suppose I am treating another person cruelly. The deictic nature of a transcendent sense of self means that the pain of that other person is more available if I am more connected with this aspect of myself. Said in a more normal language, spiritual awareness tends to connect us to the suffering of others, in other times, and in other places. In order to treat another person cruelly without restraint, different kinds of emotional reactions need to be sorted through and compartmentalized. Often this is done by fusing with judgments about the other person in a way that justifies cruelty (e.g., "he deserves it because..."). But this in turn fosters fusion with one's own self-judgments. Similarly denying the pain of others (and one's own pain occasioned by the pain of others) requires suppressive strategies applied to emotions. Fortunately, both fusion and suppressive avoidance supporting dehumanization can be undermined by a transcendent sense of self built on defusion and acceptance.

Human beings are social animals, and many if not most key human values are social. We have just argued that deictic framing inherently links psychological openness to compassion toward others. The natural tendency toward prosociality that is fostered by deictic responding can be threatened by avoidance, fusion, and the conceptualized self, but a transcendent sense of self undermines and weakens these threats. Thus human PT fosters both internal and external cooperation and prosociality. This helps explain the empirical findings about spirituality reviewed earlier. The compassion that comes from PT can be undermined but only by feeding psychological processes (e.g., avoidance and fusion) that are known to have significant psychological costs for individuals engaging in them (Hayes, Luoma, Bond, Masuda, & Lillis, 2006). The impact of spirituality is not just on compassion, connection, or prosociality, but on happiness, peace of mind, and flourishing.

In evolutionary science there is a final step needed for the evolution of prosociality and cooperation: selection by consequences and the retention of what is selected. Some of these consequences are direct—contingencies of survival, reinforcement or cultural evolution—but the same symbolic relations that allow for the development of a PT sense of self also allow for the construction of meaningful consequences *verbally*. Here we arrive at the domain of values, and in this domain as well, a transcendent sense of self is helpful.

Values are chosen qualities of ongoing patterns of behavior that establish reinforcers intrinsic to the behavior itself (Hayes et al., 2011). There is a growing empirical literature showing the impact of human values (e.g., Cohen, Garcia, Purdie-Vaughns, Apfel, & Brzustoski, 2009). Values work is key to the evolution of prosociality because it is a verbal means by which new selection criteria can be created for behavior. Relational framing abilities permit a person to construct an "IF-THEN" relation between current response patterns and expected consequences. These actions can alter what functions as a consequence for human action in a more immediate sense. Values link the qualities of patterns of actions to remote and probabilistic consequences. As a result, these qualities become immediately meaningful, essentially self-reinforcing values-based behavior.

A transcendent sense of self empowers values choices and values-based action. Deictic responding can help the person imagine consequences for others at other times and other places. This can help undermine the role of time and place in the impact of verbally constructed consequences of action. A transcendent sense of self fosters values-based action in other ways, also, such as supporting defusion and thus a sense of choice; and reducing the impact of the conceptualized self, thereby encouraging values more broadly based than narrow self-interest.

# Conclusion

Almost 30 years have passed since our first attempt to build a naturalistic account of spirituality and a transcendent sense of self (Hayes, 1984). At that time, we argued that although the content of spiritual beliefs is often not reachable by science, the experience they refer to is a natural psychological phenomenon that can be studied within a materialistic, monistic framework. More specifically, we predicted that the ability to take and change perspective on oneself was at the core of the experience of transcendence. Since the formulation of this conceptual proposition, empirical work on PT (i.e., deictic framing) has been conducted by RFT researchers in a variety of contexts demonstrating how a sense of self emerges through multiple exemplar training in deictic framing, and how such skill is necessary to identifying one's own and others' mental states and to building a sense of compassion and self-compassion. In the current chapter, we have tried to show that this growing literature can make sense of the existing data on spirituality and its impact on prosocial behavior. We have also tried to integrate these ideas with those of evolution science, attempting to provide a naturalistic account of one of the most interesting and important aspects of human functioning: spirituality.

# References

Abramson, L. Y., Seligman, M. E. P., & Teasdale, J. D. (1978). Learned helplessness in humans: Critique and reformulation. *Journal of Abnormal Psychology, 87,* 49–74.

Addis, M. E., & Jacobson, N. S. (1996). Reasons for depression and the process and out-come of cognitive-behavioral psychotherapies. *Journal of Consulting and Clinical Psychology, 64,* 1417–1424.

Alatiq, Y., Crane, C., Williams, J. M. G., & Goodwin, G. (2010). Self-organization in bipo-lar disorder: Replication of compartmentalization and self-complexity. *Cognitive Therapy and Research, 34,* 479–486.

Amsterdam, B. (1972). Mirror image reactions before age two. *Developmental Psychobiology, 5,* 297–305.

Apperly, I. A., & Butterfill, S. A. (2009). Do humans have two systems to track beliefs and belief-like states? *Psychological Review, 116,* 953–970.

Ashing, K. T., Padilla, G., Tejero, J., & Kagawa-Singer, M. (2003). Understanding the breast cancer experience of Asian American women. *Psycho-Oncology, 12,* 38–58.

Bach, P. B., & Hayes, S. C. (2002). The use of acceptance and commitment therapy to pre-vent the rehospitalization of psychotic patients: A randomized controlled trial. *Journal of Consulting and Clinical Psychology, 70,* 1129–1139.

Baer, R. (2003). Mindfulness training as a clinical intervention: A conceptual and empiri-cal review. *Clinical Psychology: Science and Practice, 10,* 125–143.

Baillargeon, R., Scott, R. M., & He, Z. (2010). False-belief understanding in infants. *Trends in Cognitive Sciences, 14,* 110–118.

Bandura, A. (1976). Self-reinforcement: Theoretical and methodological considerations. *Behaviorism, 4,* 135–155.

Bandura, A. (1982). Self-efficacy mechanism in human agency. *American Psychologist, 37*, 122–147.

Barnes-Holmes, D., Hayes, S. C., & Dymond, S. (2001). Self and self-directed rules. In S. C. Hayes, D. Barnes-Holmes, & B. Roche (Eds.), *Relational frame theory: A post-Skinnerian account of human language and cognition*. New York: Kluwer Academic/Plenum Publishers.

Barnes-Holmes, D., Hayes, S. C., Dymond, S., & O'Hora, D. (2001). Multiple stimulus relations and the transformation of stimulus functions. In S. C. Hayes, D. Barnes-Holmes, & B. Roche (Eds.), *Relational frame theory: A post-Skinnerian account of human language and cognition*. New York: Plenum.

Barnes-Holmes, D., Hayes, S. C., & Gregg, J. (2001). Religion, spirituality, and transcendence. In S. C. Hayes, D. Barnes-Holmes, & B. Roche (Eds.), *Relational frame theory: A post-Skinnerian account of human language and cognition*. New York: Plenum Press.

Barnes-Holmes, D., O'Hora, D., Roche, B., Hayes, S. C., Bissett, R. T., & Lyddy, F. (2001). Understanding and verbal regulation. In S. C. Hayes, D. Barnes-Holmes, & B. Roche (Eds.), *Relational frame theory: A post-Skinnerian account of human language and cognition*. New York: Kluwer Academic/Plenum.

Barnes-Holmes, Y., McHugh, L., & Barnes-Holmes, D. (2004). Perspective-taking and theory of mind: A relational frame account. *The Behavior Analyst Today, 5*, 15–25.

Baron-Cohen, S. (1991). Do people with autism understand what causes emotion? *Child Development, 62*, 385–395.

Baron-Cohen, S. (1994). How to build a baby that can read minds: Cognitive mechanisms in mind reading. *Cahiers de Psychologie Cognitive, 13*, 513–552.

Baron-Cohen, S., Leslie, A. M., & Frith, U. (1985). Does the autistic child have a theory of mind? *Cognition, 21*, 37–46.

Baron-Cohen, S., Leslie, A., & Frith, U. (1986). Mechanical, behavioral and intentional understanding of picture stories in autistic children. *British Journal of Developmental Psychology, 4*, 113–125.

Baron-Cohen, S., Tager-Flusberg, H., & Cohen, D. (Eds.) (2000). *Understanding other minds: Perspectives from developmental cognitive neuroscience*. Oxford University Press.

Barresi, J. (2001). Extending self-consciousness into the future. In C. Moore & K. Lemmon (Eds.), *The self in time: Developmental perspectives*. Hillsdale, NJ: Erlbaum.

Bartsch, K. (2002). The role of experience in children's developing folk epistemology: Review and analysis from the theory-theory perspective. *New Ideas in Psychology, 20*, 145–161.

Baumeister, R. F., Campbell, J. D., Krueger, J. I., & Vohs, K. D. (2003). Does high self-esteem cause better performance, interpersonal success, happiness, or healthier lifestyles? *Psychological Science in the Public Interest, 4*, 1–44.

Beck, A. T. (1964). Thinking and depression: II. Theory and therapy. *Archives of General Psychiatry, 10*, 561–571.

Beck, A. T. (1976). *Cognitive therapy and the emotional disorders*. New York: Meridian.

Beck, A. T., Rush, A. J., Shaw, B. F., & Emery, G. (1979). *Cognitive therapy of depression.* New York: Guilford Press.

Beck, J. S. (1995). *Cognitive therapy: Basics and beyond.* New York: Guilford Press.

Begeer, S., Gevers, C., Clifford, P., Verhoeve, M., Kat, K., Hoddenbach, E., et al. (2010). Theory of mind training in children with autism: A randomized controlled trial. *Journal of Autism and Developmental Disorders.* Epub ahead of print.

Bentall, R. P., Corcoran, R., Howard, R., Blackwood, N., & Kinderman, P. (2001). Persecutory delusions: A review and theoretical integration. *Clinical Psychology Review, 21,* 1143–1192.

Berger, P. L. (1999). The desecularization of the world: Resurgent and world politics. Washington, DC and Grand Rapids, MI: Ethics and Public Policy Center and William B. Eerdmans.

Bermudez, J. (1998). *The paradox of self-consciousness.* Cambridge, MA: MIT Press.

Berrios, G. E., & Markova, I. S. (2003). The self and psychiatry: A conceptual history. In T. Kircher & A. David (Eds.), *The self in neuroscience and psychiatry.* Cambridge: Cambridge University Press.

Biglan, A. (1995). *Changing cultural practices: A contextualistic framework for intervention research.* Reno, NV: Context Press.

Blackledge, J. T. (2007). Disrupting verbal processes: Cognitive defusion in acceptance and commitment therapy and other mindfulness-based psychotherapies. *The Psychological Record, 57,* 555–577.

Blackledge, J. T., & Barnes-Holmes, D. (2009), Core processes in acceptance & commitment therapy. In J. Blackledge, J. Ciarrochi, & F. Deane (Eds.), *Acceptance and commitment therapy: Contemporary theory, research, and practice.* Bowen Hills, Australia: Australian Academic Press.

Blaney, P. H. (1986). Affect and memory: A review. *Psychological Bulletin, 99,* 229–246.

Bond, F. W., & Flaxman, P. E. (2006). The ability of psychological flexibility and job control to predict learning, job performance, and mental health. *Journal of Organizational Behavior Management, 26,* 113–130.

Bowen, S., Chawla, N., Collins, S. E., Witkiewitz, K., Hsu, S., Grow, J., et al. (2009). Mindfulness-based relapse prevention for substance use disorders: A pilot efficacy trial. *Substance Abuse, 30,* 295–305.

Brewin, C. R. (2006). Understanding cognitive behaviour therapy: A retrieval competition account. *Behaviour Research and Therapy, 44,* 765–784.

Broden, M., Hall, V., & Mitts, B. (1971). The effect of self-recording on the classroom behavior of two eighth-grade students. *Journal of Applied Behavior Analysis, 4,* 191–199.

Brome, D. R., Owens, M. D., Allen, K., & Vevaina, T. (2000). An examination of spirituality in African American women in recovery from substance abuse. *Journal of Black Psychology, 26,* 470–486.

Brotherson, S. E., & Soderquist, J. (2002). Coping with a child's death: Spiritual issues and therapeutic implications. *Journal of Family Psychotherapy, 13,* 53–86.

Brown, R. (1973). *A first language: The early stages.* Cambridge, MA: Harvard University Press.

Call, J., & Tomasello, M. (2008). Does the chimpanzee have a theory of mind? 30 years later. *Trends in Cognitive Sciences, 12,* 187–192.

Campos, J., and Barrett, K. (1984). Toward a new understanding of emotions and their development. In C. E. Izard, J. Kagan, & R. Zajonc (Eds.), *Emotions, cognition, and behavior.* Cambridge: Cambridge University Press.

Carpenter, M., Nagell, K., & Tomasello, M. (1998). Social cognition, joint attention, and communicative competence from 9 to 15 months of age. *Monographs of the Society for Research in Child Development, 63.*

Carpenter, M., Pennington, B. E., & Rogers, S. J. (2002). Interrelations among social-cognitive skills in young children with autism. *Journal of Autism and Developmental Disorders, 32,* 91–106.

Carruthers, P., & Smith, P. K. (1996). *Theories of theory of mind.* Cambridge: Cambridge University Press.

Catania, A. C. (1975). The myth of self-reinforcement. *Behaviorism, 3,* 192–199.

Chandler, M. J., & Helm, D. (1984). Developmental-changes in the contribution of shared experience to social role-taking competence. *International Journal of Behavioral Development, 7,* 145–156.

Chapman, J. P., Chapman, L. J., & Kwapil, T. R. (1995). Scales for the measurement of schizotypy. In A. Raine, T. Lencz, & S. A. Mednick (Eds.), *Schizotypal personality.* Cambridge: Cambridge University Press.

Chapman, L. J., Chapman, J. P., Kwapil, T. R., Eckblad, M., & Zinser, M. C. (1994). Putatively psychosis-prone subjects 10 years later. *Journal of Abnormal Psychology, 103,* 171–183.

Charman, T. (1997). The relationship between joint attention and pretend play in autism. *Development and Psychopathology, 9,* 1–16.

Churchland, P. M. (1981). Eliminative materialism and the propositional attitudes. *Journal of Philosophy, 78,* 67–90.

Clark, D. M. (1996). Panic disorder: From theory to therapy. In P. M. Salkovskis (Ed.), *Frontiers of cognitive therapy.* New York: Guilford Press.

Clark, D. M. (1997). Panic disorder and social phobia. In D. M. Clark & C. G. Fairburn (Eds.), *Science and practice of cognitive behavior therapy.* Oxford: Oxford University Press.

Clements, W. A., & Perner, J. (1994). Implicit understanding of belief. *Cognitive Development, 9,* 377–395.

Clements, W. A., Rustin, C., & McCallum, S. (2000). Promoting the transition from implicit to explicit understanding: A training study of false belief. *Developmental Science, 3,* 88–92.

Cohen, G. L., Garcia, J., Purdie-Vaughns, V., Apfel, N., & Brzustoski, P. (2009). Recursive processes in self-affirmation: Intervening to close the minority achievement gap. *Science, 324,* 400–403.

Collins, A. M., & Quillian, M. R. (1969). Retrieval time from semantic memory. *Journal of Verbal Learning and Verbal Behavior, 8*, 240–247.

Combs, D. R., Adams, S. D., Penn, D. L., Roberts, D., Tiegreen, J., & Stem, P. (2007). Social Cognition and Interaction Training (CSIT) for inpatients with schizophrenia spectrum disorders: Preliminary findings. *Schizophrenia Research, 91*, 112–116.

Comte-Sponville, A. (2007). *The little book of atheist spirituality.* New York: Penguin.

Conway, M. A. (2005). Memory and the self. *Journal of Memory and Language, 53*, 594–628.

Conway, M. A., & Pleydell-Pearce, C. W. (2000). The construction of autobiographical memories in the self-memory system. *Psychological Review, 107*, 261–288.

Cooley, C. H. (1902). *Human nature and the social order.* New York: Scribner's.

Cooper, J. O., Heron, T. E., & Heward, W. L. (2007). *Applied behavior analysis* (2nd ed.). Upper Saddle River, NJ: Pearson.

Coopersmith, S. (1967). *The antecedents of self-esteem.* San Francisco: W. H. Freeman & Company.

Corcoran, R., Mercer, G., & Frith, C. D. (1995). Schizophrenia, symptomatology and social inference: Investigating "theory of mind" in people with schizophrenia. *Schizophrenia Research, 17*, 5–13.

Critchfield, T. S. (1993). Signal-detection properties of verbal self-reports. *Journal of the Experimental Analysis of Behavior, 60*, 495–514.

Dahl, J. C., Plumb, J. C., Stewart, I., & Lundgren, T. (2009). *The art & science of valuing in psychotherapy.* Oakland, CA · New Harbinger Publications.

Dalgleish, T., & Power, M. J. (2004). The I of the storm—relations between self and conscious emotion experience: Comment on Lambie and Marcel (2002). *Psychological Review, 111*, 812–819.

Damasio, A. (1999). *The feeling of what happens: Body and emotion in the making of consciousness.* Harcourt Brace.

Damon, W., & Hart, D. (1988). *Self-understanding in childhood and adolescence.* New York: Cambridge University Press.

David, D., & Szentagotai, A. (2006). Cognitions in cognitive-behavioral psychotherapies; toward an integrative model. *Clinical Psychology Review, 26*, 284–298.

Dawkins, R. (2006). *The God delusion.* New York: Mariner.

Dawson, G., Toth, K., Abbott, R., Osterling, J., Munson, J., & Estes, A. (2004). Defining the early social attention impairments in autism: Social orienting, joint attention, and responses to emotions. *Developmental Psychology, 40*, 271–283.

Dennett, D. C. (1978). Beliefs about beliefs. *Behavioral and Brain Sciences, 1*, 568–570.

Dennett, D. (1991). *Consciousness explained.* Little, Brown & Co.

Dennett, D. (2010). *Daniel Dennett discusses secular spirituality.* Retrieved April 29, 2011, from http://bigthink.com/danieldennett.htm.

Dickins, D. W., Singh, K. D., Roberts, N., Burns, P., Downes, J., Jimmieson, P., et al. (2001). An fMRI study of stimulus equivalence. *Neuroreport, 12*, 2–7.

Dillon, M., & Wink, P. (2007). *In the course of a lifetime: Tracing religious belief, practice, and change.* Berkeley, CA: University of California Press.

Dimaggio, G., Hermans, H. J. M., & Lysaker, P. H. (2010). Health and adaptation in a multiple self: The role of absence of dialogue and poor metacognition in clinical populations. *Theory & Psychology, 20,* 379–399.

Dimidjian, S., Hollon, S. D., Dobson, K. S., Schmaling, K. B., Kohlenberg, R. J., Addis, M. E., et al. (2006). Randomized trial of behavioral activation, cognitive therapy, and antidepressant medication in the acute treatment of adults with major depression. *Journal of Consulting and Clinical Psychology, 74,* 655–670.

Doherty, M. J. (2000). Children's understanding of homonymy: Metalinguistic awareness and false belief. *Journal of Child Language, 27,* 367–392.

Doherty, M. J. (2009). *Theory of mind: How children understand others' thoughts and feelings.* Hove, UK: Psychology Press.

Doherty, M. J. (2011). A two systems theory of social cognition: Engagement and theory of mind. In N. Eilan, H. Lerman, & J. Roessler (Eds.), *Understanding perception, causation and objectivity.* Oxford: Oxford University Press.

Doherty, M., & Perner, J. (1998). Metalinguistic awareness and theory of mind: Just two words for the same thing? *Cognitive Development, 13,* 279–305.

Doherty, M. J., & Wimmer, M. C. (2005). Children's understanding of ambiguous figures: Which cognitive developments are necessary to experience reversal? *Cognitive Development, 20,* 407–421.

Dowling, E. M., Gestsdottir, S., Anderson, P. M., von Eye, A., Almerigi, J., & Lerner, R. M. (2004). Structural relations among spirituality, religiosity, and thriving in adolescence. *Applied Developmental Science, 8,* 7–16.

Dozois, D. J. A. (2007). Stability of negative self-structures: A longitudinal comparison of depressed, remitted, and non-psychiatric controls. *Journal of Clinical Psychology, 63,* 319–338.

Dozois, D. J. A., & Beck, A. T. (2011). Cognitive therapy. In J. D. Herbert & E. M. Forman (Eds.), *Acceptance and mindfulness in cognitive behavior therapy: Understanding and applying the new therapies.* Hoboken, NJ: Wiley.

Dube, W. V., MacDonald, R. P. F., Mansfield, R. C., Holcomb, W. L., & Ahearn, W. H. (2004). Toward a behavioral analysis of joint attention. *The Behavior Analyst, 27,* 197–207.

Dymond, S., & Barnes, D. (1994). A transfer of self-discrimination response functions through equivalence relations. *Journal of the Experimental Analysis of Behavior, 62,* 251–267.

Dymond, S., & Barnes, D. (1995). A transformation of self-discrimination response functions in accordance with the arbitrarily applicable relations of sameness, more than, and less than. *Journal of the Experimental Analysis of Behavior, 64,* 163–184.

Dymond, S., & Barnes, D. (1996). A transformation of self-discrimination response functions in accordance with the arbitrarily applicable relations of sameness and opposition. *The Psychological Record, 46,* 271–300.

Dymond, S., & Barnes, D. (1997). Behavior-analytic approaches to self-awareness. *The Psychological Record, 47,* 181–200. .

Dziadosz, T., & Tustin, R. D. (1982). Self-control: An application of the generalized matching law. *American Journal of Mental Deficiency, 86,* 614–620.

Eckblad, M. L., Chapman, L. J., Chapman, J. P., & Mishlove, M. (1982). *The Revised Social Anhedonia Scale.* Unpublished test, University of Wisconsin, Madison.

English, H. B., & English, A. C. (1958). *A comprehensive dictionary of psychological and psychoanalytic terms.* New York: David McKay.

Epley, N., Morewedge, C., & Keysar, B. (2004). Perspective taking in children and adults: Equivalent egocentrism but differential correction. *Journal of Experimental Social Psychology, 40,* 760–768.

Epstein, R., Lanza, R. P., & Skinner, B. F. (1981). "Self-awareness" in the pigeon. *Science, 212,* 695–696.

Ericsson, K. A., & Simon, H. A. (1993). *Protocol analysis: Verbal reports as data* (Rev. ed.). Cambridge, MA: Bradford Books/MIT Press.

Erikson, E. H. (1968). *Identity: Youth and crisis.* New York: Norton.

Falk, D. (2004). Prelinguistic evolution in early hominins: Whence motherese? *Behavioral and Brain Sciences, 27,* 491–503.

Fannon, D., Hayward, P., Thompson, N., Green, N., Surguladze, S., & Wykes, T. (2009). The self or the voice? Relative contributions of self-esteem and voice appraisal in persistent auditory hallucinations. *Schizophrenia Research, 112,* 174–180.

Farb, N. A. S., Segal, Z. V., Mayberg, H., Bean, J., McKeon, D., Fatima, Z., et al. (2007). Attending to the present: mindfulness meditation reveals distinct neural modes of self-reference. *SCAN, 2,* 313–322.

Feinberg, I. (1978). Efference copy and corollary discharge: Implications for thinking and its disorders. *Schizophrenic Bulletin, 4,* 636–640.

Fisher, N., & Happe, F. (2005). A training study of theory of mind and executive function in children with autistic spectrum disorders. *Journal of Autism and Developmental Disorders, 35,* 757–771.

Flaxman, P. E., & Bond, F. W. (2006). Acceptance and commitment therapy (ACT) in the workplace. In R. A. Baer (Ed.), *Mindfulness-based treatment approaches: Clinician's guide to evidence base and application.* London: Elsevier Academic Press.

Fletcher, L., & Hayes, S. C. (2005). Relational frame theory, acceptance and commitment therapy, and a functional analytic definition of mindfulness. *Journal of Rational-Emotive & Cognitive-Behavior Therapy, 23,* 315–336.

Fodor, J. A. (1983). *The modularity of mind: An essay on faculty psychology.* Cambridge, MA: MIT Press.

Fodor, J. A. (1987). *Psychosemantics.* Cambridge, MA: MIT Press.

Fodor, J. A. (1992). A theory of the child's theory of mind. *Cognition, 44,* 283–296.

Fowler, D., Freeman, D., Smith, B., Kuipers, E., Bebbington, P., Bashforth, H., et al. (2006). The Brief Core Schema Scales (BCSS): Psychometric properties and associations with paranoia and grandiosity in non-clinical and psychosis samples. *Psychological Medicine, 36*, 749–759.

Friman, P. C., Hayes, S. C., & Wilson, K. G. (1998). Why behavior analysts should study emotion: The example of anxiety. *Journal of Applied Behavior Analysis, 31*, 137–156.

Frith, C. D. (1992). *The cognitive neuropsychology of schizophrenia*. Hove, UK: Lawrence Erlbaum.

Furrow, J., King, P. E., & White, K. (2004). Religion and positive youth development: Identity, meaning, and prosocial concerns. *Applied Developmental Science, 8*, 17–26.

Gallagher, H. L., & Frith, C. D. (2003). Functional imaging of 'theory of mind'. *Trends in Cognitive Sciences, 7*, 77–83.

Gallagher, S. (2000). Philosophical conceptions of the self: Implications for cognitive science. *Trends in Cognitive Sciences, 4*, 15–21.

Gallese, V., & Goldman, A. (1998). Mirror neurons and the simulation theory of mind-reading. *Trends in Cognitive Sciences, 2*, 493–501.

Gallup, G. G., Jr. (1970). Chimpanzees: Self recognition. *Science, 167*, 86–87.

Gallup, G. G. (1977). Self-recognition in primates. *American Psychologist, 32*, 329–338.

Gallup, G. G. (1998). Can animals empathize? Yes. *Scientific American Presents, 9*, 66, 68–71.

Garety, P. A., & Freeman, D. (1999). Cognitive approaches to delusions: A critical review of theories and evidence. *British Journal of Clinical Psychology, 38*, 113–154.

Gazzaniga, M. (1995). Consciousness and the cerebral hemispheres. In M. Gazzaniga (Ed.), *The cognitive neurosciences*. Boston: MIT Press.

Gazzaniga, M. (1998). *The mind's past*. New York: Basic Books.

Gentile, B., Twenge, J. M., & Campbell, W. K. (2010). Birth cohort difference in self-esteem, 1988–2008: A cross-temporal meta-analysis. *Review of General Psychology, 14*, 261–268.

Gewirtz, J. L., & Pelaez-Nogueras, M. (1992). B. F. Skinner's legacy to infant behavioral development. *American Psychologist, 47*, 1411–1422.

Gilbert, P. (2009). *The compassionate mind*. Oakland, CA: New Harbinger Publications.

Gill, C. S., Barrio Minton, C. A., & Myers, J. E. (2010). Spirituality and religiosity: Factors affecting wellness among low-income, rural women. *Journal of Counseling & Development, 88*, 293–302.

Gogate, L. J., Bahrick, L. E., & Watson, J. D. (2000). A study of multimodal motherese: The role of temporal synchrony between verbal labels and gestures. *Child Development, 71*, 878–894.

Goldiamond, I. (1976). Self-reinforcement. *Journal of Applied Behavior Analysis, 9*, 509–514.

Goldman, A. I., & Sripada, C. S. (2005). Simulationist models of face-based emotion recognition. *Cognition, 94*, 193–213.

Goldsmith, T. H. (1994). *The biological roots of human nature: Forging links between evolution and behavior.* New York: Oxford University Press.

Gomez, R. L., & Gerken, L. (2000). Infant artificial language learning and language acquisition. *Trends in Cognitive Sciences, 4,* 178–186.

Gooding, D. C., Tallent, K. A., & Matts, C. W. (2005). Clinical status of at-risk individuals 5 years later: Further validation of the psychometric high-risk strategy. *Journal of Abnormal Psychology, 114,* 170–175.

Gopnik, A. (1993). How we know our minds: The illusion of first-person knowledge of intentionality. *Behavioral and Brain Sciences, 16,* 1–14.

Gopnik, A., & Astington, J. W. (1988). Children's understanding of representational change and its relation to the understanding of false belief and the appearance-reality distinction. *Child Development, 59,* 26–37.

Gopnik, A,, & Graf, P. (1988). Knowing how you know: Young children's ability to identify and remember the sources of their beliefs. *Child Development, 59,* 1366–1371.

Gopnik, A. & Slaughter, V. (1991). Young children's understanding of changes in their mental states. *Child Development, 62,* 98–110.

Gordon, R. (1986). Folk psychology as simulation. *Mind and Language, 1,* 158–171.

Gortner, E. T., Gollan, J. K., Dobson, K. S., & Jacobson, N. S. (1998). Cognitive-behavioral treatment for depression: Relapse prevention. *Journal of Consulting and Clinical Psychology, 66,* 377–384.

Greenwald, A. G., McGhee, D. E , & Schwartz, J. L. K. (1998). Measuring individual differences in implicit cognition: The Implicit Association Test. *Journal of Personality and Social Psychology, 74,* 1464–1480.

Greenwald, A. G., & Farnham, S. D. (2000). Using the Implicit Association Test to measure self-esteem and self-concept. *Journal of Personality and Social Psychology, 79,* 1022–1038.

Grosch, J., & Neuringer, A. (1981). Self-control in pigeons under the Mischel paradigm. *Journal of the Experimental Analysis of Behavior, 35,* 3–21.

Hadwin, J., & Perner, J. (1991). Pleased and surprised: Children's cognitive theory of emotion. *British Journal of Developmental Psychology, 9,* 215–234.

Haeffel, G. J., Gibb, B. E., Metalsky, G. I., Alloy, L. B., Abramson, L. Y., Hankin, B. L., et al. (2008). Measuring cognitive vulnerability to depression: Development and validation of the cognitive style questionnaire. *Clinical Psychology Review, 28,* 824–836.

Hall, G. S. (1917). *Jesus the Christ in the light of psychology.* New York: Doubleday.

Hardy-Bayle, M. C. (1994). Organisation de l'action, phenomenes de conscience et representation mentale de l'action chez des schizophrenes. *Actualites Psychiatriques, 1,* 9–16.

Harré, R. (1989). The self as a theoretical concept. In M. Krausz (Ed.), *Relativism: Interpretation and confrontation.* Notre Dame, IN: University of Notre Dame Press.

Harris, A. H. S., & Thoresen, C. E. (2005). Forgiveness, unforgiveness, health and disease. In E. L. Worthington (Ed.), *Handbook of forgiveness.* New York: Routledge.

Harris, P. L. (1992). From simulation to folk psychology: The case for development. *Mind and Language, 7,* 120–144.

Harris, P. L., Johnson, C. N., Hutton, D., Andrews, G., & Cooke, T. (1989). Young children's theory of mind and emotion. *Cognition and Emotion, 3,* 379–400.

Hart, B., & Risley, T. (1995). *Meaningful differences in the everyday experience of young American children.* Baltimore: Paul H. Brookes Publishing.

Hart, B., & Risley, T. R. (1999). *The social world of children learning to talk.* Baltimore: Paul H. Brookes Publishing Co.

Hayes, S. C. (1984). Making sense of spirituality. *Behaviorism, 12,* 99–110.

Hayes, S. C. (1986). The case of the silent dog—Verbal reports and the analysis of rules: A review of Ericsson and Simon's *Protocol Analysis: Verbal Reports as Data. Journal of the Experimental Analysis of Behavior, 45,* 351–363.

Hayes, S. C. (1993). Why environmentally based analyses are necessary in behavior analysis. *Journal of the Experimental Analysis of Behavior, 60,* 461–463.

Hayes, S. C. (1995). Knowing selves. *The Behavior Therapist, 18,* 94–96.

Hayes, S. C. (2002). Buddhism and acceptance and commitment therapy. *Cognitive and Behavioral Practice, 9,* 58–66.

Hayes, S. C., Barnes-Holmes, D., & Roche, B. (2001). *Relational frame theory: A post-Skinnerian account of human language and cognition.* New York: Plenum Press.

Hayes, S. C., Bissett, R. T., Korn, Z., Zettle, R. D., Rosenfarb, I. S., Cooper, L. D., et al. (1999). The impact of acceptance versus control rationales on pain tolerance. *The Psychological Record, 49,* 33–47.

Hayes, S. C., & Brownstein, A. J. (1986). Mentalism, behavior-behavior relations, and a behavior-analytic view of the purposes of science. *The Behavior Analyst, 9,* 175–190.

Hayes, S. C., & Gifford, E. V. (1997). The trouble with language: Experiential avoidance, rules, and the nature of verbal events. *American Psychological Society, 8,* 170–173.

Hayes, S. C., Gifford, E. V., & Hayes, G. J. (1998). Moral behavior and the development of verbal regulation. *Behavior Analyst, 21,* 253–279.

Hayes, S. C., Luoma, J. B., Bond, F., Masuda, A., & Lillis, J. (2006). Acceptance and commitment therapy: Model, processes and outcomes. *Behaviour Research and Therapy, 44,* 1–25.

Hayes, S. C., & Plumb, J. C. (2007). Mindfulness from the bottom up: Providing an inductive framework for understanding mindfulness processes and their application to human suffering. *Psychological Inquiry, 18,* 242–248.

Hayes, S. C., Strosahl, K. D., & Wilson, K. G. (1999). *Acceptance and commitment therapy: An experiential approach to behavior change.* New York: Guilford Press.

Hayes, S. C., Strosahl, K., & Wilson, K. G. (2011). *Acceptance and commitment therapy: The process and practice of mindful change* (2nd ed.). New York: Guilford Press.

Hayes, S. C., & Wilson, K. G. (1993). Some applied implications of a contemporary behavior analytic account of verbal events. *The Behavior Analyst, 16,* 283–301.

Hayes, S. C., Wilson, K. G., Gifford, E. V., Bissett, R., Piasecki, M., Batten, S. V., et al. (2004). A preliminary trial of twelve-step facilitation and acceptance and commitment therapy with polysubstance-abusing methadone-maintained opiate addicts. *Behavior Therapy, 35,* 667–688.

Hayes, S. C., Wilson, K. G., Gifford, E. V., Follette, V. M., & Strosahl, K. (1996). Experiential avoidance and behavioral disorders: A functional dimensional approach to diagnosis and treatment. *Journal of Consulting and Clinical Psychology, 64,* 1152–1168.

Hayes, S. C., Zettle, R. D., & Rosenfarb, I. (1989). Rule-following. In S. C. Hayes (Ed.), *Rule-governed behavior: Cognition, contingencies, and instructional control.* New York: Plenum Press.

Hazlett-Stevens, H., & Borkovec, T. D. (2001). Effects of worry and progressive relaxation on the reduction of fear in speech phobia: An investigation of situational exposure. *Behavior Therapy, 32,* 503–517.

Heagle, A. I., & Rehfeldt, R. A. (2006). Teaching perspective-taking skills to typically developing children through derived relational responding. *Journal of Early and Intensive Behavior Intervention, 3,* 1–34.

Heal, J. (1986). Replication and functionalism. In J. Butterfield (Ed.), *Language, mind, and logic.* Cambridge: Cambridge University Press.

Helbig-Lang, S., & Petermann, F. (2010). Tolerate or eliminate? A systematic review on the effects of safety behavior across anxiety disorders. *Clinical Psychology: Science and Practice, 17,* 218–233.

Higgins, E. T. (1987). Self-discrepancy: A theory relating self and affect. *Psychological Review, 94,* 319–340.

Hineline, P. N. (1984). When we speak of knowing. *The Behavior Analyst, 6,* 183–186.

Hirsh-Pasek, K., & Treiman, R. (1982). Doggerel: Motherese in a new context. *Journal of Child Language, 9,* 229–237.

Hofmann, S. G. (2008). Common misconceptions about cognitive mediation of treatment change: A commentary to Longmore and Worrell (2007). *Clinical Psychology Review, 28,* 67–70.

Hofmann, S. G., & Asmundson, G. J. G. (2008). Acceptance and mindfulness-based therapy: New wave or old hat? *Clinical Psychology Review, 28,* 1–16.

Holder, M. D., Coleman, B., & Wallace, J. M. (2010). Spirituality, religiousness, and happiness in children aged 8–12 years. *Journal of Happiness Studies, 11,* 131–150.

Hollon, S. D., DeRubeis, R. J., Shelton, R. C., Amsterdam, J. D., Salomon, R. M., O'Reardon, J. P., et al. (2005). Prevention of relapse following cognitive therapy vs. medications in moderate to severe depression. *Archives of General Psychiatry, 62,* 417–422.

Hood, R. W., Hill, P. C., & Spilka, B. (2009). *The psychology of religion: An empirical approach* (4th ed.). New York: Guilford Press.

Horan, W. P., Brown, S. A., & Blanchard, J. J. (2007). Social anhedonia and schizotypy: The contribution of individual differences in affective traits, stress and coping. *Psychiatry Research, 149,* 147–156.

Houtman, D., & Aupers, S. (2007). The spiritual turn and the decline of tradition: The spread of post-Christian spirituality in 14 Western countries, 1981–2000. *Journal for the Scientific Study of Religion, 46*, 305–320.

Howlin, P., Baron-Cohen, S., & Hadwin, J. (1999). *Teaching children with autism to mind-read: A practical guide*. Chichester, England: Wiley.

Hume, D. (1739). *A treatise of human nature*. Clarendon Press (reprinted, 1975).

Ingram, R. E. (1990). Self-focused attention in clinical disorders: Review and a conceptual model. *Psychological Bulletin, 107*, 156–176.

Isaksen, J., & Holth, P. (2009). An operant approach to teaching joint attention skills to children with autism. *Behavioral Interventions, 24*, 215–236.

Jacobson, N. S., Dobson, K. S., Truax, P. A., Addis, M. E., Koerner, K., Gollan, J. K., et al. (1996). A component analysis of cognitive-behavioral treatment for depression. *Journal of Consulting and Clinical Psychology, 64*, 295–304.

James, W. (1890). *Principles of psychology* (Vol. 1). New York: Henry Holt and Co.

James, W. (1891a). *The principles of psychology* (Vol. 1). Cambridge, MA: Harvard University Press.

James, W. (1891b). *The principles of psychology* (Vol. 2). Cambridge, MA: Harvard University Press.

James, W. (1896/1958). *Talks to teachers*. New York: Norton.

James, W. (1902). *The varieties of religious experience*. New York: Longmans, Green & Co.

James, W. (1910). *Psychology: The briefer course*. New York: Holt.

Janeck, A. S., Calamari, J. E., Riemann, B. C., & Heffelfinger, S. K. (2003). Too much thinking about thinking?: Metacognitive differences in obsessive-compulsive disorder. *Journal of Anxiety Disorders, 17*, 181–195.

Jarrett, R. B., Vittengl, J. R., Doyle, K., & Clark, L. A. (2007). Changes in cognitive content during and following cognitive therapy for recurrent depression: Substantial and enduring, but not predictive of change in depressive symptoms. *Journal of Consulting and Clinical Psychology, 75*, 432–446.

Jenkins, J. M., & Astington, J. W. (1996). Cognitive factors and family structure associated with theory of mind development in young children. *Developmental Psychology, 32*, 18–70.

Johnson, M. W., & Bickel, W. K. (2002). Within-subject comparison of real and hypothetical money rewards in delay discounting. *Journal of the Experimental Analysis of Behavior, 77*, 129–146.

Kabat-Zinn, J. (1982). An outpatient program in behavioral medicine for chronic pain patients based on the practice of mindfulness meditation: Theoretical considerations and preliminary results. *General Hospital Psychiatry, 4*, 33–47.

Kayser, N., Sarfati, Y., Besche-Richard, C., & Hardy-Bayle, M.-C. (2006). Elaboration of a rehabilitation method based on a pathogenetic hypothesis of "theory of mind" impairment in schizophrenia. *Neuropsychological Rehabilitation, 16*, 83–95.

Keller, H., Chasiotis, A., & Runde, B. (1992). Intuitive parenting programs in German, American, and Greek parents of 3-month-old infants. *Journal of Cross-Cultural Psychology, 23*, 510–520.

Kelley, W. T., Macrae, C. N., Wyland, C., Caglar, S., Inati, S., & Heatherton, T. F. (2002). Finding the self? An event-related fMRI study. *Journal of Cognitive Neuroscience, 14*, 785–794.

Kerestes, M., Youniss, J., & Metz, E. (2004). Longitudinal patterns of religious perspective and civic integration. *Applied Developmental Science, 8*, 39–46.

Kinderman, P., & Bentall, R. P. (1996). Self-discrepancies and persecutory delusions: Evidence for a model of paranoid ideation. *Journal of Abnormal Psychology, 105*, 106–113.

Klein, S. B. (2010). The self: As a construct in psychology and neuropsychological evidence for its multiplicity. Wiley Interdisciplinary Reviews. *Cognitive Science, 1*, 172–183.

Klein, S. B., Cosmides, L., Costabile, K. A., & Mei, L. (2002). Is there something special about the self? A neuropsychological case study. *Journal of Research in Personality, 36*, 490–506.

Klin, A., Volkmar, F. R., & Sparrow, S. S. (1992). Autistic social dysfunction: Some limitations of the theory of mind hypothesis. *Journal of Child Psychology and Psychiatry, 33*, 861–876.

Kloo, D., & Perner, J. (2008). Training social and executive control competence. *Mind, Brain and Education, 2*, 122–127.

Knoll, M., & Charman, T. (2000). Teaching false belief and visual perspective taking skills in young children: Can a theory of mind be trained? *Child Study Journal, 30*, 273–303.

Kochanska, G. (1997). Mutually responsive orientation between mothers and their young children: Implications for early socialization. *Child Development, 67*, 94–112.

Kochanska, G. (2002). Mutually responsive orientation between mothers and their young children: A context for the early development of conscience. *Current Directions in Psychological Science, 11*, 191–195.

Kochanska, G., & Aksan, N. (2004). Development of mutual responsiveness between parents and their young children. *Child Development, 75*, 1657–1676.

Kochanska, G., & Aksan, N. (2006). Children's conscience and self-regulation. *Journal of Personality, 74*, 1587–1617.

Kochanska, G., Aksan, N., Prisco, T. R., & Adams, E. E. (2008). Mother-child and father-child mutually responsive orientation in the first 2 years and children's outcomes at preschool age: Mechanisms of influence. *Child Development, 79*, 30–44.

Kochanska, G., & Murray, K. T. (2000). Mother-child mutually responsive orientation and conscience development: From toddler to early school age. *Child Development, 71*, 417–431.

Kwapil, T. R. (1998). Social anhedonia as a predictor of the development of schizophrenia-spectrum disorders. *Journal of Abnormal Psychology, 107*, 558–565.

Lane, S. D., Cherek, D. R., Lieving, L. M., & Tcheremissine, O. V. (2005). Marijuana effects on human forgetting functions. *Journal of the Experimental Analysis of Behavior, 83*, 67–83.

Langdon, R., & Coltheart, M. (1999). Mentalising, schizotypy and schizophrenia. *Cognition, 71*, 43–71.

Langdon, R., & Coltheart, M. (2001). Visual perspective-taking and schizotypy: Evidence for a simulation-based account of mentalizing in normal adults. *Cognition, 82*, 1–26.

Langdon, R., Coltheart, M., Ward, P. B., & Catts, S.V. (2001). Visual and cognitive perspective-taking impairments in schizophrenia: A failure of allocentric simulation? *Cognitive Neuropsychiatry, 6*, 241–269.

Lattal, K. A. (1975). Reinforcement contingencies as discriminative stimuli. *Journal of the Experimental Analysis of Behavior, 23*, 241–246.

Lattal, K. A., & Doepke, K. J. (2001). Correspondence as conditional stimulus control: Insights from experiments with pigeons. *Journal of Applied Behavior Analysis, 34*, 127–144.

Leach, M. M., & Lark, R. (2004). Does spirituality add to personality in the study of trait forgiveness? *Personality and Individual Differences, 37*, 147–156.

Leary, M. R. (2004). *The curse of the self: Self-awareness, egotism, and the quality of human life*. New York: Oxford University Press.

Lee, H. (1960). *To kill a mockingbird*. New York: Harper Collins.

LeGrand, D., & Ruby, P. (2009). What is self-specific? Theoretical investigation and critical review of neuroimaging results. *Psychological Review, 116*, 252–282.

Leslie, A. M. (1987). Pretense and representation: The origins of "theory of mind". *Psychological Review, 94*, 412–426.

Leuba, J. H. (1912). *A psychological study of religion: Its origin, function, and future*. New York: Macmillan.

Levin, M. E., & Hayes, S. C. (2009). ACT, RFT, and contextual behavioral science. In J. T. Blackledge, J. Ciarrochi, & F. P. Deane (Eds.), *Acceptance and commitment therapy: Contemporary research and practice*. Sydney: Australian Academic Press.

Lewis, C., & Osborne, A. (1990). Three-year-olds' problems with false belief: Conceptual deficit or linguistic artifact? *Child Development, 61*, 1514–1519.

Lewis, M., & Brooks-Gunn, J. (1979). *Social cognition and the acquisition of self*. New York: Plenum Press.

Lewis, V., & Boucher, J. (1988). Spontaneous, instructed, and elicited play in relatively able autistic children. *British Journal of Developmental Psychology, 6*, 325–339.

Linehan, M. M. (1993). *Cognitive behavioral treatment of borderline personality disorder*. New York: Guilford Press.

Linehan, M. M., Comtois, K. A., Murray, A. M., Brown, M. Z., Gallop, R. J., Heard, et al. (2006). Two-year randomized controlled trial and follow-up of dialectical behavior therapy vs therapy by experts for suicidal behaviors and borderline personality disorder. *Archives of General Psychiatry, 63*, 757–766.

Linville, P. W. (1985). Self-complexity and affective extremity: Don't put all of your eggs in one cognitive basket. *Social Cognition, 3*, 94–120.

Linville, P. W. (1987). Self-complexity as a cognitive buffer against stress-related illness and depression. *Journal of Personality and Social Psychology, 52*, 663–676.

Lloyd, K. E. (2002). A review of correspondence training: Suggestions for a revival. *The Behavior Analyst, 25*, 57–73.

Lowe, F. C. (1979). Determinants of human operant behavior. In M. D. Zeiler & P. Harzem (Eds.), *Reinforcement and the organization of behavior*. New York: John Wiley.

Luciano, C., Valdivia-Salas, S., & Ruiz, F. (2011). *Integrating the dimensions of the self and behavior regulation*. Manuscript submitted for publication.

Luciano, C., Valdivia-Salas, S., Cabello-Luque, F., & Hernandez, M. (2009). Developing self-directed rules. In R. A. Rehfeldt & Y. Barnes-Holmes (Eds.), *Derived relational responding: Applications for learners with autism and other developmental disabilities*. Oakland, CA: New Harbinger Publications.

Lyons, G. C. B., Deane, F. P., & Kelly, P. J. (2010). Forgiveness and purpose in life as spiritual mechanisms of recovery from substance use disorders. *Addiction Research & Theory, 18*, 528–543.

Maccoby, E. E. (1980). *Social development: Psychological growth and the parent-child relationship*. New York: Harcourt Brace Jovanovich.

MacDonald, R., Anderson, J., Dube, W. V., Geckeler, A., Green, G., Holcomb, W., et al. (2006). Behavioral assessment of joint attention: A methodological report. *Research in Developmental Disabilities, 27*, 138–150.

MacKinnon, K., Newman-Taylor, K., & Stopa, L. (2011). Persecutory delusions and the self: An investigation of implicit and explicit self-esteem. *Journal of Behavior Therapy and Experimental Psychiatry, 42*, 54–64.

Macrae, C. N., Heatherton, T. F., & Kelley, W. M. (2004). A self less ordinary: The medial prefrontal cortex and you. In M. S. Gazzaniga (Ed.), *The cognitive neurosciences III*. Cambridge, MA: MIT Press.

Markus, H. (1990). Unresolved issues of self-representation. *Cognitive Therapy and Research, 14*, 241–253.

Markus, H., & Nurius, P. (1986). Possible selves. *American Psychologist, 41*, 954–969.

Maslow, A. H. (1954). *Motivation and personality*. New York: Harper and Row.

Maslow, A. H. (1964). *Religions, values, and peak-experiences*. Ohio State University Press.

Matheis, E. N., Tulsky, D. S., & Matheis, R. J. (2006). The relation between spirituality and quality of life among individuals with spinal cord injury. *Rehabilitation Psychology, 51*, 265–271.

McCracken, L. M., & Yang, S-Y. (2006). The role of values in a contextual cognitive-behavioral approach to chronic pain. *Pain, 123*, 137–145.

McCullough, M. E., Bono, G., & Root, L. M. (2007). Rumination, emotion, and forgiveness: Three longitudinal studies. *Journal of Personality and Social Psychology, 92*, 490–505.

McHugh, L. (2004). *Integrating relational frame theory and theory of mind: An empirical investigation* (Unpublished doctoral thesis). National University of Ireland, Maynooth.

McHugh, L., Barnes-Holmes, Y., & Barnes-Holmes, D. (2004a). Perspective-taking as relational responding: A developmental profile. *The Psychological Record, 54,* 115–144.

McHugh, L., Barnes-Holmes, Y., & Barnes-Holmes, D. (2004b). Understanding perspective-taking, false belief, and deception from a behavioural perspective. *The Irish Psychologist, 30,* 142–147.

McHugh, L., Barnes-Holmes, Y., & Barnes-Holmes, D. (2009). Understanding and training perspective taking as relational responding. In R. A. Rehfeldt & Y. Barnes-Holmes (Eds.), *Derived relational responding: Applications for learners with autism and other developmental disabilities.* Oakland, CA: New Harbinger Publications.

McHugh, L., Barnes-Holmes, Y., Barnes-Holmes, D., & Stewart, I. (2006). False belief as generalised operant behavior. *The Psychological Record, 56,* 341–364.

McHugh, L., Barnes-Holmes, Y., Barnes-Holmes, D., Stewart, I., & Dymond, S. (2007). Deictic relational complexity and the development of deception. *The Psychological Record, 57,* 517–531.

McHugh, L., Barnes-Holmes, Y., Barnes-Holmes, D., Whelan, R., & Stewart, I. (2007). Knowing me, knowing you: Deictic complexity in false-belief understanding. *Psychological Record, 57,* 533–542.

McHugh, L., Barnes-Holmes, Y., O'Hora, D., & Barnes-Holmes, D. (2004). Perspective-taking: A relational frame analysis. *Experimental Analysis of Human Behavior Bulletin, 22,* 4–10.

McHugh, L., Simpson, A., & Reed, P. (2010). Mindfulness as a potential intervention for stimulus over-selectivity in older adults. *Research in Developmental Disabilities, 31,* 178–184.

Mead, G. H. (1934). *Mind, self and society.* Charles W. Morris (Ed.). Chicago: University of Chicago.

Meins, E., & Fernyhough, C. (1999). Linguistic acquisitional style and mentalising development: The role of maternal mind-mindedness. *Cognitive Development, 14,* 363–380.

Meltzoff, A. N. (2002). Imitation as a mechanism of social cognition: Origins of empathy, theory of mind, and the representation of action. In U. Goswami (Ed.), *Handbook of childhood cognitive development.* Oxford: Blackwell Publishers.

Mennin, D. S. (2005). Emotion and the acceptance-based approaches to the anxiety disorders. In S. M. Orsillo & L. Roemer (Eds.), *Acceptance and mindfulness-based approaches to anxiety: Conceptualization and treatment.* New York: Springer Science + Business Media.

Michael, J. (1993). Establishing operations. *The Behavior Analyst, 16,* 191–206.

Miller, J., Fletcher, K., & Kabat-Zinn, J. (1995). Three-year follow-up and clinical implications of a mindfulness-based stress reduction intervention in the treatment of anxiety disorders. *General Hospital Psychiatry, 17,* 192–200.

Miller, W. R., & Thoresen, C. E. (2003). Spirituality, religion, and health: An emerging research field. *American Psychologist, 58,* 24–35.

Mischel, W. (1974). Processes in delay of gratification. In L. Berkowitz (Ed.), *Advances in experimental social psychology* (Vol. 7). New York: Academic Press.

Moerk, E. L. (1983). *The mother of Eve—As a first language teacher.* Norwood, NJ: Ablex.

Moerk, E. L. (1986). Environmental factors in early language acquisition. In G. J. Whitehurst (Ed.), *Annals of child development* (Vol. 3): JAI Press.

Moerk, E. L. (1989). The LAD was a lady and the tasks were ill-defined. *Developmental Review, 9,* 21–57.

Moerk, E. L. (1990). Three-term contingency patterns in mother-child verbal interactions during first-language acquisition. *Journal of the Experimental Analysis of Behavior, 54,* 293–305.

Moerk, E. L. (2000). *The guided acquisition of first language skills.* Stamford, CT: Ablex.

Morales, M., Mundy, P., Delgado, C. E. F., Yale, M., Messinger, D., Neal, R., et al. (2000). Responding to joint attention across the 6- through 24-month age period and early language acquisition. *Journal of Applied Developmental Psychology, 21,* 283–298.

Moscovitch, D. A. (2009). What is the core fear in social phobia? A new model to facilitate individualized case conceptualization and treatment. *Cognitive and Behavioral Practice, 16,* 123–134.

Muir, W. M. (1996). Group selection for adaptation to multiple-hen cages: Selection program and direct responses. *Poultry Science, 75,* 447–458.

Mukamel, R., Ekstrom, A. D., Kaplan, J., Iacoboni, M., & Fried, I. (2010). Single-neuron responses in humans during execution and observation of actions. *Current Biology, 20,* 750–756.

Mundy, P., Block, J., Delgado, C., Pomares, Y., Vaughn Van Hecke, A., & Parlade, M. V. (2007). Individual differences and the development of joint attention in infancy. *Child Development, 78,* 938–954.

Mundy, P., Sigman, M., & Kasari, C. (1994). Joint attention, developmental level, and symptom presentation in autism. *Development and Psychopathology, 6,* 389–401.

Myers, D. G. (2000). *The American paradox: Spiritual hunger in an age of plenty.* New Haven, CT: Yale University Press.

Neisser, U. (1988). Five kinds of self-knowledge. *Philosophical Psychology, 1,* 35–59.

Neisser, U., & Fivush, R. (1994). *The remembering self: Construction and accuracy in the self-narrative.* Cambridge University Press.

Nelson, J. (2009). *Psychology, religion, and spirituality.* New York: Springer.

Neuringer, A. (1981). Self-experimentation: A call for change. *Behaviorism, 9,* 79–94.

Neuringer, A. (1986). Can people behave "randomly"?: The role of feedback. *Journal of Experimental Psychology: General, 115,* 62–75.

Newton, P., Reddy, V., & Bull, R. (2000). Children's everyday deception and performance on false-belief tasks. *British Journal of Developmental Psychology, 18,* 297–317.

Nisbett, R. E., & Wilson, T. D. (1977a). The halo effect: Evidence for unconscious alteration of judgments. *Journal of Personality & Social Psychology, 35,* 250–256.

Nisbett, R. E., & Wilson, T. D. (1977b). Telling more than we can know: Verbal reports of mental processes. *Psychological Review, 84,* 231–259.

Northoff, G., & Bermpohl, F. (2004). Cortical midline structures and the self. *Trends in Cognitive Sciences, 8,* 102–106.

Novak, G. (1996). *Developmental psychology: Dynamical systems and behavior analysis.* Reno, NV: Context Press.

Novak, G. (1998). Behavioral systems theory. *Mexican Journal of Behavior Analysis, 24,* 100–112.

Novak, G. (1999). Skills learning in behavioral epigenesis. *Behavioral Development Bulletin, 8,* 17–20.

Novak, G., & Pelaez, M. (2004). *Child and adolescent development: A behavioral systems approach.* Thousand Oaks, CA: Sage Publications.

Novak, G., & Scott-Klingbord, S. (1998, May). *Incidental teaching of stimulus equivalency to infants.* Paper presented at the Association for Behavior Analysis, Tampa, FL.

O'Hora, D., & Barnes-Holmes, D. (2004). Instructional control. Developing a relational frame analysis. *International Journal of Psychology and Psychological Therapy, 4,* 263–284.

Okamoto, S., Tanaka, M., & Tomonaga, M. (2004). Looking back: The 'representational mechanism' of joint attention in an infant chimpanzee (*Pan troglodytes*). *Japanese Psychological Research, 46,* 236–245.

O'Leary, S. G., & Dubey, D. R. (1979). Applications of self-control procedures by children: A review. *Journal of Applied Behavior Analysis, 12,* 449–465.

Oman, D., Hedberg, J., Downs, D., & Parsons, D. (2003). A transcultural spiritually based program to enhance caregiving self-efficacy: A pilot study. *Complementary Health Practice Review, 8,* 201–224.

O'Neill, D. K. (1996). Two-year-old children's sensitivity to a parent's knowledge state when making requests. *Child Development, 67,* 659–677.

O'Neill, D. K., Astington, J. W., & Flavell, J. H. (1992). Young children's understanding of the role that sensory experiences play in knowledge acquisition. *Child Development, 63,* 474–490.

Onishi, K. H., & Baillargeon, R. (2005). Do 15-month-old infants understand false beliefs? *Science, 308,* 255–258.

Ostrom, E. (2009). A general framework for analyzing sustainability of social-ecological systems. *Science, 325,* 419–422.

Pack, A. A., & Herman, L. M. (2004). Bottlenosed dolphins (*Tursiops truncatus*) comprehend the referent of both static and dynamic human gazing and pointing in an object-choice task. *Journal of Comparative Psychology, 118,* 160–171.

Paez-Blarrina, M., Luciano, C., Gutierrez-Martinez, O., Valdivia, S., Ortega, J., & Rodriguez-Valverde, M. (2008). The role of values with personal examples in altering the functions of pain: Comparison between acceptance-based and cognitive-control-based protocols. *Behaviour Research and Therapy, 46,* 84–97.

Papousek, H., & Papousek, M. (1987). Intuitive parenting: A dialectic counterpart to the infant's integrative competence. In J. D. Osofsky (Ed.), *Handbook of infant development* (2nd ed.). New York: Wiley.

Parrot, L. (1987). Rule-governed behavior: An implicit analysis of reference. In S. Modgil & C. Modgil (Eds.), *B.F. Skinner: Consensus and Controversy.* Philadelphia: Falmer Press.

Pelaez, M. (2009). Joint attention and social referencing in infancy as precursors of derived relational responding. In R. A. Rehfeldt & Y. Barnes-Holmes (Eds.), *Derived relational responding: Applications for learners with autism and other developmental disabilities.* Oakland, CA: New Harbinger Publications.

Pelaez-Nogueras, M., & Gewirtz, J. L. (1997). The context of stimulus control in behavior analysis. In D. M. Baer & E. M. Pinkston (Eds.), *Environment and behavior.* Boulder, CO: Westview Press.

Penn, D. L., Spaulding, W. D., Reed, D., & Sullivan, M. (1996). The relationship of social cognition to ward behavior in chronic schizophrenia. *Schizophrenia Research, 20,* 327–335.

Penn, D. C., & Povinelli, D. J. (2007). On the lack of evidence that chimpanzees possess anything remotely resembling a 'theory of mind.' *Philosophical Transactions of the Royal Society, B, 362,* 731–744.

Pepper, S. C. (1942). *World hypotheses: A study in evidence.* Berkeley, CA: University of California Press.

Perner, J. (1991). *Understanding the representational mind.* Cambridge, MA: MIT Press.

Perner, J., Leekam, S. R., Myers, D., Davis, S., & Odgers, N. (1998). Misrepresentation and referential confusion: Children's difficulty with false beliefs and outdated photographs. Available http://cogprints.org/708/ (accessed 20th January 2011).

Perner, J., Leekam, S., & Wimmer, H. (1987). Three year olds' difficulty with false belief. The case for a conceptual deficit. *British Journal of developmental Psychology, 5,* 125–137.

Perner, J., Stummer, S., Sprung, M., & Doherty, M. (2002). Theory of mind finds its Piagetian perspective: Why alternative naming comes with understanding belief. *Cognitive Development, 17,* 1451–1472.

Perner, J., & Wimmer, H. (1985). John thinks that Mary thinks that: Attribution of 2nd-order beliefs by 5-year-old to 10-year-old children. *Journal of Experimental Child Psychology, 39,* 437–471.

Peskin, J. (1992). Ruse and representations: On children's ability to conceal information. *Developmental Psychology, 28,* 84–89.

Peskin, J., & Ardino, V. (2003). Representing the mental world in children's social behavior: Playing hide-and-seek and keeping a secret. *Social Development, 12,* 496–512.

Peterson, C. M., & Siegal, M. (1999). Representing inner worlds: Theory of mind in autistic, deaf, and normal hearing children. *Psychological Science, 10,* 126–129.

Piaget, J. (1970). *Structuralism.* New York: Harper & Row.

Pitman, C. A., & Shumaker, R. W. (2009). Does early care affect joint attention in great apes (*Pan troglodytes, Pan paniscus, Pongo abelii, Pongo pygmaeus, Gorilla gorilla*)? *Journal of Comparative Psychology, 123*, 334–341.

Platek, S. M., Critton, S. R., Myers, T. E., & Gallup, G. G. (2003). Contagious yawning: The role of self-awareness and mental state attribution. *Cognitive Brain Research, 17*, 223–227.

Polkinghorne, D. E. (2001). The self and humanistic psychology. In K. J. Schneider, J. F. T. Bugental, & J. F. Pierson (Eds.), *The handbook of humanistic psychology*. Thousand Oaks, CA: Sage Publications.

Potter, H. (2007). Battered Black women's use of religious services and spirituality for assistance in leaving abusive relationships. *Violence against Women, 13*, 262–284.

Potter, J., & Wetherell, M. (1987). *Discourse and social psychology: Beyond attitudes and behaviour*. London: Sage. ‹

Povinelli, D. J. (1998). Can animals empathize? *Scientific American Presents: Exploring Intelligence, 9*, 67, 72–75.

Povinelli, D. J., & Vonk, J. (2003). Chimpanzee minds: Suspiciously human? *Trends in Cognitive Sciences, 7*, 157–160.

Power, M. J. (2007). The multistory self: Why the self is more than the sum of its autoparts. *Journal of Clinical Psychology, 63*, 187–198.

Power, M. J., de Jong, F., & Lloyd, A. (2002). The organization of the self-concept in bipolar disorders: An empirical study and replication. *Cognitive Therapy and Research, 26*, 553–561.

Pratt, C., & Bryant, P. (1990). Young children understand that looking leads to knowing (so long as they are looking into a single barrel). *Child Development, 61*, 973–982.

Premack, D., & Woodruff, G. (1978). Does the Chimpanzee have a theory of mind? *Behavioral and Brain Sciences, 1*, 515–526.

Pyszczynski, T., & Greenberg, J. (1987). Self-regulatory perseveration and the depressive self-focusing style: A self-awareness theory of reactive depression. *Psychological Bulletin, 102*, 122–138.

Rachlin, H., & Green, L. (1972). Commitment, choice and self-control. *Journal of the Experimental Analysis of Behavior, 17*, 15-22.

Rachlin, H., Raineri, A., & Cross, D. (1991). Subjective probability and delay. *Journal of the Experimental Analysis of Behavior, 55*, 233–244.

Raine, A. (1991). The SPQ: A scale for the assessment of schizotypal personality based on *DSM-III-R* criteria. *Schizophrenia Bulletin, 17*, 55–64.

Random House Dictionary of the English Language. (1966). New York: Random House.

Ray, B. A. (1969). Selective attention: The effects of combining stimuli which control incompatible behavior. *Journal of the Experimental Analysis of Behavior, 12*, 539–550.

Reeve, H. K., & Hölldobler, B. (2007). The emergence of a superorganism through intergroup competition. *Proceedings of the National Academy of Sciences, 104*, 9736–9740.

Regnerus, M. D., Smith, C., & Fritsch, M. (2003). Religion in the lives of American adolescents: A review of the literature. *Research Report of the National Study of Youth and Religion, Number 3.* Chapel Hill, NC: National Study of Youth and Religion.

Rehfeldt, R. A., & Barnes-Holmes, Y. (Eds.). (2009). *Derived relational responding: Applications for learners with autism and other developmental disabilities.* Oakland, CA: New Harbinger Publications.

Rehfeldt, R. A., Dillen, J. E., Ziomek, M. M., & Kowalchuk, R. K. (2007). Assessing relational learning deficits in perspective-taking in children with high-functioning autism spectrum disorder. *The Psychological Record, 57,* 23–47.

Repacholi, B. M., & Gopnik, A. (1997). Early reasoning about desires: Evidence from 14- and 18-month-olds. *Developmental Psychology, 33,* 12–21.

Risley, T. R., & Hart, B. (1968). Developing correspondence between the non-verbal and verbal behavior of preschool children. *Journal of Applied Behavior Analysis, 1,* 267–281.

Roberts, S., & Neuringer, A. (1998). Self-experimentation. In K. A. Lattal & M. Perone (Eds.), *Handbook of human operant research methods.* New York: Plenum.

Robinson, E. J., & Mitchell, P. (1995). Masking of children's early understanding of the representational mind: Backwards explanation versus prediction. *Child Development, 66,* 1022–1039.

Roche, B., & Barnes, D. (1997). A transformation of respondently conditioned stimulus function in accordance with arbitrarily applicable relations. *Journal of the Experimental Analysis of Behavior, 67,* 275–300.

Roemer, L., & Orsillo, S. M. (2009). *Mindfulness- and acceptance-based behavioral therapies in practice.* New York: Guilford Press.

Rogers, C. (1961). *On becoming a person: A therapist's view of psychotherapy.* London: Constable.

Rogers, T. B., Kuiper, N. A., & Kirker, W. S. (1977). Self-reference and the encoding of personal information. *Journal of Personality and Social Psychology, 35,* 677–688.

Roof, W. C. (1993). *A generation of seekers: The spiritual journeys of the baby boom generation.* San Francisco: Harper.

Rosales-Ruiz, J., & Baer, D. M. (1997). Behavioral cusps: A developmental and pragmatic concept for behavior analysis. *Journal of Applied Behavior Analysis, 30,* 533–544.

Rosenbaum, M. S., & Drabman, R. S. (1979). Self-control training in the classroom: A review and critique. *Journal of Applied Behavior Analysis, 12,* 467–485.

Ruby, P., & Decety, J. (2004). How would you feel versus how do you think she would feel? A neuroimaging study of perspective taking with social emotions. *Journal of Cognitive Neuroscience, 16,* 988–999.

Ruffman, T. (1996). Do children understand the mind by means of simulation or a theory? Evidence from their understanding of inference. *Mind & Language, 11,* 388–414.

Ruffman, T., Garnham, W., Import, A., & Connolly, D. (2001). Does eye gaze indicate implicit knowledge of false belief? Charting transitions in knowledge. *Journal of Experimental Child Psychology, 80,* 201–224.

Ruffman, T., & Keenan, T. R. (1996). The belief-based emotion of surprise: The case for a lag in understanding relative to false belief. *Developmental Psychology, 32*, 40–49.

Ruffman, T., & Perner, J. (2005). Do infants really understand false belief? Response to Leslie. *Trends in Cognitive Sciences, 9*, 462–463.

Ruiz, F. J. (2010). A review of acceptance and commitment therapy (ACT) empirical evidence: Correlational, experimental psychopathology, component and outcome studies. *International Journal of Psychology and Psychological Therapy, 10*, 125–162.

Rutter, M., Bailey, A., & Lord, C. (2004). *SCQ: Social Communication Questionnaire.* Western Psychological Services: Los Angeles, CA.

Sarfati, Y., Hardy-Bayle, M. C., Nadel, J., Chevalier, J. F., & Widlocher, D. (1997). Attribution of mental states to others by schizophrenic patients. *Cognitive Neuropsychiatry, 2*, 1–17.

Sarfati, Y., Passerieux, C., & Hardy-Bayle, M. C. (2000). Can verbalization remedy the theory of mind deficit in schizophrenia? *Psychopathology, 33*, 246–251.

Schiffman, J., Lam, C. W., Jiwatram, T., Ekstrom, M., Sorensen, H., & Mednick, S. (2004). Perspective-taking deficits in people with schizophrenia spectrum disorder: A prospective investigation. *Psychological Medicine, 34*, 1581–1586.

Schlinger, H. D. (1990). A reply to behavior analysts writing about rules and rule-governed behavior. *The Analysis of Verbal Behavior, 8*, 77–82.

Schultz, J. M., Tallman, B. A., & Altmaier, E. M. (2010). Pathways to posttraumatic growth: The contributions of forgiveness and importance of religion and spirituality. *Psychology of Religion and Spirituality, 2*, 104–114.

Segal, Z. V. (1988). Appraisal of the self-schema construct in cognitive models of depression. *Psychological Bulletin, 103*, 147–162.

Segal, Z. V., Bieling, P., Young, T., MacQueen, G., Cooke, R., Martin, L., et al. (2010). Antidepressant monotherapy vs sequential pharmacotherapy and mindfulness-based cognitive therapy, or placebo, for relapse prophylaxis in recurrent depression. *Archives of General Psychiatry, 67*, 1256–1264.

Segal, Z. V., & Muran, J. C. (1993). A cognitive perspective on self-representation in depression. In Z. V. Segal & S. J. Blatt (Eds.), *The self in emotional distress: Cognitive and psychodynamic perspectives.* New York: Guilford Press.

Segal, Z. V., Williams, J. M. G., & Teasdale, J. D. (2002). *Mindfulness-based cognitive therapy for depression: A new approach for preventing relapse.* New York: Guilford Press.

Selman, R. L. (1980). *The growth of interpersonal understanding.* New York: Academic Press.

Shavelson, R. J., & Marsh, H. W. (1986). On the structure of self-concept. In R. Schwarzer (Ed.), *Anxiety and cognitions.* Hillsdale, NJ: Erlbaum.

Shimoff, E., Catania, A. C., & Matthews, B. A. (1981). Uninstructed human responding: Sensitivity of low-rate performance to schedule contingencies. *Journal of the Experimental Analysis of Behavior, 36*, 207–220.

Showers, C. J. (1992). Compartmentalization of positive and negative self-knowledge: Keeping bad apples out of the bunch. *Journal of Personality and Social Psychology, 62*, 1036–1049.

Showers, C. J., Abramson, L. Y., & Hogan, M. E. (1998). The dynamic self: How the content and structure of the self-concept change with mood. *Journal of Personality and Social Psychology, 75,* 478–493.

Showers, C. J., Limke, A., & Zeigler-Hill, V. (2004). Self-structure and self-change: Applications to psychological treatment. *Behavior Therapy, 35,* 167–184.

Sidman, M. (1960). *Tactics of scientific research.* New York: Basic Books.

Sidman, M. (1971). Reading and auditory-visual equivalences. *Journal of Speech and Hearing Research, 14,* 5–13.

Siegal, M., & Beattie, K. (1991). Where to look first for children's knowledge of false beliefs. *Cognition, 38,* 1–12.

Skinner, B. F. (1935). Two types of conditioned reflex and a pseudo type. *Journal of General Psychology, 12,* 66–77.

Skinner, B. F. (1938). *The behavior of organisms: An experimental analysis.* New York: Appleton-Century.

Skinner, B. F. (1945). The operational analysis of psychological terms. *Psychological Review, 52,* 270–277.

Skinner, B. F. (1953). *Science and human behavior.* New York: Macmillan.

Skinner, B. F. (1957). *Verbal behavior.* New York: Appleton-Century-Crofts.

Skinner, B. F. (1969). *Contingencies of reinforcement.* New York: Appleton-Century-Crofts.

Skinner, B. F. (1974). *About behaviorism.* London: Penguin.

Skinner, B. F. (1988). In A. C. Catania, & S. Harnad (Eds.), *The selection of behavior: The operant behaviorism of B. F. Skinner: Comments and consequences.* New York: Cambridge University Press. (Original work published 1981)

Smith, C., Denton, M. L., Fans, R., & Regnerus, M. (2002). Mapping American adolescent religious participation. *Journal for the Scientific Study of Religion, 41,* 597–612.

Sodian, B., Taylor, C., Harris, P. L., & Perner, J. (1991). Early deception and the child's theory of mind: False trails and genuine markers. *Child Development, 62,* 468–483.

Southgate, V., Senju, A., & Csibra, G. (2007). Action anticipation through attribution of false belief by 2-year-olds. *Psychological Science, 18,* 587–592.

Sparrow, S. S., Balla, D. A., & Cicchetti, D. V. (1984). *Vineland Adaptive Behavior Scales: Interview editions, Survey form manual.* Circle Pines, MN: American Guidance Service.

Steele, D. L., & Hayes, S. C. (1991). Stimulus equivalence and arbitrarily applicable relational responding. *Journal of the Experimental Analysis of Behavior, 56,* 519–555.

Tarbox, J., Tarbox, R. S. F., & O'Hora, D. (2009). Nonrelational and relational instructional control. In R. A. Rehfeldt & Y. Barnes-Holmes (Eds.), *Derived relational responding: Applications for learners with autism and other developmental disabilities.* Oakland, CA: New Harbinger Publications.

Tate, D. G., & Forchheimer, M. (2002). Quality of life, life satisfaction, and spirituality: Comparing outcomes between rehabilitation and cancer patients. *American Journal of Physical Medicine and Rehabilitation, 81,* 400–410.

Taylor, B. A., & Hoch, H. (2008). Teaching children with autism to respond to and initiate bids for joint attention. *Journal of Applied Behavior Analysis, 41*, 377–391.

Taylor, M. (1988). Conceptual perspective taking: Children's ability to distinguish what they know from what they see. *Child Development, 59*, 703–718.

Taylor, M., & Carlson, S. M. (1997). The relation between individual differences in fantasy and theory of mind. *Child Development, 68*, 436–455.

Taylor, M., Carlson, S. M., Maring, B., Gerow, L. E., & Charley, C. (2004). The characteristics and correlates of high fantasy in school-aged children: Imaginary companions, impersonation, and social understanding. *Developmental Psychology, 40*, 1173–1187.

Teasdale, J. D., Segal, Z. V., Williams, J. M. G., Ridgeway, V. A., Soulsby, J. M., & Lau, M. A. (2000). Preventing relapse/recurrence in major depression by mindfulness-based cognitive therapy. *Journal of Consulting and Clinical Psychology, 68*, 615–623.

Thelen, E., & Ulrich, B. D. (1991). Hidden Skills (Serial No. 233 ed. Vol. 36). *Monographs of the Society for Research in Child Development*. Society for Research in Child Development.

Thompson, T. (2008). Self-awareness: Behavior analysis and neuroscience. *The Behavior Analyst, 31*, 137–144.

Tomasello, M. (2003). *Constructing a language: A usage-based theory of language acquisition*. Cambridge, MA: Harvard University Press.

Tomasello, M. (2008). *Origins of human communication*. Cambridge, MA: MIT Press.

Tomasello, M., Call, J., & Hare, B. (2003). Chimpanzees understand psychological states— the question is which ones and to what extent. *Trends in Cognitive Sciences, 7*, 153–156.

Tomasello, M., & Herrmann, E. (2010). Ape and human cognition: What's the difference? *Current Directions in Psychological Research, 19*, 3–8.

Törneke, N. (2010). *Learning RFT: An introduction to relational frame theory and its clinical applications*. Oakland, CA: New Harbinger Publications.

Törneke, N., Luciano, C., & Valdivia, S. (2008). Rule-governed behavior and psychological problems. *International Journal of Psychology and Psychological Therapy, 8*, 141–156.

Tryon, W. W., & Misurell, J. R. (2008). Dissonance induction and reduction: A possible principle and connectionist mechanism for why therapies are effective. *Clinical Psychology Review, 28*, 1297–1309.

Vilardaga, R. (2009). A relational frame theory account of empathy. *The International Journal of Behavioral Consultation and Therapy, 5*, 178–184.

Vilardaga, R., Estevez, A., Levin, M. E., & Hayes, S. C. (2011). Deictic relational responding, empathy and experiential avoidance as predictors of social anhedonia: Further contributions from relational frame theory. *The Psychological Record*.

Villatte, M., Monestes, J. L., McHugh, L., Freixa i Baque, E., & Loas, G. (2008). Assessing deictic relational responding in social anhedonia: A functional approach to the development of Theory of Mind impairments. *International Journal of Behavioral Consultation and Therapy, 4*, 360–373.

Villatte, M., Monestes, J. L., McHugh, L., Freixa i Baque, E., & Loas, G. (2010a). Adopting the perspective of another in belief attribution: Contribution of relational frame theory to the understanding of impairments in schizophrenia. *Journal of Behavior Therapy and Experimental Psychiatry, 41*, 125–134.

Villatte, M., Monestes, J. L., McHugh, L., Freixa i Baque, E., & Loas, G. (2010b). Assessing perspective taking in schizophrenia using relational frame theory. *The Psychological Record, 60*, 413–424.

Vittengl, J. R., Clark, L. A., Dunn, T. W., & Jarrett, R. B. (2007). Reducing relapse and recurrence in unipolar depression: A comparative meta-analysis of cognitive-behavioral therapy's effects. *Journal of Consulting and Clinical Psychology, 75*, 475–488.

Vogeley, K., Bussfeld, P., Newen, A., Herrmann, S., Happe, F., Falkai, P., et al. (2001). Mind reading: Neural mechanisms of theory of mind and self-perspective. *NeuroImage, 14*, 170–181.

Wade, M. J., Bijma, P., Ellen, E. D., & Muir, W. M. (2010). Group selection and social evolution in domesticated animals. *Evolutionary Applications, 3*, 453–465.

Wagenaar, W. A. (1972). Generation of random sequences by human subjects: A critical survey of the literature. *Psychological Bulletin, 77*, 65–72.

Wallace, J. M., Jr., Forman, T. A., Caldwell, C. H., & Willis, D. S. (2003). Religion and U.S. secondary school students: Current patterns, recent trends, and socio-demographic correlates. *Youth & Society, 35*, 98–125.

Watson, D. L., & Tharp, R. G. (2006). *Self-directed behavior: Self-modification for personal adjustment*. Belmont, CA: Wadsworth.

Weil, T. M., Hayes, S. C., & Capurro, P. (2011). Establishing a deictic relational repertoire in young children. *The Psychological Record, 61*, 371–390.

Wellman, H., Cross, D., & Watson, J. K. (2001). Meta-analysis of Theory-of-Mind development: The truth about false belief. *Child Development, 72*, 655–684.

Whalen, C., & Schreibman, L. (2003). Joint attention training for children with autism using behavior modification procedure. *Journal of Child Psychology and Psychiatry, 44*, 456–468.

Wilber, K. (1997). An integral theory of consciousness. *Journal of Consciousness Studies, 4*, 71–92.

Williams, J. M. G., Watts, F. N., MacLeod, C., & Mathews, A. (1997). *Cognitive psychology and emotional disorders* (2nd ed.). Chichester, UK: Wiley.

Williams, L. M. (2006). *Acceptance and commitment therapy: An example of third-wave therapy as a treatment for Australian Vietnam veterans with posttraumatic stress disorder* (Unpublished dissertation). Charles Stuart University, Bathurst, New South Wales.

Wilson, D. S. (2003). *Darwin's cathedral: Evolution, religion, and the nature of society*. Chicago: University of Chicago Press.

Wilson, D. S. (2007). *Evolution for everyone: How Darwin's theory can change the way we think about our lives*. New York: Delta.

Wilson, D. S., & Wilson, E. O. (2007). Rethinking the theoretical foundation of sociobiology. *The Quarterly Review of Biology, 82*, 327–348.

Wilson, K. G., & DuFrene, T. (2008). *Mindfulness for two: An acceptance and commitment therapy approach to mindfulness in psychotherapy.* Oakland, CA: New Harbinger Publications.

Wilson, K. G., Hayes, S. C., Gregg, J., & Zettle, R. D. (2001). Psychopathology and psychotherapy. In S. C. Hayes, D. Barnes, & B. Roche (Eds.), *Relational frame theory: A post-Skinnerian account of human language and cognition.* New York: Plenum Press.

Wimmer, H., Hogrefe, G. J., & Perner, J. (1988). Children's understanding of informational access as source of knowledge. *Child Development, 59*, 386–396.

Wimmer, H., & Mayringer, H. (1998). False belief understanding in young children: Explanations do not develop before predictions. *International Journal of Behavioral Development, 22*, 403–422.

Wimmer, H., & Perner, J. (1983). Beliefs about beliefs: Representation and constraining function of wrong beliefs in young children's understanding of deception. *Cognition, 13*, 103–128.

Wisco, B. E. (2009). Depressive cognition: Self-reference and depth of processing. *Clinical Psychology Review, 29*, 382–392.

Wolman, B. J. (1973). *Dictionary of behavioral science.* New York: Van Nostrand Reinhold.

Yeats, K. O., & Selman, R. L. (1989). Social competence in the schools: Towards an integrative development model for intervention. *Developmental Review, 9*, 64–100.

Yirmiya, N., Erel, O., Shaked, M., & Salomonica-Levi, D. (1998). Meta-analyses comparing Theory of Mind abilities of individuals with autism, individuals with mental retardation, and normally developing individuals. *Psychological Bulletin, 124*, 283–307.

Young, J. E., Klosko, J. S., & Weishaar, M. E. (2003). *Schema therapy: A practitioner's guide.* New York: Guilford Press.

Youngblade, L. M., & Dunn, J. (1995). Individual differences in young children's pretend play with mother and sibling: Links to relationships and understanding of other people's feeling and beliefs. *Child Development, 66*, 1472–1492.

Zaitchik, D. (1990). When representations conflict with reality: The preschooler's problem with false beliefs and "false" photographs. *Cognition, 35*, 41–68.

Zettle, R. D., & Hayes, S. C. (1982). Rule-governed behavior: A potential theoretical framework for cognitive behavioral research and therapy. In P. C. Kendall (Ed.), *Advances in cognitive behavioral research and therapy.* New York: Academic Press.

Zettle, R. D., & Hayes, S. C. (2002). Brief ACT treatment of depression. In F. Bond & W. Dryden (Eds.), *Handbook of brief cognitive behavior therapy.* Chichester, England: Wiley.

Zinnbauer, B. J., Pargament, K. I., Cole, B., Rye, M. S., Butter, E. M., Belavich, T. G., et al. (1997). Religion and spirituality: Unfuzzying the fuzzy. *Journal for the Scientific Study of Religion, 36*, 549–564.

Zuriff, G. E. (1986). *Behaviorism: A conceptual reconstruction.* New York: Columbia University Press.

**Editor Louise McHugh, PhD,** is a faculty member in the school of psychology at University College Dublin. Her research interests are centered on the experimental analysis of language and cognition from a behavior analytic and relational frame theory perspective, including the development of perspective-taking and the process-level investigation of behavioral and cognitive psychotherapies, such as acceptance and commitment therapy.

**Editor Ian Stewart, PhD,** is a faculty member in the department of psychology at the National University of Ireland, Galway. His research focuses on the analysis of language and cognition using relational frame theory. His articles have been published in over forty international peer-reviewed journals and he is coauthor of *The Art and Science of Valuing in Psychotherapy.*

Foreword writer **Mark Williams, PhD,** is professor of clinical psychology and Wellcome Principal Research Fellow at Oxford University, UK. He is a fellow of the Academy of Medical Sciences and the British Academy. Williams is also author of many books and articles on the psychology of depression and depression treatment, with a focus on mindfulness-based approaches.

# Index

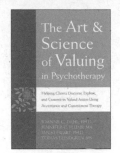

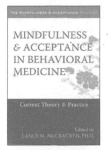